DANGEROUS THINKING IN THE AGE OF THE NEW AUTHORITARIANISM

Critical Interventions
Politics, Culture, and the Promise of Democracy

A Series from Paradigm Publishers

Edited by Henry A. Giroux, Susan Searls Giroux, and Kenneth J. Saltman

DANGEROUS THINKING IN THE AGE OF THE NEW AUTHORITARIANISM

HENRY A. GIROUX

Taylor & Francis Group

LONDON AND NEW YORK

First published 2015 by Paradigm Publishers

Published 2016 by Routledge
2 Park Square, Milton Park, Abingdon, Oxon OX14 4RN
711 Third Avenue, New York, NY 10017, USA

Routledge is an imprint of the Taylor & Francis Group, an informa business

Cataloging-in-Publication Data Available from the Library of Congress

ISBN 13: 978-1-61205-863-4 (hbk)
ISBN 13: 978-1-61205-864-1 (pbk)
ISBN 978-1-61205-865-8 (library ebook)

To those teachers, young people, and workers who chose to think critically and act courageously.

To Arshad and Freda.

To Susan, Chris, and Danielle.

Contents

Contents

Section 3: Reclaim the Radical Imagination: Politics beyond Hope

Acknowledgments

⊹

I want to thank Susan Searls Giroux for her insights, support, and ability to extend the conversation further than I could have imagined. Her editorial skills are unparalleled, and I am thankful that she was able to take the time to edit many of the chapters in this book, especially with her busy schedule. My graduate students Tyler Pollard, Jennifer Fisher, and Clorinde Peters have been enormously helpful in pushing me to think through a number of important issues. I want to thank my colleagues and friends David L. Clark and Lindsay Fitzclarence for their comments and the generous amount of time they have been willing to give to reading this work. As usual, my assistant, Maya Sabados, has been indispensable in editing and reading endless drafts of every chapter. My editors at *Truthout*—Victoria Harper, Leslie Thatcher, and Maya Schenwar—have provided me with unwavering support in publishing my work there, some of which is included in this book. I am enormously grateful to Dean Birkenkamp, who has been my editor for longer than I can remember. He is one of the great independent publishers in the United States, and in my mind he is a national hero for his willingness to struggle to make publishing mean something in dark times. Highly modified versions of some of these articles have been published in *E-International Relations, Boundary 2, Thesis 11, Cultural Studies, Policy Futures in Education, Tikkun, Fast Capitalism, Tidal Basin Review,* and *Arena Magazine.*

SECTION I
Orwell and Huxley's America

I
Between Orwell and Huxley
America's Plunge into Dystopia

ֆ

In spite of their differing perceptions of the architecture of the totalitarian superstate and how it exercises power and control over its residents, George Orwell and Aldous Huxley shared a fundamental conviction. They both argued that the established democracies of the West were moving quickly toward a historical moment when they would willingly relinquish the noble promises and ideals of liberal democracy and enter that menacing space where totalitarianism perverts the modern ideals of justice, freedom, and political emancipation. Both believed that Western democracies were devolving into pathological states in which politics was recognized in the interest of death over life and justice. Both were unequivocal in the shared understanding that the future of civilization was on the verge of total domination—or what Hannah Arendt called "dark times."

While Neil Postman and other critical descendants have pitted Orwell and Huxley against each other because of their distinctively separate notions of a future dystopian society,[1] I believe that the dark shadow of authoritarianism that shrouds American society like a thick veil can be lifted by re-examining Orwell's prescient dystopian fable *1984*, as well as Huxley's *Brave New World*, in light of contemporary neoliberal ascendancy. Rather than pit their dystopian visions against each other, it might be more productive to see them as complementing each other, especially at a time when, to quote Antonio Gramsci, "The old world is dying and the new world struggles to be born; in this interregnum a great variety of morbid symptoms appear."[2]

Both authors provide insight into the merging of the totalitarian elements that constitute a new and more hybridized form of authoritarian control, appearing less as fiction than a threatening portent of the unfolding twenty-first century. Consumer fantasies and authoritarian control; "Big Brother" intelligence agencies and the voracious seductions of privatized pleasures; the rise of the punishing state, which criminalizes an increasing number of behaviors and invests in institutions that incarcerate and are organized principally for the production of violence; the collapse of democratic public spheres into narrow, market-driven orbits of privatization—these now constitute the new order of authoritarianism.

Orwell's Big Brother has more recently found a new incarnation in the revelations of government lawlessness and corporate spying by whistleblowers such as Chelsea Manning, Jeremy Hammond, and Edward Snowden.[3] All of these individuals revealed a government that lied about its intelligence operations, illegally spied on millions of people who were not considered terrorists or had committed no crime, and collected data from every conceivable electronic source to be stored and potentially used to squelch dissent, blackmail people, or just intimidate those who fight to make corporate and state power accountable.[4] Orwell offered his readers an image of the modern state in which privacy was no longer valued as a civil virtue and a basic human right, nor perceived as a measure of the robust strength of a healthy and thriving democracy. In Orwell's dystopia the right to privacy had come under egregious assault, but more than that, such ruthless transgressions of privacy pointed to something more sinister than the violation of individual rights. The claim to privacy, for Orwell, represented a moral and political principle by which to assess the nature, power, and severity of an emerging totalitarian state. Orwell's warning was intended to shed light on the horrors of totalitarianism, the corruption of language, the production of a pervasive stupidity, and the endless regimes of state spying imposed on citizens in the mid-twentieth century. Orwell opened a door for all to see a "nightmarish future" in which everyday life becomes harsh, an object of state surveillance, and control—a society in which the slogan "ignorance becomes strength"—morphs into a guiding principle of mainstream media, education, and the culture of politics.

Huxley shared Orwell's concern about ignorance as a political tool of the elite, enforced through surveillance and the banning of books, dissent, and critical thought itself. But Huxley believed that social control and the propagation of ignorance would be introduced by those in power through the political tools of pleasure and distraction. Huxley thought that this might take place through the use of drugs and genetic engineering. But the real drugs and social planning of late modernity are found in an entertainment and public pedagogy industry that trades in pleasure and idiocy—most evident in the merging of neoliberalism, celebrity culture, and the control of commanding cultural apparatuses extending from Hollywood movies and video games to mainstream television, news, and the social media.

Orwell's Big Brother of 1984 has been upgraded in the 2015 edition. As Zygmunt Bauman points out, if the older Big Brother presided over traditional enclosures such as military barracks, prisons, schools, and "countless other big and small panopticons," the updated Big Brother is concerned with not only inclusion and the death of privacy but also the suppression of dissent and the widening of the politics of exclusion.[5] Keeping people out is the extended face of Big Brother, who now patrols borders, hospitals, and other public spaces in order to spot "the people who do not fit in the places they are in, banishing them from . . . 'where they belong,' or better still never allowing them to come anywhere near in the first place."[6]

This is the Big Brother that pushes youthful protests out of the public spaces they attempt to occupy. This is the hypernationalistic Big Brother clinging to notions of racial purity and American exceptionalism as a driving force in creating a country that has come to resemble an open-air prison for the dispossessed. This is the Big Brother whose split personality portends the dark authoritarian universe of the 1 percent, with their control over the economy and use of paramilitarized police forces on the one hand, and on the other their retreat into gated communities manned by SWAT-like security forces. Fear and isolation constitute an updated version of Big Brother. Fear is now managed and buttressed by normalizing the neoliberal claim that it be accepted as a general condition of society, dealt with exclusively as an individual consideration, disassociated from the politics and moral panics endemic to an authoritarian society, and used to mobilize the individual's fear of the other. In the surveillance state, fear is misplaced from the political sphere to the personal concern with the fear of surviving, of not getting ahead, of unemployment, and of the danger posed by the growing legions of alien others. As the older order dies and a new one struggles to be born, Gramsci's vision rightly identifies a liminal space that has given rise to monsters, all too willing to kidnap, torture, and spy on law-abiding citizens while violating civil liberties.[7] He is also right in suggesting that while such an interregnum offers no political guarantees, it does provide, or at least gestures toward, reimagining "what is to be done," how it might be done, and who is going to do it.[8]

Orwell's 1984 continues to serve as a brilliant and important metaphor for mapping the expansive trajectory of global surveillance, authoritarianism, and the suppression of dissent that has characterized the first decades of the new millennium. The older modes of surveillance to which Orwell pointed—including his warnings regarding the dangers of microphones and giant telescreens that watch and listen—are surprisingly limited when compared with the varied means now available for spying. Orwell would be astonished by this contemporary, refashioned Big Brother given the threat that the new surveillance state poses because of its reach, and the alleged "advance" of technologies that far outstretch anything he could have imagined, technologies that pose a much greater threat to both the personal privacy of citizens *and* the control exercised by sovereign power.

As Marjorie Cohn has similarly indicated, "Orwell never could have imagined that the National Security Agency (NSA) would amass metadata on billions of our phone calls and 200 million of our text messages every day. Orwell could not have foreseen that our government would read the content of our emails, file transfers, and live chats from the social media we use."[9] Snowden, Cohn, and other critics are correct about the dangers of the state's infringement of privacy rights, but their analysis should be taken further by linking the issue of citizen surveillance with the rise of "networked societies," global flows of power, and the emergence of a totalitarian ethos that defies even state-based control.[10] For Orwell, domination was state imposed and bore the heavy hand of unremitting repression and a smothering language that eviscerated any appearance of dissent, erased historical memory, and turned the truth into its opposite. For Orwell, individual freedom was at risk under the heavy hand of state terrorism.

In Orwell's world individual freedom and privacy were under attack from outside forces. For Huxley, in contrast, freedom and privacy were willingly given up as part of the seductions of a soft authoritarianism, with its vast machinery of manufactured needs, desires, and identities. This new mode of persuasion seduced people into chasing commodities, and infantilized them through the mass production of easily digestible entertainment, disposable goods, and new scientific advances in which any viable sense of agency was undermined. The conditions for critical thought dissolved into the limited pleasures of instant gratification wrought through the use of technologies and consuming practices that dampened, if not obliterated, the very possibility of thinking itself. Orwell's dark image is the stuff of government oppression, whereas Huxley's is the stuff of distractions, diversions, and the transformation of privacy into a cheap and sensational performance for public display. Neil Postman, writing in a different time and worried about the destructive anti-intellectual influence of television, sided with Huxley and believed that repression was now on the side of entertainment and the propensity of the American public to amuse itself to death.[11] His attempt to differentiate Huxley's dystopian vision from Orwell's is worth noting:

> Orwell warns that we will be overcome by an externally imposed oppression. But in Huxley's vision, no Big Brother is required to deprive people of their autonomy, maturity and history. As he saw it, people will come to love their oppression, to adore the technologies that undo their capacities to think. What Orwell feared were those who would ban books. What Huxley feared was that there would be no reason to ban a book, for there would be no one who wanted to read one. Orwell feared those who would deprive us of information. Huxley feared those

who would give us so much that we would be reduced to passivity and egoism. Orwell feared that the truth would be concealed from us. Huxley feared the truth would be drowned in a sea of irrelevance. Orwell feared we would become a captive culture. Huxley feared we would become a trivial culture, preoccupied with some equivalent of the feelies, the orgy porgy, and the centrifugal bumblepuppy. As Huxley remarked in *Brave New World Revisited*, the civil libertarians and rationalists who are ever on the alert to oppose tyranny "failed to take into account man's almost infinite appetite for distractions." In *1984*, Huxley added, people are controlled by inflicting pain. In *Brave New World*, they are controlled by inflicting pleasure. In short, Orwell feared that what we hate will ruin us. Huxley feared that what we love will ruin us.[12]

Echoes of Huxley's insights play out in the willingness of millions of people who voluntarily hand over personal information whether in the service of the strange sociality prompted by social media or in homage to the new surveillance state. New surveillance technologies employed by major service providers now focus on diverse consumer populations who are targeted in the collection of endless amounts of personal information as they move from one site to the next, one geopolitical region to the next, and across multiple screens and digital apparatuses. As Ariel Dorfman points out, "Social media users gladly give up their liberty and privacy, invariably for the most benevolent of platitudes and reasons,"[13] all the while endlessly shopping online, updating Facebook, and texting. Indeed, surveillance technologies are now present in virtually every public and private space—such as video cameras in streets, commercial establishments, workplaces, and even schools, as well as the myriad scanners at entry points of airports, retail stores, sporting events, and so on. They function as control mechanisms that become normalized through their heightened visibility. So, too, our endless array of personal devices that chart, via GPS tracking, our every move, our every choice, our every pleasure.

At the same time, Orwell's warning about Big Brother applies not simply to an authoritarian-surveillance state but also to commanding financial institutions and corporations that have made diverse modes of surveillance a ubiquitous feature of daily life. Corporations use the new technologies to track spending habits and to collect data points from social media so as to provide us with consumer goods that match our desires, to employ facial recognition technologies to alert store salespersons to our credit ratings, and so it goes. Heidi Boghosian points out that if omniscient state control in Orwell's *1984* is embodied by the two-way television sets present in each home, then in "our own modern adaptation, it is symbolized by the location-tracking cell phones we willingly carry in our pockets and the microchip-embedded clothes we wear on our bodies."[14] In this instance, the surveillance state is one that not only listens, watches, and gathers massive amounts of information through data mining, allegedly for the purpose of identifying "security threats." It also acculturates the public into accepting the intrusion of commercial surveillance technologies—and, perhaps more vitally, the acceptance of privatized, commodified values—into all aspects of their lives. In other words, the most dangerous repercussions of a near total loss of privacy involve more than the unwarranted collecting of information by the government: we must also be attentive to the ways in which being spied on has become not only *normalized* but even enticing, as corporations up the pleasure quotient for consumers who use new digital technologies and social networks—not least of all by and for simulating experiences of community.

Many individuals, especially young people, now run from privacy and increasingly demand services in which they can share every personal facet of their lives. While Orwell's vision touches upon this type of control, there is a notable difference that he did not foresee. According to Pete Cashmore, while Orwell's "Thought Police tracked you without permission, some consumers are now comfortable with sharing their every move online."[15] The state and corporate cultural apparatuses now collude to socialize everyone—especially young people—into a regime of security and commodification in which their identities, values, and desires are inextricably tied to a culture of commodified addictions, self-help, therapy, and social indifference. Intelligence networks now inhabit the world of major corporations such as Disney and the Bank of America as well as the secret domains of the NSA, FBI, and fifteen other intelligence agencies. As Edward Snowden's revelations about the PRISM program revealed, the NSA has also collected personal data from "the world's largest Internet companies—Facebook, Yahoo!, Apple, Google—as well as extensive efforts by Microsoft to provide the agency with access to its communications platforms such as Outlook."[16] According to a senior lawyer for the NSA, the Intenet companies "were fully aware of the surveillance agency's widespread collection of data."[17]

The fact is that Orwell's and Huxley's ironic representations of the modern totalitarian state—along with their implied defense of a democratic ideal rooted in the right to privacy and the right to be educated in the capacity to be autonomous and critical thinkers—have been transformed and mutilated almost beyond recognition by the material and ideological registers of a worldwide neoliberal order. Just as we can envision Orwell's and Huxley's dystopian fables morphing over time from "realistic novels" into a "real-life documentary," and now into a form of "reality TV," privacy and freedom have been radically altered in an age of permanent, nonstop global exchange and circulation. That is, in the current moment, the right to privacy and freedom has been usurped by the seductions of a narcissistic culture and casino capitalism's unending desire to turn every relationship into an act of commerce and to make all aspects of daily life subject to market forces under watchful eyes of both government and corporate regimes of surveillance. In a world devoid of care, compassion, and protection, personal privacy and freedom are no longer connected and resuscitated through its connection to public life, the common good, or a vulnerability born of the recognition of the frailty of human life. Culture loses its power as the bearer of public memory, civic literacy, and the lessons of history in a social order in which the worst excesses of capitalism are left unchecked and a consumerist ethic "makes impossible any shared recognition of common interests or goals."[18] With the rise of the punishing state along with a kind of willful amnesia taking hold of the larger culture, we see little more than a paralyzing fear and apathy in response to the increasing exposure of formerly private spheres to data mining and manipulation, while the concept of privacy itself has all but expired under a "broad set of panoptic practices."[19] With individuals more or less succumbing to this insidious cultural shift in their daily lives, there is nothing to prevent widespread collective indifference to the growth of a surveillance culture, let alone an authoritarian state.

The worst fears of Huxley and Orwell merge into a dead zone of historical amnesia as more and more people embrace any and every new electronic device regardless of the risks it might pose in terms of granting corporations and governments increased access to and power over their choices and movements. Detailed personal information flows from the sphere of entertainment to the deadly serious and integrated spheres of capital accumulation and policing as they are collected and sold to business and government agencies who track the populace for either commercial purposes or for fear of a possible threat to the social order and its established institutions of power. Power now imprisons not only bodies under a regime of surveillance and a mass incarceration state but also subjectivity itself as the threat of state control is now coupled with the seductions of the new forms of passivity-inducing soma: electronic technologies, a pervasive commodified landscape, and a mind-numbing celebrity culture.

Underlying these everyday conveniences of modern life, as Boghosian documents in great detail, is the growing Orwellian partnership between the militarized state and private security companies in the United States. Each day, new evidence surfaces pointing to the emergence of a police state that has produced ever more sophisticated methods for surveillance in order to enforce a mass suppression of the most essential tools for democratic dissent: "the press, political activists, civil rights advocates and conscientious insiders who blow the whistle on corporate malfeasance and government abuse."[20] As Boghosian points out, "By claiming that anyone who questions authority or engages in undesired political speech is a potential terrorist threat, this government-corporate partnership makes a mockery of civil liberties."[21] Nowhere is this more evident than in American public schools, where youth are being taught that they are a generation of suspects, subject to the presence of armed police and security guards, drug-sniffing dogs, and an array of surveillance apparatuses that chart their every move—not to mention in some cases how they respond emotionally to certain pedagogical practices.

Whistleblowers are not only punished by the government: their lives are also turned upside down in the process by private surveillance agencies and major corporations, which now work in tandem. For instance, the Bank of America assembled fifteen to twenty bank officials and retained the law firm of Hunton and Williams in order to devise "various schemes to attack WikiLeaks and Greenwald whom they thought were about to release damaging information about the bank."[22] It is worth repeating that Orwell's vision of surveillance and the totalitarian state look mild next to the emergence of a corporate-private-state surveillance system that can tap into every conceivable mode of communication, collect endless amounts of metadata to be stored in vast intelligence storage sites around the country, and potentially use that data to repress any vestige of dissent.[23]

As Huxley anticipated, any critical analysis must move beyond documenting abuses of power to addressing how contemporary neoliberal modernity has created a social order in which individuals become complicit with authoritarian practices. That is, how is the loss of freedom internalized? What and how do state- and corporate-controlled institutions, cultural apparatuses, social relations, and policies contribute to making a society's plunge into self-generating dark times, as Huxley predicted? Put differently, what is the educative nature of a repressive politics, and how does it function to secure the consent of the American public? And, most important, how can it be challenged and under what circumstances?

The nature of repression has become more porous, employing not only brute force but also dominant modes of education, persuasion, and authority. Aided by a public pedagogy produced and circulated through a machinery of consumption and public relations tactics, a growing regime of repression works through the homogenizing forces of the market to support the widespread embrace of an authoritarian culture. Relentlessly entertained by spectacle, people not only become numb to violence and cruelty but also begin to identify with an authoritarian worldview. As David Graeber suggests, the police "become the almost obsessive objects of imaginative identification in popular culture . . . watching movies, or viewing TV shows that invite them to look at the world from a police point of view."[24] But it is not just the spectacle of violence that ushers individuals into a world in which brutality becomes a primary force for mediating relations as well as the ultimate source of pleasure; there is also the production of an unchecked notion of individualism that both dissolves social bonds and removes any viable notion of agency from the landscape of social responsibility and ethical consideration. Absorbed in privatized orbits of consumption, commodification, and display, Americans vicariously participate in the toxic pleasures of the authoritarian state. Violence has become the organizing force of a society driven by a noxious notion of privatization in which it becomes difficult for ideas to be lifted into the public realm. Under such circumstances, politics is eviscerated because it now supports a market-driven view of society that has turned its back on the idea that "humanity is never acquired in solitude."[25] This violence against the bonds of sociality undermines and dissolves the nature of social obligations as freedom becomes an exercise in self-development rather than social responsibility. This upending of the social and critical modes of agency mimics not just the death of the radical imagination but also a notion of banality made famous by Hannah Arendt, who argued that at the root of totalitarianism is a kind of thoughtlessness, an inability to think, and a type of outrageous indifference in which "there's simply the reluctance ever to imagine what the other person is experiencing."[26]

By integrating insights drawn from both Huxley and Orwell, it becomes necessary for any viable critical analysis to take a long view, contextualizing the contemporary moment as a new historical conjuncture in which political rule has been replaced by corporate sovereignty, consumerism becomes the only obligation of citizenship, and the only value that matters is exchange value. Precarity has replaced social protections provided by the state, just as the state cares more about building prisons and infantilizing the American public than it does about providing all of its citizens with quality educational institutions, health care, and other social rights. America is not just dancing into oblivion, as Huxley suggested; it is also being pushed into the dark recesses of an authoritarian state. Orwell wrote dystopian novels, but he believed that the sheer goodness of human nature would in the end be enough for individuals to develop modes of collective resistance that he could only imagine in the midst of the haunting specter of totalitarianism.

Huxley was more indebted to Kafka's notion of destabilization, despair, and hopelessness. For Huxley, the subject had lost a sense of agency and had become the product of a scientifically manufactured form of idiocy and conformity. Progress had been transformed into its opposite, and science needed to be liberated from itself. Where Huxley fails, as Theodor Adorno has pointed out, is that he has no sense of resistance. According to Adorno, "The weakness of Huxley's entire conception is that it makes all its concepts relentlessly dynamic but nevertheless arms them against the tendency to turn into their own opposites."[27] Hence, the forces of resistance are not simply underestimated but rendered impotent. The authoritarian nature of the corporate-state surveillance apparatus and security system, with its "urge to surveil, eavesdrop on, spy on, monitor, record, and save every communication of any sort on the planet,"[28] can be fully understood only when its ubiquitous tentacles are connected to wider cultures of control and punishment, including security-patrolled corridors of public schools, the rise in supermax prisons, the hypermilitarization of local police forces, the justification of secret prisons and state-sanctioned torture abroad, and the increasing labeling of dissent as an act of terrorism in the United States.[29] This is part of Orwell's narrative, but it does not go far enough.

The new authoritarian corporate-driven state deploys more subtle tactics to depoliticize public memory and promote the militarization of everyday life. Alongside efforts to defund public and higher education and to attack the welfare state, a wide-ranging assault is being waged across the culture on all spheres that encourage the public to hold power accountable. If these public institutions are destroyed, there will be few sites left in which to nurture the critical formative cultures capable of educating people to challenge the range of injustices plaguing the United States and the forces that reproduce them. One particular challenge comes from the success of neoliberal tyranny to dissolve those social bonds that entail a sense of responsibility toward others and form the basis for political consciousness. Under the new authoritarian state, perhaps the gravest threat one faces is not simply being subject to the dictates of what Quentin Skinner calls "arbitrary power," but failing to respond with outrage when "my liberty is also being violated, and not merely by the fact that someone is reading my emails but also by the fact that someone has the power to do so should they choose."[30] The situation is dire when people seem no longer interested in contesting such power. It is precisely the poisonous spread of a broad culture of political indifference that puts at risk the fundamental principles of justice and freedom that lie at the heart of a robust democracy. The democratic imagination has been transformed into a data machine that marshals its inhabitants into the neoliberal dreamworld of babbling consumers and armies of exploitative labor whose ultimate goal is to accumulate capital and initiate individuals into the brave new surveillance/punishing state that merges Orwell's Big Brother with Huxley's mind-altering soma.

Nothing will change unless people begin to take seriously the subjective underpinnings of oppression in the United States and what it might require to make such issues meaningful in order to make them critical and transformative. As Charles Derber has explained, knowing "how to express possibilities and convey them authentically and persuasively seems crucially important" if any viable notion of resistance is to take place.[31] The current regime of authoritarianism is reinforced through a new and pervasive sensibility in which people surrender themselves to both the capitalist system and a general belief in its call for security. It does not simply repress independent thought but constitutes new modes of thinking through a diverse set of cultural apparatuses ranging from the schools and media to the Internet. The fundamental question in resisting the transformation of the United States into a twenty-first-century authoritarian society must concern the educative nature of politics—that is, what people believe and how their individual and collective dispositions and capacities to be either willing or resistant agents are shaped.

What will American society look like in a hundred years? For Huxley, it may well mimic a nightmarish image of a world in which ignorance is a political weapon and pleasure a form of control, offering nothing more than the swindle of fulfillment, if not something more self-deluding and defeating. Orwell, more optimistically, might see a more open future and history disinclined to fulfill itself in the image of the dystopian society he so brilliantly imagined. He believed in the power of those living under such oppression to imagine otherwise, to think beyond the dictates of the authoritarian state and to offer up spirited forms of collective resistance, being willing to reclaim the reigns of political emancipation. For Huxley, there was hope in a pessimism that had exhausted itself; for Orwell optimism had to be tempered by a sense of educated hope. History is open and only time will tell who was right.

2
Thinking Dangerously in an Age
of Political Betrayal

<del>∽</del>

> Thinking is not the intellectual reproduction of what already exists anyway. As long as it doesn't break off, thinking has a secure hold on possibility. . . . Open thinking points beyond itself.
>
> —*Theodor Adorno*

> There are no dangerous thoughts for the simple reason that thinking itself is such a dangerous enterprise. . . . Nonthinking is even more dangerous.
>
> —*Hannah Arendt*

Thinking has become dangerous in the United States and the symptoms are everywhere. For instance, the 2012 Texas GOP party platform not only supported corporal punishment in schools but also stated: "We oppose teaching of Higher order Thinking Skills [because they] have the purpose of challenging the student's fixed beliefs and undermining parental control."[1] Similarly, the results of what might be called the push toward pedagogical ignorance and the assault on reason can also be found in a number of states including Tennessee, Arkansas, Florida, Georgia, and Indiana, which allow the teaching of creationism in their state's classrooms.[2] A glaring example of the pedagogy of ignorance and assault on critical thinking can be found in one Denver, Colorado, public school system. In August 2014 the newly elected conservative Jefferson Country school board called for revamping curriculum for the district's Advanced Placement history courses on the grounds that they were teaching acts of civil disobedience, which they labeled as unpatriotic.

As part of the newly revised curriculum, the board argued for course materials that would "promote citizenship, patriotism, essentials and benefits of the free-market system, respect for authority and respect for individual rights."[3] Julie Williams, one of the conservative board members behind the call for such revisions, provided a glimpse of the reactionary politics driving the attempted reforms. According to Williams, history is currently being taught with "an emphasis on race, gender, class, ethnicity grievance, and American-bashing while simultaneously omitting the most basic structure and philosophical elements considered essential to the understanding of American History for generations."[4] Essential in this case means a history that is cleansed of conflicts, politics, ideology, and struggle. At the same time the Texas State Board of Education made the motive for the attack on the teaching of AP US history even more obvious in passing a resolution stipulating that the curriculum be rewritten "in a transparent manner to accurately reflect U.S. history without a political bias."[5]

Political bias has become a right-wing code word for stripping knowledge of any critical content, taming intellectual inquiry, and imposing a pedagogy that turns schools into dead zones of the imagination. This is a depoliticized history stripped of historical consciousness and public memory, one that emphasizes the teaching of facts while justifying a deadening pedagogy of memorization. This is not just a pedagogy of ignorance whose hidden curriculum is the teaching of political and intellectual conformity, it is also an assault on the critical imagination and those historical struggles that have challenged social, economic, and racial injustices in the name of creating a more substantial democracy.

Celebrating ignorance has no place in American education, nor does the pedagogy of repression that reproduces it. Governance steeped in ignorance is, in part, related to the degree of civic and political illiteracy the larger public is all too willing to inhabit. And such illiteracy, with its dismantling of the possibility of critical thought, appears widespread and dangerously conducive to those antidemocratic formative cultures that breed ethically deprived monsters and a politics of savage authoritarianism. Leni Riefenstahl, the infamous and brilliant filmmaker who produced *Triumph of the Will* as a celebration of Hitler's Third Reich, stated in a conversation with John Pilger that her propaganda films were successful not only because they were supported by Hitler's government but also because of a "submissive void" among both the larger German population and intellectuals in general. In such societies, reform means submission, regression, conformity, and the depoliticization of language, history, and agency.[6] What the attack on dangerous thinking suggests, to paraphrase George Orwell, is that one does not have to live in an overtly totalitarian country to be corrupted by the formative culture that makes it possible.

The attacks on history, critical pedagogy, and dissent cited above indicate a merging of a naked stupidity, a manufactured ignorance, and an assault on critical thought, if not reason itself. There is nothing serendipitous about the cultivation and celebration of ignorance and civic literacy as the organizing principles of much of the corporate media and the discourse of corporate and ruling elites. For example, the Walton family, Bill and Melinda Gates, Silicon Valley optical entrepreneur David Welch, the Koch brothers, the Republican Party, and a host of other financial and corporate elites have a common interest in destroying public education, imposing a pedagogy of repression, replacing public schools with charter schools, destroying teachers' unions, and privatizing the education system. They are petrified of public schools that might promote critical thinking, unsettle the commonplace assumptions that students rely on, and encourage students to become active and engaged citizens. Such a pedagogy is considered both dangerous and a threat to those right-wing antireformers who want to turn schools into high-tech training centers while producing students who revel in conformity and obedience, and conveniently refuse to hold power accountable.[7]

But the dark money of the financial elite does not only produce manufactured ignorance; it also works hard to expand the reach of the surveillance state, suppress dissent, destroy academic freedom, and debase all forms of resistance aimed at embracing democratic relations, values, and policies.[8] Critical thought has not only become dangerous under casino capitalism and the long reach of religious fundamentalism in America, but it has been elevated to the equivalent of a major social evil. In Orwell's 1984, dissenters were disgraced because they allegedly betrayed Big Brother. While Orwell's depiction of a fascist future may appear too extreme to take seriously, the United States has entered a period in which student protesters are brutally attacked by the police, whistleblowers like Edward Snowden are defined as traitors, and critical journalists such as Glenn Greenwald, Chris Hedges, and Amy Goodman, along with public intellectuals such as Noam Chomsky and Cornell West, are discredited in the mainstream media through the use of jingoistic invective, personal condemnations, and ad hominem criticisms. As Sonali Kolhatkar observes: "Many of the tactics adopted by today's so-called objective journalists to keep dissenters ... in line are consistent with Orwell's dark fantasies. By discrediting those who speak out, it is possible to dismiss the substance of their criticisms. But, as Orwell famously wrote, 'in a time of universal deceit, telling the truth is a revolutionary act.'"[9]

Historically, there is a long tradition of punishing intellectuals, journalists, and activists who have questioned the practices of established power brokers, dominant economic policies, and US actions abroad. Of course, historical analysis and critical thinking after 9/11 became especially dangerous as state power was reconfigured in the interest of expanding state apparatuses of repression such as the Department of Homeland Security, intensified domestic surveillance by the NSA and other intelligence agencies, the passing of the USA Patriot Act, the Military Commissions Act, and the egregious National Defense Authorization Act, which allows the military to detain individuals for an indefinite period of time without recourse to legal defense or trial. Colleges and universities were viewed by many right-wingers as the weak link in the war against terrorism.[10] Hence it came as no surprise that professors who took up critical issues in their classrooms that unsettled and held accountable any commonsense assumption that questioned the Iraq War, the doctrine of permanent war, and the legal illegalities that emerged from the war on terrorism were condemned for teaching propaganda.

For instance, the former governor of Colorado called for the firing of Professor Ward Churchill because of an essay he wrote shortly after 9/11 in which he condemned US foreign policy. Additionally, former US congressman Anthony Weiner from New York called for the firing of Joseph Massad, a Columbia University professor who has been critical of Israeli policies against Palestinians. More recently, the trustees and chancellor at the University of Illinois at Urbana revoked a contract to hire Professor Steven Salaita because of some tweets he wrote criticizing the Israeli government for its bombing of Gaza.[11] Under the guise of patriotic correctness, conservatives successfully promoted a number of campaigns to fire prominent academics such as Massad, Churchill, and Salaita because of their opposition to both Israel's policies toward the Palestinians and the explicitly imperialist politics of US foreign policy, while completely ignoring the quality of their intellectual scholarship.[12] Such attacks also took place in the mainstream media. One example that stands out took place when *New York Times* columnist Thomas Friedman called upon the State Department to draw up a blacklist of those critics he calls "excuse makers," which included those who believe that US actions are at the root cause of violence. According to Friedman, "These excuse makers are just one notch less despicable than the terrorists and also deserve to be exposed."[13] This kind of McCarthyite babble had become so commonplace in the United States that it was championed by a famous columnist in the *New York Times,* one of the world's leading newspapers. Challenging the current conservative wisdom—that is, holding views at odds with official orthodoxy—has now become the grounds for being labeled un-American, dismissed from one's job, or put on a government blacklist. Malinda Smith commenting on the post-9/11 suppression of critical thinking, and echoing John Le Carre's observation that "we entered a new, Orwellian world," observes:

> In the moment after 9/11 it became both politically dangerous and intellectually unsafe to try to assess the broader historical and political meaning, however shape-shifting, of the terrorist attacks. Critical thinking about historical and contemporary forms of political violence and terrorism—or even the tactics and strategies of the Bush administration—became traitorous acts . . . . Critical thinking, alternative opinions, appeals to historical understanding became suspect. . . . Historical thinking and understanding, at least that which fell outside the official orthodoxy of 9/11 as unprecedented and the United States as exceptional, became criminal, subversive, unpatriotic, and even against Western civilization.[14]

What is often ignored in the reporting of such overt displays of repression and ignorance, especially since the 1980s, is that religious and ideological fundamentalism are at the root of a right-wing political movement to miseducate young people, keep the American public ignorant, and hasten a return to the Gilded Age. Just in case students disagree with this retreat into ignorance, one freshman Tea Party state representative in Arizona is pushing a loyalty oath bill in which "public high school students in Arizona will have to 'recite an oath supporting the U.S. Constitution' to receive a graduation diploma."[15] But ignorance is not simply a matter of pedagogy, willful stupidity, panic-stricken blindness, or the suppression of dissent; it also drives a great deal of state and federal policy. For example, the Koch brothers–financed American Legislative Exchange Council (ALEC), a corporate-funded lobby that aggressively attends to the interests of the financial elite and the corporate sector, "hit the ground running in 2013, pushing 'models bills' mandating the teaching of climate change denial in public school systems."[16] Under the appeal to balanced teaching, ALEC is pushing legislation in which evidence-based arguments provided by and published by scientists in academic journals is "balanced" by the insertion into public school curricula of the unscientific opinions of climate change deniers. At the same time, policy-makers at the state level define a return to the Dark Ages as progress. As John Atcheson observes:

> For example, North Carolina law-makers recently passed legislation against sea level rise. A day later, the Virginia legislature required that references to global warming, climate change and sea level rise be excised from a proposed study on sea level rise. Last year, the Texas Department of Environmental Quality, which had commissioned a study on Galveston Bay, cut all references to sea level rise— the main point of the study. We are, indeed, at an epochal threshold. As Stephen Colbert so aptly put it: if your science gives you results you don't like, pass a law saying that the result is illegal. Problem solved. Except it isn't. Wishing reality away, doesn't make it go away. Pretending that the unreal is real doesn't make it real.[17]

Bobby Jindal, the current governor of Louisiana, once warned his fellow Republican Party members to no obvious avail that they "must stop being the stupid party."[18] As Chomsky points out, right-wing extremists, financial elite, and corporate behemoths have taken over the machineries of state and federal government. They constitute not only the "stupid party" but are aggressive in their attempts to build a servile and stupid nation "in the interests of their short-term gain."[19] Chomsky writes:

> For those whom Adam Smith called the "Masters of Mankind," it is important that we must become the stupid nation in the interests of their short-term gain, damn the consequences. These are essential properties of contemporary market fundamentalist doctrines. ALEC and its corporate sponsors understand the

importance of ensuring that public education train children to belong to the stupid nation, and not be misled by science and rationality.[20]

Manufactured stupidity is never enough to suppress critical thinking, dissent, and organized resistance. It is always accompanied by state repression and the squelching of dissent. Hence, it is not surprising that the legacy of the suppression of dissent extending from the McCarthy era of the 1950s to the post-9/11 period of repression still haunts the United States, especially at a time when anti-intellectualism runs rampant throughout the mainstream media, celebrity culture, popular entertainment, and the political landscape. Moreover, the current war against reason, rationality, and the ethical and radical imagination do more than bear the traces of such historically informed repression. Ignorance, stupidity, thoughtlessness, and anti-intellectualism have become both dominant features of American politics and life and symptomatic of an embrace of anti-Enlightenment ideologies, the rise of a poisonous religious fundamentalism, and the emergence of a culture of conformity that have become the DNA of American politics and society.

Purging critical thought and public memory goes hand in hand with the suppression of dissent. And this is not an antidemocratic process limited to the United States. As Helen Gao points out, post-Tiananmen China has worked hard to create a neoliberal depoliticization of Chinese youth through a combination of political repression and by emphasizing through all state apparatuses that students focus on "their personal well-being, rather than the larger issues that bedevil the society."[21] Under such circumstances, public memory is cleansed of any protests, especially memories of the demonstrations at Tiananmen Square, as well as the purging of the activities of well-known dissenters such as Chen Guangcheng and Ai Weiwei, whose struggles against the Chinese government are well known. Goa believes that the ideological campaign coupled with the fear of state violence has produced a generation of young people who see "censorship more as a nuisance of daily life, something to be begrudgingly endured, rather than an infringement on their freedom of speech."[22] Moreover, she argues that this is a generation that cares more about graduating "from top Chinese universities and working at state banks and government-owned enterprises."[23]

Fred Inglis, writing about the conservative drive to impose a neoliberal model of education in the United Kingdom, cites David Browne, an advisor to David Cameron, as an example of the use of "lethally menacing" categories overloaded with what he calls a "military certainty" to disparage dissent among academics who, as he puts it, are "setting dangerous precedents."[24] Browne is worth quoting at length. He writes that many universities may

encounter high performing employees, who, although academically brilliant, have the potential to damage their employer's brand. This could be through outspoken opinion or general insubordination. Irrespective of how potentially valuable these employees may be to their institutions, the reality is that, in consistently accepting unacceptable behaviour, institutions may be setting dangerous precedents to other employees that such conduct will be accommodated. From a risk perspective, it is also much harder to justify a dismissal, or other sanction, if similar conduct has gone unpunished before.[25]

Inglis is certainly right in pointing to Browne's remarks as "blandly assured" in all of its "Miltonic repulsiveness."[26] Both the repression of critical thinking and its ghastly authoritarian consequences are on full display here and provide a signpost of those antidemocratic forces that unite China, the United Kingdom, and the United States, in spite of their ideological differences.

Intensifying the current anti-intellectualism in the United States and many other countries is the emergence of a digitized world that is at odds with contemplation, thoughtfulness, and the slowing down of time necessary to work through complex thoughts, reasoned analyses, and critical exchange. Silicon Valley has emerged as the model of the new heteropia with its "teenage dress codes ... its willingness to trade in realty for the miniature screen of the cell phone," and its notion of change that is as empty and lacks any vision beyond creating high-tech products that connect change to a frictionless world filled with an endless barrage of computer products.[27] In a 24/7 society that thrives on speed, sensation, and a general withdrawal from intimacy and long-term commitments, thoughtfulness, difficult knowledge, informed thinking, and the notion of the literate mind appear to have become tragic casualties. The new web technologies with their emphasis on velocity, efficiency, and the overabundance of data blur the lines between fact and opinion, news and entertainment. Moreover, they produce a glut of overstimulation and increasingly have to rely on "sensationalism and willful hyperbole to grab people's attention."[28] Gary Standing provides an astute analysis of the triumph of speed over contemplation in the new digital age. He writes:

> This digital living is damaging the long-term memory consolidation process that is the basis for what generations of humans have come to regard as intelligence, the capacity to reason through complex processes and to create new ideas and ways of imagining. . . . The digitised world has no respect for contemplation or reflection; it delivers instant stimulation and gratification, forcing the brain to give most attention to short-term decisions and reactions. . . . The literate mind—with its respect for the deliberative potential of "boredom," of time standing still, for reflective contemplation and a systematic linking of the past, present and an imagined future—is under threat from the constant bombardment of electronically prompted adrenalin rushes.[29]

But there is more at stake than the crisis of thinking; there is also the crisis of historical and political agency. Neoliberalism's emphasis on self-interest, privatization, and commodification plays a powerful pedagogical role in informing the anti-intellectual use of this new technology and the social media it embraces, which more often than not aggressively legitimates a politics born of an inward-looking obsession and a cynical reveling in the embrace of hopelessness. In such a world, adulthood becomes more difficult not simply to imagine but to inhabit. As A. O. Scott observes, this retreat from adult responsibility is largely part of a "strategy of evasion."[30] The idiocy of Hollywood cinema and celebrity culture makes this digression possible especially in an age, as Scott points out, in which "we devolve from Lenny Bruce to Adam Sandler, from 'Catch-22' to 'The Hangover,' from 'Goodbye, Columbus' to 'The Forty-Year-Old Virgin.'"[31] Scott is only partly right, since there is more going on here than a kind of manufactured infantilization of the culture; there is also the widespread use of the entertainment industry—from movies and reality TV to video games—to depoliticize young people by turning them into full-time consumers and digital device addicts, stripping them of any sense of critical agency and social responsibility.

Neoliberalism's culture of individual responsibility, self-help, self-interest, and inward-looking gaze, with its all-embracing affective, privatizing, and ideological spaces of consumption, has no interest in connecting private troubles to larger public issues or, for that matter, producing visions, hopes, and public spheres in which politics becomes both inspiring and energizing, offering up an ethical imagination that enables one to find a place in the world. Unfortunately, the strangulating economic conditions that young people now find themselves in make them all the more susceptible to neoliberalism's antipolitics. When coupled with an age of precarity and endless uncertainty in which young people have few decent jobs, are strangulated by debt, face a future of career-less jobs, and are isolated, young people have little room for politics because they are more concerned with trying to survive than with engaging in political struggles, or imagining a different future. Under such circumstances, thinking and informed action become more difficult and politics becomes eviscerated.

Accordingly, it seems imperative to remind ourselves once again of how important critical thought as a crucible for thinking analytically can be, both as a resource and as an indispensable tool of civic engagement. If critical thought, sometimes disparaged as theory, gets a bad name, it is not because it is inherently dogmatic, jargonistic, or rigidly specialized, but because it is often abused or because it becomes a tool of irrelevancy—a form of theoreticism in which theory becomes an end in itself. This abuse of critical thought appears to have a particularly strong hold in the humanities, especially among many graduate students in English departments who succumb to surrendering their own voices to class projects and dissertations filled with obtuse jargon associated with the most fashionable theorists of the moment. Such work is largely rewarded less for its originality than for the fact that it threatens no one.

What is sad about the issue of losing one's voice is that this loss is the first step in the triumph of formalism over substance. Endnotes become more important than content, ideas lose their grip on reality, and fashion becomes a rationale for discarding historical scholarship and the work of older (unfashionable) public intellectuals, such as C. W. Mills, Ellen Willis, Angela Davis, Paul Sweezy, Stanley Aronowitz, or even James Baldwin. Reflection no longer challenges the demands of common sense. Instead, it is mangled under a suffocating pastiche of borrowed quotations and gives way to "the incontestable demands of quiet acceptance."[32] The truth of an event is not open to public discussion or engaged scholarship. All that remains is the fog of jargon and the haze of political and moral indifference.

At the same time there are many students who find the esoteric language associated with dangerous thinking and critical thought to be too difficult to master or engage. The latter points to the fact that some theories may be useless because they are too impenetrable to decipher, or there are theories that support bad practices, such as high-stakes testing, creationism, faith-based evidence, the spanking of children, incarcerating children as adults, and other assumptions and policies that are equally poisonous. Stephen Pinker is not far from the truth in making a case for both clarity and the importance of producing critical knowledge. He writes:

> Fog comes easily to writers; it's the clarity that requires practice. The naïve realism and breezy conversation in classic style are deceptive, an artifice constructed through effort and skill. Exorcising the curse of knowledge is no easier. It requires more than just honing one's empathy for the generic reader. . . . Our indifference to how we share the fruits of our intellectual labors is a betrayal of our calling to enhance the spread of knowledge. In writing badly, we are wasting each other's time, sowing confusion and error, and turning our profession into a laughingstock.[33]

Theory is not inherently good or bad. Its meaning and efficacy are rooted in a politics of usefulness, accessibility, and whether it can be used resourcefully to articulate frameworks and tools that deepen the possibility of self-reflection, critical thought, and a sense of social responsibility. On the positive side, theory is crucial for finding better forms of knowledge, essential to understanding how contexts are made and remade, and indispensable for charting the relations between language, representations, everyday life, and the machineries of power and politics. But theory must avoid becoming a purely academic exercise reduced to academia and legitimized through an appeal to the devices of professionalism. At its best, theory not only takes a detour through everyday life but also provides the groundwork for understanding how reality is continually constructed, struggled over, and often transformed. Theory in this case is not just about how power is enacted but how those who hold the potential to wield power can better understand their own sense of individual and social agency. Theory at its best is not simply about privileged discourses but about the relationship between meaning and effect. The difficulty of theory is less a reason to dismiss it than to understand the pedagogical challenges it poses in getting students and others to think deeply and thoughtfully about the ideas, values, and social relations that shape their lives.

When theory is removed from broader social forces, it turns in on itself and becomes a form of theoreticism; and, no longer taking seriously the need to make something meaningful in order to make it critical, it sabotages its informative and liberating potential by becoming an end in itself. For instance, theory fails when it grasps the forces at work in the world but simply reproduces them as they are. When theory loses itself in its own performative unfolding and divorces itself from a sense of intervention driven by conscience, urgency, and a deep commitment to justice, it becomes hollow. Theory is also injurious when it is used to legitimate modes of inquiry and research that are bought out by corporations, the military, and other state and private institutions to validate dangerous products, policies, and social practices.

Theory has no guarantees, and like any other mode of thought it has to be problematized, critically engaged, and judged in terms of its interests, effects, and value as part of a broader enhancement of human agency and democratization. The claim that theory is more important than practice or that practice has no need of theory reproduces a binary that is as false as it is politically useless. The call to activism as a marker of identity, especially when it disdains theory and reduces all politics to a kind of crude, unthinking instrumentalism, is as poisonous as modes of theorizing that collapse into a firewall of jargon and distance from the world. There is a great deal of this kind of crude politics on the left.[34] Theory and practice mutually inform each other and are mutually determining, though privileging one over the other cancels out that ever-present dialectic.

Theory never has to compromise itself to be accessible. On the contrary, theorists simply need to learn how to elevate their ideas into the public realm and, in doing so, need to discover how to address multiple audiences in ways that invite learning, reflection, and dialogue rather than cancel them out. The notion that theory is by default obscure, arcane, and obtuse to the point of utter unintelligibility is highly exaggerated, and an easy fallback position for those who could care less about the pedagogical principles at work in adjusting theory to the context in which it intervenes.

At its best, theory, thinking dangerously, and critical thought have the power to shift the questions, provide the tools for offering historical and relational contexts, and "push at the frontiers ... of the human imagination."[35] Stuart Hall is right in insisting that theory is crucial "to change the scale of magnification. . . . to break into the confusing fabric that 'the real' apparently presents, and find another way in. So it's like a microscope and until you look at the evidence through the microscope, you can't see the hidden relations."[36] In this instance, theory functions as a critical resource when it can intervene in the "continuity of commonsense, unsettle strategies of domination," and work to promote strategies of transformation.[37] As Adorno observes, "Theory speaks for what is not narrow-minded—and commonsense most certainly is."[38] As such, theory is not only analytical in its search for understanding and truth, it is also critical and subversive, always employing modes of self and social critique necessary to examine its own grounds and those poisonous fundamentalisms in the larger society haunting the body politic. As Michael Payne observes, theory should be cast in the language of hints, dialogue, and an openness to other positions, rather than be "cast in the language of orders."[39]

It is important to note that defending critical thought, thinking dangerously, and theory is not the same as solely mounting a defense of academics as public intellectuals or the university as the only site of critical thought, though both are important. When defined this way, theory is easily dismissed as an academic exercise and practice mediated through an impenetrable and often incomprehensible vocabulary. Theory and the frameworks it supports are just one important political register that keeps alive the notion that critical reflection and thought are necessary not only to address the diverse symbolic and material realities of power but also for engaging in informed action willing to address important social issues. In this respect, as Lawrence Grossberg has brilliantly argued, theory is a crucial tool that enables one to respond to and provide a better understanding of problems as they emerge in a variety of historical and distinctive contexts.[40] Hence, theory becomes a toolbox that guides the work of many artists, journalists, and other cultural workers in a variety of public spheres who are well aware that their work has consequences when translated into daily life and must be the object of self-reflection.[41] Paraphrasing Grossberg, theory is not about simply the production of meaning but also the making of effects. At the same time, critical thought functions to "lift ... human beings above the evidence of our senses and sets appearances apart from the truth."[42] Salmon Rushdie gestures toward the political necessity of critical thought, informed action, and its effects by insisting: "It's a vexing time for those of us who believe in the right of artists, intellectuals and ordinary, affronted citizens to push boundaries and take risks and so, at times, to change the way we see the world."[43] As Hannah Arendt noted, thoughtfulness, the ability to think reflectively and critically, is a fundamental necessity in a functioning democracy. And the formative cultures that make such thinking possible along with the spaces in which dialogue, debate, and dissent can flourish are essential to producing critically literate and actively engaged citizens. This is especially true at a time when, as Jonathan Crary points out,

"Mechanisms of command and effects of normalization [have] penetrated almost everywhere," and they have become "internalized in a more comprehensive, micrological way than the disciplinary power of the nineteenth and much of the twentieth century."[44] Evidence of this neoliberal disdain for critical reflection was recently reported in the *New York Times* under the byline "No Time to Think."[45] According to Kate Murphy, a study conducted by the University of Virginia reported that a majority of participants in the investigation found it so unpleasant to be alone in a room with their thoughts for more than six to fifteen minutes that they "began self-administrating electric shocks when left alone to think." In this case, thinking is not only viewed as a drain on one's time, but is so painful as to promote a form of self-destructiveness. There is more at work here than what might be called the atrophy of critical thought, self-reflection, and theory; there is also the degeneration of agency itself.

Theory is at its weakest and most oppressive when it supports a common-sense understanding of the framing mechanisms that guide the actions of human beings. One consequence is that it disavows dialogue and critique, and shapes knowledge and ideas into fixed and absolute meanings. It also shuts down analysis and poisons the culture with an orthodoxy that limits critical agency to following the orders of others. As such, it is transformed into a pedagogical parasite on the body of democracy. This is quite different than a call for theory and critical thought that practice rigorous analytic work enabling students, intellectuals, artists, and journalists to be attentive to how they function as individual and social agents. Bad theory is also at fault for failing to address and engage the layered and complex social, political, economic, and cultural forces that not only shape our desires, values, and modes of identification but also guide and direct the commanding ideologies and institutions of society. As a form of intellectual inquiry, theory thrives in those public spaces that both legitimate the world of ideas and refuse to separate them from addressing the major troubles of our time. At the same time, it is an important register, if not reminder in such perilous times, for determining, as Judith Butler observes, "not only the question of whether certain kinds of ideas and positions can be permitted in public space, but how public space is itself defined by certain kinds of exclusions, certain emerging patterns of censoriousness and censorship."[46]

Rather than being a mechanistic enterprise, offering formulas and recipes, theory should provide the frameworks and tools for what it means to be a thoughtful, judicious, layered, complex, and critical thinker willing to engage in communicative and collective action. Theory does not resemble the discourse of blind action, a stripped-down instrumental rationality, or the vision of accountants. Nor, in this instance, does theory become an end in itself, an ossified discourse that defines itself to the degree to which it removes itself from the world and vanishes in a black hole of irrelevancy and opaqueness. Theory as a critical enterprise is about both a search for the truth and a commitment to the practice of freedom. Not one or the other but both. Theory should be used both to understand and engage the major upheavals people face and to connect such problems to larger political, structural, and economic issues. In addition, theory is invaluable as a response to particular problems, allowing intellectuals, artists, academics, students, and others to connect their intellectual work and critical inquiries to the daily realities and struggles of a world in upheaval, one that is moving quickly into the clutches of a new type of authoritarianism.

America has moved a great distance away from the critical theories of thinkers such as Sigmund Freud, Jacques Derrida, Theodor Adorno, Edward Said, Herbert Marcuse, Leo Lowenthal, Ellen Willis, and Simone de Beauvoir. At the current historical moment, critical thinking is utterly devalued, viewed either as a nostalgic leftover of the weighty ideological and political battles that characterized the period roughly extending from the 1960s to the late 1980s, or theory is dismissed as the province of overly privileged and pampered academics.[47] Critical ideas and concepts in support of equality, justice, freedom, and democracy, in particular, have lost their material and political grounding and have become sound bites, either scorned by mainstream politicians or appropriated only to be turned into their opposite. Unfortunately for the promise of democracy, those who advocate theory and critical thought in the service of civic courage, engaged citizenship, and social responsibility are now viewed as eggheads, elitists, or traitors. In this instance, theory is disdained and used as a form of self-sabotage, reduced to politically illiterate narratives couched in the discourse of critical thinking. How else to explain the disingenuous portrayal in the mainstream press of George Will, Thomas Friedman, and David Brooks as public intellectuals, despite the fact that they trade in a kind of ersatz theory? In the latter case, theory becomes a weapon used to empty language of any meaning, employed primarily to make war on the possibility of real communication, all the while reinforcing the ideology of demagogues.

If theory once inspired critical practice both in and out of the university, it seems that the heyday of critically informed thinking is over. As higher education has become corporatized, teaching and learning are increasingly defined through the metrics of commerce and profit, while students are viewed largely as consumers. Critical thought and dangerous thinking are now viewed as beyond the pale of market considerations, and thereby seen as having little value. This is particularly true since the radical right has not only taken seriously the notion that pedagogy and changing consciousness are the essence of politics but also developed cultural apparatuses outside of the university that function as powerful forms of public pedagogy in promoting the values of a number of fundamentalisms—including religious, educational, and market-driven ideologies. Culture for the right-wing has always been a crucial site of power in the modern world, and they have used this machinery of public pedagogy to create market-addicted subjects who appear hopelessly captive to the illiterate ideologies and slogans pumped out of Fox News, right-wing talk radio, and the editorial section of the *Wall Street Journal*. Ideas matter in this instance, but not in the service of freedom or justice.

Sound bites now pass for erudite commentary and merge with the banality of celebrity culture, which produces its own self-serving illiteracy and cult of privatization and consumerism. Moreover, as the power of communication and language wanes, collapsing into the seepage of hateful discourses, the eager cheerleaders of casino capitalism along with the ever-present antipublic intellectuals dominate the airwaves and screen culture in order to aggressively wage a war against all public institutions, youth, women, immigrants, unions, poor minorities, the homeless, gays, workers, the unemployed, poor children, and others. In this instance, thinking degenerates into forms of ideological boosterism, and the crucial potential of thinking to serve as a dynamic resource disappears from the American cultural and academic landscapes. When thinking itself becomes dangerous, society loses its ability to question itself and paves the way for authoritarian regimes of power.

The success of conservatives in colonizing, if not undermining, any model of critical reflection often takes place by reducing thought to a matter of common sense while supporting rampant forms of anti-intellectualism—most evident in the Republican Party's recent war on evidence-based arguments, science, and reason itself. At the same time, the success on the part of right-wing ideologues, conservative foundations, and antipublic intellectuals to shape domestic and foreign policy and gain the support of most Americans for doing so speaks to a roundly successful pedagogical and political strategy to manipulate public opinion while legitimating the rise of an authoritarian state. At the least, this war on reason and politics raises serious questions about the failure of the academy to counter such views. In particular, it raises questions about the alienating nature of what passes for critical thought, theory, and informed commentary in the academy. Moreover, the issue here is not whether intellectuals can use theory to solve the myriad problems facing the United States and the larger world, but what role critical thought plays in various sites in developing the formative culture that produces critical modes of agency and makes democracy possible. What must be remembered is that totalitarianism destroys those zones of memory and experience that offer up alternative views of the world and the struggles that accompany them, and participates fully in what Cornelius Castoriadis called "the shameful degradation of the critical function."[48]

The assault on critical thought is taking place in a variety of spheres, including higher education, especially at a time when corporatism, a mad empiricism, and market-driven ideologies are the dominant forces at work in defining what counts as labor, research, pedagogy, journalism, and learning. The notion that thinking dangerously produces forms of literacy in which knowledge is related to issues of agency, public values, and social problems is quickly disappearing from higher education and other sites. For example: Republican governors in states such as Texas, Maine, and Florida are defunding those fields of study in higher education that cannot be measured in economic terms, while redefining the mission of the university as merely an adjunct of corporations, the military-industrial complex, and government intelligence agencies.

Unfortunately, higher education houses an increasing number of intellectuals who have slipped into diverse forms of unprincipled careerism in which matters of critical thought have less to do with politics and power, or social justice for that matter, than with a kind of arcane cleverness—a sort of ineffectual performance that allows them to threaten no one. This probably sounds harsh, but personally I have seen this trend growing since the 1980s and actually believe that it has a lot do with the cultural capital and investment in careerism that many academics now bring to the academy and to their roles as intellectuals—partly a response to the corporatization of the university. These are middle- and ruling-class intellectuals on the move, always looking for new opportunities, all too willing to be quiet, safe, and ready and eager for the next promotion. In addition, too many academics are giving in to the seductions and rewards of corporate power, and are complicit in destroying theory and critical thought as tools that enable faculty and students to relate the self to others, public values, and the demands of a robust democracy. Of course, what often happens in this case is that by not having any viable vision or sense of the political, for that matter, such academics do an incredible injustice to their roles as potential public intellectuals and to critical thought itself. As Larry Grossberg once put it, they are clueless in taking up the challenge of theorizing the political and politicizing theory.

What is troubling about this state of affairs is that theorizing the politics of the twenty-first century may be the most important challenge facing the academy and any other public sphere committed to critical thinking, thoughtfulness, dialogue, and the radical imagination. If we lose control of those spheres that cultivate the knowledge and skills necessary for rigorous analysis, along with a culture of questioning, it will become more and more difficult for students and others to question authority, challenge common-sense assumptions, and hold power accountable. Thinking, theory, and ideas become critical and transformative when they become meaningful and have some purchase on peoples' lives. They also play a powerful role in shaping the formative cultures necessary to keep the spirit of democracy alive in a society. Theory or general frameworks of thought are always at work in what we say and practice. The question is whether we are aware of them, and whether they constitute a hidden dimension of thought or function as critically engaged frameworks. But the so-called abuse of theory and critical thought in the academy is not simply the fault of errant professionalism and careerism. Defining theory and dangerous thinking as part of a critical pedagogy and emancipatory project becomes increasingly difficult for part-time faculty and those not on the tenure line who are harnessed with the increased pressures posed by the corporate university coupled with the market-driven production of an ongoing culture of uncertainty, insecurity, and fear that makes the black hole of despair more paralyzing and crippling.

Killing the imagination and the quest for truth is not too difficult when faculty are struggling to survive the tasks of teaching too many courses, receiving poverty wages for their teaching, laboring under savage debts, and excluded from the power relations that govern their time. Under such circumstances, time becomes a burden rather than a luxury to be used to enable one to be self-reflective, thoughtful, and capable of critically examining the assumptions and institutions that shape our lives. Of course, at the same time, there are still a number of public intellectuals—including Cornell West, Stanley Aronowitz, Gayatri Spivak, and Dorothy Roberts—who use theory to address a range of social problems both in- and outside of the university, including issues such as right-wing fundamentalism, the attack on the welfare state, racism in America, and a host of other issues. Moreover, there has been a resurgence of public intellectuals in- and outside the academy who are refiguring the role of dangerous thinking as critical and central pedagogical elements in fashioning a new language for politics, one that begins with the question of what a democracy should look like and in whose interests it should operate. Such intellectuals refuse the notion that any appeal to theory automatically makes them suspect. All of these intellectuals accept the notion that thinking becomes critical when it "brings theory into the focus of analysis by refusing to accept its authority without proof, by making visible the grounds on which authority is claimed to be revealed, and, eventually, by questioning those grounds . . . . Theory is an activity rather than a body of knowledge ... in that it produces practices" and refuses to be satisfied with the world as it is.[49]

On the other side, the diatribes against theory and dangerous thinking by the press, media, and so forth can be construed as a kind of resentment, the product of a turf war, a defense of neoliberal fundamentalism, or an expression of ignorance and anti-intellectualism in the service of power. Of course, it is all these and more, but I think that one important issue highlighted by Bob McChesney and others lies in the corporatizing of the media and its ongoing refusal to address important problems with intellectual rigor and theoretical depth—not to mention any simple honesty (Fox being the most obvious and horrible example).[50] The dominant media have become lap dogs to corporate power, serving largely as a source of entertainment, hate, and militarism, all provided in ways that resemble barking commands. Public spaces are simply being eaten up and turned into offshoots of what Fox News and right-wing talk hate radio have become—toxic advertisements for various elements of right-wing and fundamentalist discourses.

Of course, there are alternative public spheres, and one should never underestimate the power of resistance, even in times such as ours, but the colonizing of alternative views, ideas, and knowledge available to people constitutes not only a crisis of theory and critical thought but also a crisis of pedagogy and democracy itself. This is not new, but it has become more intensified and dangerous. In the current historical conjuncture, serious questions have to be raised about what role artists, intellectuals, journalists, writers, and other cultural workers might play in challenging the authoritarian state while deepening and expanding the process of democratization. One answer might be found in the important work of people such as Edward Said, Pierre Bourdieu, Arundhati Roy, Noam Chomsky, Cornel West, Naomi Klein, Stanley Aronowitz, and Bill Mckibben, who have provided important work in this regard.

One important function of dangerous thinking is that it foregrounds the responsibility of artists, intellectuals, academics, and others who use it. Mapping the full range of how power is used and how it can be made accountable represents a productive pedagogical and political use of theory. Theorizing the political, economic, and cultural landscapes is central to any form of political activism and suggests that theory is like oxygen. That is: a valuable resource that one has to become conscious of in order to realize how necessary it is. Where we should take pause is when academic culture uses critical thought in the service of ideological purity and, in doing so, transforms pedagogy into forms of poisonous indoctrination for students. Critical thought in this case ossifies from a practice to a form of political dogmatism. The cheerleaders for casino capitalism disdain critical theory and thought because they contain the possibility of politicizing everyday life and exposing those savage market-driven ideologies, practices, and social relations that hide behind an appeal to common sense. Both the fetishism of thinking and its dismissal are part of the same coin—the overall refusal to link conception and practice, agency and intervention, all aggravated by neoliberalism's hatred of all things critical, social, and public.

While there is more than enough evidence to distrust the appeal to democracy, especially in light of how the term is utterly debased at all levels of mainstream politics and in the culture in general, I think it is a term with a long legacy of struggle and needs to be reclaimed and fought over rather than abandoned. Derrida is particularly instructive in his insistence on distinguishing between the reality and promise of democracy—a distinction that points to democracy as a signpost that anticipates something better and in so doing offers a political and moral referent to think and act otherwise. I also think that the left and liberals have lost sight of the power of "democracy" as a term that can bring together a variety of diverse struggles, thus providing a referent for moving beyond particularized struggles while not abandoning them.

As part of an appeal to radical democracy, I think it is crucial for educators and other cultural workers to find ways to talk about the social contract as a means of invoking what John Rawls once called "the infrastructure of justice," while affirming freedom as a constitutive part of the social, rather than in opposition to the social. Young people have raised serious questions about what a democracy looks like and whom it might serve. Critically interrogating the meaning, reality, misappropriation, and promise of democracy, along with the necessary agents to have it come into fruition, is an important political task.

The right-wing in its various guises has so devalued any democratic notion of the social and critical thought that it has become difficult to think in terms outside the survival-of-the-fittest ethic and culture of malice that now dominates reality TV, the bullies who set policy in Washington, and the sycophants who are media cheerleaders for Obama, the bankers, and corporate America. Fortunately, we have a number of brave souls in and out of the academy who refuse to give up the language of democracy—from Harvey Kay and Chris Hedges to the indomitable and courageous Bill Moyers.

Needless to say, ideas without institutions in which they can be nurtured tend to fall to the margins of society. That is all the more reason to defend public and higher education and all of those public spheres where democratic ideas, values, and practices are taken seriously, and intellectual rigor becomes the norm rather than a side show. Think of the informed critical writing and interviews one can find in Truthout, Salon, CounterPunch, Monthly Review Zine, Democracy Now, TomDispatch.com, and a range of other online sites that refuse prescriptions and barking commands. These are the new cultural apparatuses of freedom for the twenty-first century, and they need to be defended in the name of dangerous forms of thinking that are self-reflective, infused with democratic values, and expand the public good.

Critical thought and thinking dangerously are not just about reading texts and screen culture closely, or for that matter using abstract models of language to explain the arc of history, politics, and human behavior. They are also about the frameworks we develop in terms of how we deal with power, treat one another, and develop a sense of compassion for others and the planet. I was so taken a few years ago by a similar sentiment reflected in a story that Jürgen Habermas told about being at Herbert Marcuse's side as he was dying, and being moved by Marcuse's last few words: "I know wherein our most basic value judgments are rooted—in compassion, in our sense of the suffering of others."[51] While it makes little sense to be trapped in a kind of ossified intellectual rigor, there is no excuse to believe that action uninformed by theory is anything but an expression of thoughtlessness.

We live in an era when conservatives and the financial elite collapse public concerns into private interests, define people largely as consumers, and consider everyone as potential terrorists. Moreover, the apostles of neoliberal capitalism militarize and commodify the entire society, consider youth as nothing more than a source of profit, define education as training, undermine the welfare state in favor of a warfare state, and define democracy as synonymous with the language of capital. We live in a period that the late Gil Scott-Herron once called "winter in America." As the forces of authoritarianism sweep over every major institution in America, the time for widespread resistance and radical democratic change has never been so urgent. We are beginning to see glimpses of such struggles in the resurgence of the Occupy Movement and the massive street demonstrations protesting the killing of African Americans such as Eric Garner and Tamir Rice. Such change will not come unless the call for political and economic change is matched by a change in subjectivity, consciousness, and the desire for a better world. This is, in part, a theoretical challenge and supports individual and collective efforts to reconfiguring those public spheres where theory can emerge and be refined into modes of critique, understanding, and collective action. As a mode of resistance, dangerous thinking is the basis for a formative and pedagogical culture of questioning and politics that takes seriously how knowledge can become central to the practice of freedom, justice, and democratic change. At a time of lowered expectations, thinking dangerously raises the bar and points to making the impossible, once again, all the more possible.

3
Data Storms and the Tyranny of Manufactured Forgetting

꩜

For in the world in which we live it is no longer merely a question of the decay of collective memory and declining consciousness of the past, but of the aggressive [assault on] whatever memory remains, the deliberate distortion of the historical record, the invention of mythological pasts in the service of the powers of darkness.

—Yose Hayim Yerushalmi[1]

All reification is forgetting.

—Herbert Marcuse[2]

The current mainstream debate regarding the crisis in Iraq and Syria offers a near-perfect example of both the death of historical memory and the collapse of critical thinking in the United States. It also signifies the emergence of a profoundly antidemocratic culture and discourse of manufactured ignorance, cruelty, and social indifference. Surely, historical memory is under assault when the dominant media give airtime to the incessant war-mongering of politicians such as John McCain and Lindsay Graham and retro pundits such as Bill Kristol, Douglas Feith, Condoleezza Rice, and Paul Wolfowitz—not one of whom has any credibility, given how they have worked to legitimate the unremitting web of lies and deceit that provided cover for the disastrous US invasion of Iraq under the Bush/Cheney administration.

History repeats itself in the recent resurgence of calls for US military interventions in Syria and Iraq. And such repetitions of history undoubtedly shift from tragedy to farce as former vice president Dick Cheney once again becomes a leading pundit calling for military solutions to the current crises in the Middle East, in spite of his established reputation for hypocrisy, lies, corporate cronyism, defending torture, and abysmal policy-making under the Bush administration. The resurrection of Dick Cheney, the Darth Vader of the twenty-first century, as a legitimate source on the current crisis in Syria and Iraq is a truly monumental display of historical amnesia and moral dissipation.[3] As Thom Hartmann observes, Cheney bears a large responsibility for the Iraq War, which "was the single biggest foreign policy disaster in recent—or maybe even all—of American history. It cost the country around $4 trillion, killed hundreds of thousands of innocent civilians, left 4,500 Americans dead, and turned what was once one of the more developed countries in the Arab World into a slaughterhouse."[4] What room is there for historical memory in an age "when the twin presiding deities are irony and violence"?[5]

Missing from the commentaries by the mainstream media regarding the current situation in Iraq is any historical context that would offer a critical account of the disorder plaguing the Middle East. A resurrection of historical memory in this moment could provide important lessons regarding the present crisis. What is clear in this case is that a widespread avoidance of the past has become not only a sign of the appalling lack of historical knowledge in contemporary American culture but also a deliberate political weapon used by the powerful to keep people passive and blind to the truth. Of course, there are many factors currently contributing to this production of ignorance and the lobotomizing of individual and collective agency.

Such factors extend from the idiocy of celebrity and popular culture and the dumbing down of American schools to the transformation of the mainstream media into a deadly mix of propaganda and entertainment. The latter is particularly crucial as the collapse of journalistic standards that could inform the onslaught of information finds its counterpart in a government wedded to state secrecy and the aggressive prosecution of whistleblowers,[6] the expanding use of state secrecy, the corruption of political language,[7] the disregard for truth, all of which have contributed to a growing culture of political and civic illiteracy.[8] The knowledge and value deficits that produce such detrimental forms of ignorance not only crush the critical and ethical imagination, critical modes of social interaction, and political dissent, but also destroy those public spheres and spaces that promote thoughtfulness, thinking, and critical dialogue, and serve as "guardians of truths as facts," as Hannah Arendt once put it.[9]

The blight of rampant consumerism, unregulated finance capital, and weakened communal bonds is directly related to the culture's production of atomized, isolated, and utterly privatized individuals who have lost sight of the fact that "humanity is never acquired in solitude."[10] Under the reign of neoliberalism, space, time, and even language have been subject to the forces of privatization and commodification. Public space has been replaced by malls and a host of commercial institutions. Commodified and privatized, public space is now regulated through exchange values rather than public values, just as communal values are replaced by atomizing and survival-of-the-fittest market values. Time is no longer connected to long-term investments, the development of social capital, and goals that benefit young people and the public good. On the contrary, time is now connected to short-term investments and quick financial gains. More broadly, time is now defined by "the non-stop operation of global exchange and circulation,"[11] and the frenetic reproduction and perpetuation of an impoverished celebrity and consumer culture that both depoliticizes people and narrows their potential for critical thought, agency, and social relations to an investment in shopping and other market-related activities.

As I mentioned in Chapter 1, in the age of casino capitalism, time itself has become a burden more than a condition for contemplation, self-reflection, and the cultivation of thoughtful and compassionate social relations. The extended arc of temporal relations in which one could imagine long-term investments in the common good has given way to a notion of time in which the horizon of time is contained within the fluctuating short-term investments of the financial elite and their militant drive for profits at any price. What is lost in this merging of time and the dictates of neoliberal capital are the most basic elements of being human, along with the formative culture and institutions necessary to develop a real, substantive democracy. As Christian Marazzi observes:

> Taking time means giving each other the means of inventing one's future, freeing it from the anxiety of immediate profit. It means caring for oneself and the environment in which one lives, it means growing up in a socially responsible way. [Taking time means] questioning the meaning of consumption, production, and investment [so as to not] reproduce the preconditions of financial capitalism, the violence of its ups and downs, the philosophy according to which "time is everything, man is nothing." For man [*sic*] to be everything, we need to reclaim the time of his existence.[12]

Death and disposability are the new signposts of a society in which historical memory is diminished and ethical evaluations become derided as figments of a liberal past. Dispossession and depoliticization are central to the discourse of neoliberalism, in which language is central to molding identities, desires, values, and social relationships. As Doreen Massey observes, under neoliberalism the public is urged to become consumers, customers, and highly competitive, while being taught that the only interests that matter are individual interests, almost always measured by monetary considerations.[13] Under such circumstances, social and communal bonds have been shredded, important modes of solidarity attacked, and a neoliberal war machine has been waged against any institution that embraces the values, practices, and social relations endemic to a democracy.

This retreat into private silos has resulted in the inability of individuals to connect their personal suffering with larger public issues. Thus detached from any concept of the common good or viable vestige of the public realm, they are left to face alone a world of increasing precarity and uncertainty in which it becomes difficult to imagine anything other than how to survive. Under such circumstances, there is little room for thinking critically and acting collectively in ways that are imaginative and courageous.

Surely, the celebration and widespread prevalence of ignorance in American culture does more than merely testify "to human backwardness or stupidity"; it also "indicates human weakness and the fear that it is unbearably difficult to live beset by continuous doubts."[14] Yet, what is often missed in analysis of political and civic illiteracy as the new normal is the degree to which these new forms of illiteracy not only result in an unconscious flight from politics but also produce a moral coma that supports modern systems of terror and authoritarianism. Civic illiteracy is about more than the glorification and manufacture of ignorance on an individual scale: it is producing a nationwide crisis of agency, memory, and thinking itself.

How else to explain, for instance, a major national newspaper's willingness to provide a platform for views that express an unchecked hatred of women—as when the *Washington Post* published George Will's column in which he states that being a rape victim is now "a coveted status that confers privileges"?[15] Will goes on to say that accusations of rape and sexual violence are not only overblown, but that many women who claim they were raped are "delusional."[16] There is a particular type of aggressive ignorance here that constitutes a symbolic assault on women, while obscuring the underlying conditions that legitimate sexual violence in the United States. Will expresses more concern over what he calls the "pesky arithmetic,"[17] used to determine the percentage of women actually raped on campuses, than the ever-increasing incidence of sexual assaults on women in colleges, the military, and a wide variety of other private and public spheres. Ignoring a slew of evidence about the increasing amount of sexual violence on campuses and reports indicating that most colleges are "ill prepared to evaluate an allegation so serious that, if proved in a court of law, would be a felony, with a likely prison sentence," Will conceals his ignorance and moral irresponsibility in the mantle of a suffocating indignation.[18]

The clueless George Will, evidently angry about the growing number of women who are reporting the violence waged against them, draws on the persuasive utility of mathematical data as a way to bolster a shockingly misogynist argument and flee from any sense of social and moral responsibility. While such expressions of resentment make Will appear as an antediluvian, privileged white man who is truly delusional, he is typical of an expanding mass of pundits who live in a historical void and for whom emotion overtakes reason. Increasingly, it appears that the American media no longer require that words bear any relationship to truth or to a larger purpose other than peddling rigid and archaic ideologies designed to shock and stupefy audiences.

Clearly, the attack on reason, evidence, science, and critical thought has reached perilous proportions in the United States. A number of political, economic, social, and technological forces now work to distort reality and keep people passive, unthinking, and unable to act in a critically engaged manner. Politicians, right-wing pundits, and large swaths of the American public embrace positions that support creationism, capital punishment, torture, and the denial of human-engineered climate change, any one of which not only defies human reason but stands in stark opposition to evidence-based scientific arguments. Reason now collapses into opinion, as thinking itself appears to be both dangerous and antithetical to understanding ourselves, our relations to others, and the larger state of world affairs. Under such circumstances literacy disappears, not just as the practice of learning skills but also as the foundation for taking informed action. Divorced from any sense of critical understanding and agency, the meaning of literacy is narrowed to completing basic reading, writing, and numeracy tasks assigned in schools. Literacy education is similarly reduced to strictly methodological considerations and standardized assessment, rooted in test taking and deadening forms of memorization, and becomes far removed from forms of literacy that would impart an ability to raise questions about historical and social contexts.

Literacy, in a critical sense, should always ask what it might mean to use knowledge and theory as a resource to address social problems and events in ways that are meaningful and expand democratic relations. I have commented on the decline of critical literacy elsewhere, and it is worth repeating:

> I don't mean illiterate in the sense of not being able to read, though we have far too many people who are functionally illiterate in a so-called advanced democracy, a point that writers such as Chris Hedges, Susan Jacoby, and the late Richard Hofstadter made clear in their informative books on the rise of anti-intellectualism in American life. I am talking about a different species of ignorance and anti-intellectualism. It is a form of illiteracy that points less to the lack of technical skills and the absence of certain competencies than to a deficit in the realms of politics—one that subverts both critical thinking and the notion of literacy as both critical interpretation and the possibility of intervention in the world. This type of illiteracy is not only incapable of dealing with complex and contested questions; it is also an excuse for glorifying the principle of self-interest as a paradigm for understanding politics. This is a form of illiteracy marked by the inability to see outside of the realm of the privatized self, an illiteracy

in which the act of translation withers, reduced to a relic of another age. The United States is a country that is increasingly defined by [an educational] deficit, a chronic and deadly form of civic illiteracy that points to the failure of both its educational system and the growing ability of anti-democratic forces to use the educational force of the culture to promote the new illiteracy. As this widespread illiteracy has come to dominate American culture, we have moved from a culture of questioning to a culture of shouting and in doing so have restaged politics and power in both unproductive and anti-democratic ways.[19]

Needless to say, as John Pilger has pointed out, what is at work in the death of literacy and the promotion of ignorance as a civic virtue is a "confidence trick" in which "the powerful would like us to believe that we live in an eternal present in which reflection is limited to Facebook, and historical narrative is the preserve of Hollywood."[20] Among the "materialized shocks" of the ever-present spectacles of violence, the expanding states of precarity, and the production of the atomized, repressed, and disconnected individual, narcissism reigns supreme. "Personal communication tends to all meaning," even as moral decency and the "agency of conscience" wither.[21]

How else to explain the endless attention-seeking in our self-absorbed age; a culture that accepts cruelty toward others as a necessary survival strategy; a growing "economics of contempt" that maligns and blames the poor for their condition rather than acknowledging injustices in the social order; or the paucity of even the most rudimentary knowledge among the American public about history, politics, civil rights, the Constitution, public affairs, politics, and other cultures, countries, and political systems?[22] Political ignorance now exists in the United States on a scale that seems inconceivable: for example, "only 40 percent of adults know that there are 100 Senators in the U.S. Congress," and a significant number of Americans believe that the Constitution designated English as the country's official language and Christianity as its official religion.[23]

What is particularly disturbing is the way in which there has been a resurgence of a poisonous form of technical rationality in American culture, or what I call the return of data storms that uncritically amass metrics, statistics, and empirical evidence at the expense of knowledge that signals the need for contextualization and interpretation in support of public values, the common good, and the ethical imagination. Data storms make an appeal to a decontextualized and allegedly pure description of facts, and what Herbert Marcuse called a "misplaced concreteness," one that was particularly "prevalent in the social sciences, a pseudo-empiricism which ... tended to make the objectivity of the social sciences a vehicle of apologetics and defense of the status quo."[24]

Data storms point to a world in which algorithmic regulation and infinite feedback loops are coupled with the metrics of efficiency so as to produce the sordid attempt to transcend politics. Within this depoliticized discursive universe produced by the masters of Silicon Valley, every relationship is judged within "the linguistic swamp of efficiency and innovation," far removed from political benchmarks.[25] In the new language of data fundamentalists, desired outcomes are all that matter, and such outcomes are defined not by ideology, politics, or power, at least not consciously, but by the need for stability. What is frightening in this form of digital empiricism is how it reproduces a disconnect of politics from its ends, as if the "how of politics [is not as] important as the what of politics," though the former often shapes the latter.[26] Most people want decent schools, health care, and security, but how decent is defined and who delivers such services are not simply data-gathering issues but also ideological and political considerations. Given the current neoliberal assault on public goods and social provisions along with the data-obsessed power of the surveillance state, it is not difficult to imagine how the data being collected on everyone will be used in the name of efficiency to eliminate any viable notion of the common and public good.

As politics is subordinated to a kind of algorithmic authoritarianism with its emphasis on technique, efficiency, and desired outcomes, data will be used to ruthlessly individualize the social by making all people ultimately responsible for their fate, however connected their lives may be to larger structural and policy considerations. Data storms are the modus operandi of what Evgeny Morozov calls the new authoritarian emphasis on metrics, measurement, and feedback, bent on replacing the welfare state's emphasis on political, personal, and social rights with a totalitarian algorithmic state. The algorithmic state makes politics banal and empties citizenship and agency of any viable meaning. Hence, it has no interest in fighting existing social evils as much as it promotes a growing cult of resilience—arguing for individual initiative to replace any collective struggle aimed at correcting larger structural and systemic problems that individuals face. The security–permanent warfare state views the welfare state as a hindrance to neoliberal power and does everything it can to eliminate the public spheres that support it, the democratic values that legitimate it, and the intellectuals who speak in its favor.

Individual fate, character, responsibility, and resilience have become the ideological mantras of the algorithmic neoliberal state. This points to what Brad Evans calls "insecure by design,"[27] in which, as I have argued elsewhere, "the catastrophes and social problems produced by the financial elite and mega corporations now become the fodder of an individualized politics, a space of risk in which one can exhibit fortitude and a show of hyper masculine toughness."[28] Control by the financial and corporate elite is predicated on convincing the American public that the only solutions they face to the staggering economic, political, and social problems that bear down on them are individual, and can be resolved only through singular acts of fortitude, assuming responsibility for oneself, and exercising a noble sense of character. This is the politics of technocratic neoliberal rubbish fed by the cult of data, resilience, privatization, deregulation, commodification, and fear.[29] It fails to acknowledge, as William Easterly reminds us, that major social problems such as poverty are not going to be solved through either individual initiatives or technical solutions. On the contrary, he argues that what the technocratic approach ignores regarding how to solve the crisis of poverty and massive inequality around the globe is "the unchecked power of the state against poor people without rights."[30]

This obsession with metrics feeds an insatiable desire for control and lives in an eternal present, removed from matters of justice and historical memory. The novelist Anne Lamott is right in arguing that the "headlong rush into data is overshadowing 'everything great and exciting that someone like me would dare to call grace. What this stuff steals is our aliveness . . . . Grids, spreadsheets and algorithms take away the sensory connection to our lives, where our feet are, what we're seeing, all the raw materials of life, which by their very nature are disorganized.' Metrics, she said, rob individuals of the sense that they can choose their own path, 'because if you're going by the data and the formula, there's only one way.'"[31]

Not only is this mode of rationality antithetical to other modes of reasoning that recognize and value what cannot be measured as being essential to life as well as democratic values and social relations, but it also carries the weight of a deadly form of masculine logic wedded to toxic notions of control, violence, and ideological purity.[32] It is a form of rationality that serves the interests of the rich, corporations, and government bureaucrats and obscures modes of thinking that are more capacious and reflective in their capacity to address broader conceptions of identity, citizenship, and nonmarket values such as love, trust, and fidelity.

It bears repeating: reality is now shaped by the culture's infatuation with a narrow, depoliticizing rationality, or what Frankfurt School theorist Max Horkheimer called instrumental reason. Needless to say, this obsession with metrics, technological fetishism, surveillance, and control poses a threat far greater than anything the Frankfurt School theorists could have imagined. Bruce Feiler, writing in the *New York Times,* argues that not only are we awash in data, but words and "unquantifiable arenas like history, literature, religion, and the arts are receding from public life, replaced by technology, statistics, science, and math. Even the most elemental form of communication, the story, is being pushed aside by the list."[33] Historical memory and public space are indeed the first casualties in this reign of ideological tyranny, which models agency only on consumerism and value only on exchange value. The cult of the measurable is enthralled by instant evaluation, and fervently believes that data hold the key to our collective fate. John Steppling sums up the authoritarian nature of this ideological colonization and monopoly of the present. He writes:

Today, the erasure of space is linked to the constant hum of data information, of social networking, and of the compulsive repetition of the same. There is no space for accumulation in narrative. Emotional or intellectual accumulation is destroyed by the hyper-branded reality of the Spectacle. So, the poor are stigmatized for sleep. It is a sign of laziness and sloth. Of lassitude and torpor. The ideal citizen is one at work all the time. Industrious and attentive to the screen image or the sound of command. Diligence has come to mean a readiness to obey. A culture of shaming and reprimand is based on a model of reality in which there is no history to reflect upon. Today's mass culture only reinforces this. The "real" is a never changing present. Plots revolve around the idea of disrupting this present, and then returning to this present. Actual tragedy, Chernobyl or Bhopal or Katrina, are simply ignored in terms of their material consequences. What matters are events that disrupt the Empire's carefully constructed present reality.[34]

It gets worse. Within this reality, endlessly hawked by a neoliberal brand of authoritarianism, people are turned into nothing more than "statistical units." Individuals and marginalized groups are all but stripped of their humanity, thereby clearing the way for the growth of a formative culture that allows individuals to ignore the suffering of others and to "escape from unbearable human dilemmas. . . . Statistics become more important than real human life."[35]

Zygmunt Bauman and David Lyons have connected the philosophical implications of experiencing a reality defined by constant measurement to how most people now allow their private expressions and activities to be monitored by the authoritarian security-surveillance state.[36] No one is left unscathed. In the current historical conjuncture, neoliberalism's theater of cruelty joins forces with new technologies that can easily "colonize the private" even as it holds sacrosanct the notion that any "refusal to participate in the technological innovations and social networks (so indispensable for the exercise of social and political control) . . . becomes sufficient grounds to remove all those who lag behind in the globalization process (or have disavowed its sanctified idea) to the margins of society."[37] Inured to data gathering and number crunching, the country's slide into authoritarianism has become not only permissible but also participatory—bolstered by a general ignorance of how a market-driven culture induces all of us to sacrifice our secrets, private lives, and very identities to social media, corporations, and the surveillance state.[38]

As I have mentioned in Chapter 2, the new digital technologies and social networks have created a rising tide of information broken up into bites and decontextualized facts, and have accelerated the public's addiction to speed, overstimulation, short attention spans, and the celebration of multitasking, which degrades the ability to focus on a particular task. Bombarded by huge amounts of information, it is not surprising that Americans have a growing tendency to forgo complex arguments, which are canceled out by the impulse for instant information, gratification, and a flight from adult responsibilities. As Jaron Lanier writes in *You Are Not a Gadget*, digital culture is dominated by trivia, gossip, and the brutality of an ethos of mob rule and a discourse of cruelty hidden behind the dark curtain of a cowardly anonymity.[39] The reduction of communication to data has created new forms of infantilism that have mushroomed into a depoliticizing practice that enables a flight from social responsibility and an extended immersion into a digital culture dominated by the mind-set of immature adolescents. Lanier argues strongly that the Internet is a kind of "pseudo world" that resembles a "Peter Pan Fantasy of being a child forever, without the responsibilities of adulthood."[40] The Internet and the digital landscape it creates are composed of

> wave after wave of juvenilia, with rooms of "M.I.T. Ph.D. engineers not seeking cancer cures or sources of safe drinking water for the underdeveloped world but schemes to send little digital pictures of teddy bears and dragons between adult members of social networks."[41]

Ignorance finds an easy ally in various elements of popular culture, such as the spectacle of reality TV, further encouraging the embrace of a culture in which it is no longer possible to translate private troubles into public concerns. On the contrary, reveling in private issues now becomes the grounds for celebrity status, promoting a new type of confessional in which all that matters is interviewing oneself endlessly and performing private acts as fodder for public consumption. Facebook "likes," lists of "friends," and other empty data reduce our lives to numbers that now define who we are. Technocratic rationality rules while thoughtful communication withers, translated into data without feeling, meaning, or vision. Lacking any sense of larger purpose, it is not surprising that individuals become addicted to outrageous entertainment and increasingly listen to and invest their hopes in politicians and hate-mongers who endlessly lie, trade in deceit, and engage in zombie-like behavior, destroying everything they touch.

The abuse one finds in a society addicted to violence finds its counterpart in a digital culture in which bullying, "aggression, abuse and contempt are now the normal currency of debate among strangers on blogs" and a range of other sites such as in the comments sections that follow posted articles.[42] In a world driven by data, the ethical imagination becomes simply another source of information and withers just as the Internet increasingly closes down debate and thoughtful exchange for a kind of narcissistic freedom in which people believe they have the right to say anything they want regardless of how stupid, cruel, or hateful it might be. Is it any wonder that serious problems such as poverty, inequality, health care, and education are now largely viewed "as problems in search of a technical solution"?[43] Of course, the confessional society does more than produce its own private data storm and exhibit a narcissistic obsession with performing publicly the most personal and intimate elements of the self; it also allows one to flee from any sense of moral responsibility or genuine friendship. Moreover, it is complicit with a surveillance state in which, as Zygmunt Bauman observes, "social networks offer a cheaper, quicker, more thorough and altogether easier way to identify and locate current or potential dissidents than any of the traditional instruments of surveillance … a true windfall for every dictator and his secret services."[44]

The reign of ignorance now produces a flood of discourse that clouds understanding and offers up disingenuous politicians and antipublic intellectuals who constantly interview themselves as they move through diverse media sites. Under such circumstances, evil becomes banal or commonplace, as Arendt pointed out, setting the stage for fascism when it becomes difficult to listen to or understand how others might be experiencing the world. That is, a society of ignorance that idealizes obedience and embraces a culture of cruelty and oppression has moved dangerously close to the kind of total moral collapse that gives rise to authoritarian regimes.

It does not seem unreasonable to conclude at this point that critical thinking as a mode of reasoning is nearing extinction in both the wider society and the sphere of public school education in the United States. Stanley Aronowitz has written that critical thought has lost its contemplative character and "has been debased to the level of technical intelligence, subordinate to meeting operational problems."[45] Nowhere is this more obvious than in the reactionary reforms being pushed on public schooling. Obama's educational policies along with the Common Core curriculum created by Bill Gates are devoid of any critical content and reduce pedagogy to the dictates of instrumental standards alone. Education subjected to endless empirical assessment results only in a high-stakes testing mania—a boon, of course, for the test industries, but a devastating loss for teacher and student autonomy. In this instance, student achievement and learning are reduced to data that are completely divorced from "the inequalities of race, class, and educational opportunity reflected in … test scores."[46]

Under the auspices of quality control, the cult of data and high-stakes testing becomes a signpost for empirical madness and number crunching run amok. "Teaching to the test" more often than not results in miseducating students while undermining any possibility of expanding their sense of wonder, imagination, critique, and social responsibility. Left unchecked, instrumental rationality parading as educational reform will homogenize all knowledge and meaning, as it becomes a machine for proliferating forms of civic and social death, deadening the spirit with the weight of dead time and a graveyard of useless testing pedagogies. What does this have to do with the suppression of historical consciousness and the death of politics in the broader culture? The answer becomes clearer when we analyze the relationships among critical thinking, historical consciousness, and the notions of social and self-emancipation.

If we think of emancipation as both a mode of critical understanding and a form of action designed to overthrow structures of domination, we can begin to illuminate the interplay between historical consciousness, critical thinking, and emancipatory behavior. At the level of understanding, critical thinking represents the ability to step beyond commonsense assumptions and to be able to evaluate them in terms of their genesis, development, and purpose. Such thinking should not be viewed simply as a form of progressive reasoning; it must be considered in itself as a fundamental political act. In this perspective, critical thinking becomes a mode of reasoning that, as Merleau-Ponty points out, is embedded in the realization that "I am able," meaning that one can use individual capacities and collective possibilities "to go beyond the created structures in order to create others."[47] Critical thinking as a political act means that human beings must emerge from their own "submersion and acquire the ability to intervene in reality as it is unveiled."[48] Not only does this instill a sense that they must work with others to actively shape history, but it also means that they must "escape" from their own history—that is, the history that society has designated for them.

As Jean-Paul Sartre writes, "You become what you are in the context of what others have made of you."[49] This is a crucial point, and one that links critical agency and historical consciousness. Under such circumstances, history becomes crucial in order to understand the traditions that have shaped our individual biographies and relationships with other human beings. This critical attentiveness to one's own history and culture represents an important element in examining the socially constructed sources underlying one's formative processes. To become aware of the processes of historical self-formation initiates an important beginning in breaking apart the taken-for-granted assumptions that legitimize social injustice and existing institutional arrangements. Therefore, critical thinking demands a form of hermeneutic understanding that is historically grounded. Similarly, it must be stressed that the capacity for a historically grounded critique is inseparable from those conditions that foster collective communication and critical dialogue. In this case, such conditions take as a starting point the need to delegitimize the culture of neoliberalism and the socioeconomic structure it supports, particularly what might be called a pernicious notion of instrumental rationality, with its one-sided emphasis on mathematical utility, numbers, data, and cult of the empirical.

Schools play a crucial, but far from straightforward, role in reproducing the culture of ignorance and instrumental rationality, though they are not alone, as the popular media in its traditional and newer digital formats have become a powerful educational force throughout the culture. Furthermore, the mechanisms of social control—such as high-stakes testing—that increasingly characterize school life are not new developments, despite what their proponents would claim for them. They are rooted in the modern conditions that have functioned to transform human needs as well as buttress dominant social and political institutions. Put another way, the prevailing mode of technocratic and instrumental rationality that permeates both the schools and the larger society has not just been tacked on to the existing social order as a recent innovation. It has developed historically over the last century and with particular intensity since the end of the 1970s; consequently, it deeply saturates our collective experiences, practices, and routines. Thus, to overcome the culture of instrumental rationality means that educators, artists, intellectuals, and others will have to construct alternative social formations and worldviews that transform both the consciousness as well as the deep vital structures of schools and the larger American public. Put bluntly, education and the changing of habits, consciousness, desires, and knowledge must be viewed as both an educational task and central to any viable notion of politics.

As a pedagogical challenge, progressives of various ideological stripes might engage in the political task of making power visible by raising fundamental questions such as: What counts as knowledge? How is this knowledge produced and legitimized? Whose interests does this knowledge serve? Who has access to this knowledge? How is this knowledge distributed and reproduced in the classroom and wider society? What kinds of social relationships are being produced at the level of everyday life in schools, the workplace, and other sites and may parallel or disrupt the social relations in the wider society? How do the prevailing forms of public pedagogy and empirical methodological frenzy serve to legitimize existing knowledge and practices?

Questions such as these, which focus on the production, distribution, and legitimation of knowledge, values, desires, and subjectivities, should be related to the institutional arrangements of the larger society. Moreover, these questions should be analyzed as part of a larger understanding of why so many people participate in their own oppression; why they accept the values of an authoritarian society; and why they are willing to embrace as common sense the cutthroat values, practices, and policies of neoliberalism, regardless of the misery caused by its malignant blend of social austerity and unchecked casino capitalism. In other words, these are questions that should provide the foundation for engaging the educative nature of politics as it disseminates its messages through all those cultural apparatuses that are actively engaged in producing subjectivities amenable to the dictates of an authoritarian society. It is important to recognize that these questions can help teachers, students, young people, workers, artists, intellectuals, and others to identify, understand, and generate those pivotal social processes needed to encourage the American public to become active participants in the search for knowledge and meaning—a search designed to foster, rather than suppress, critical thinking and social action.

Central to such a culture of questioning is the necessity to address the fact that the cult of instrumental rationality in America has no language for relating the self to public life, social responsibility, or the demands of citizenship. It has nothing to say about what institutions should achieve to support democracy, and why they too often fail. Instrumental reason erases the crucial question of how knowledge is related to self-definition and weakens the ability of individuals to raise questions about how knowledge works to secure particular forms of power and desire.

While it is true that critical thinking will not in and of itself change the nature of existing society, engaging in an intellectual struggle with the death-driven rationality that now fuels neoliberal capitalism will set the foundation for producing generations of young people who might launch a larger social movement. Such a movement will enable new forms of struggle, and, it can be hoped, a new future in which questions of justice, dignity, equality, and compassion matter. The relationship between the wider culture of instrumental rationality, commodification, and privatization and the wider practices of public pedagogy is, in essence, a relationship between ideology and social control. The dynamic at work in this relationship is complex and diverse. To begin to understand that dynamic as a pedagogical and political issue is to understand that history is not predetermined, but waiting to be seized.

The culture of instrumental rationality has undermined the critical nature of the civic and the political; reduced education to a narrow focus on mathematical utility; weakened the democratic purpose of schooling and other institutions; and undermined the role of educators, artists, and other cultural workers who are engaged and critical public intellectuals. Given the importance of education in and out of schools in providing the formative culture necessary for students and others to develop the capacities for connecting reason and freedom, ethics and knowledge, and learning to social change, progressives must reclaim education as an emancipatory project deeply rooted in the goal of expanding the possibilities of critical thought, agency, and democracy itself.

Such a task is about reclaiming the Enlightenment emphasis on freedom, reason, and informed hope, as well as engaging education as a crucial site of struggle, one that cannot be frozen in the empty, depoliticizing ignorance that supports an oppressive culture of instrumental rationality. Near the end of her life, Hannah Arendt argued that thinking is the essence of politics because she recognized that no politics could be visionary if it did not provide the foundation for human beings to become literate, critical agents. Thinking is a dangerous activity, especially in dark times like the historical moment we currently inhabit. But, for Arendt, what she called "nonthinking" is the real peril, in that it allows tyranny to take root, and history to repeat itself again and again. She wrote:

And to think always means to think critically. And to think critically is always to be hostile. Every thought actually undermines whatever there is of rigid rules, general convictions, et cetera. Everything which happens in thinking is subject to a critical examination of whatever there is. That is, there are no dangerous thoughts for the simple reason that thinking itself is such a dangerous enterprise. . . . Nonthinking is even more dangerous. I don't deny that thinking is dangerous, but I would say not thinking, *ne pas reflechir c'est plus dangereux encore* [not thinking is even more dangerous].[50]

No democratic society can survive with a configuration of power, institutions, and politics dedicated to keeping people ignorant while exploiting their needs, labor, desires, and hopes for a better future. Dependency and vulnerability are now viewed as a weakness, even as the public services and public servants that might alleviate people's distress are defined as gratuitous costs by the neoliberal state. American democracy is losing ground against an onslaught of neoliberal forces in every realm, not only in the realm of politics. As historical memory is erased, critical thought is crushed by a sterile instrumental rationality under the guise of mass information and a data storm. The formative cultures and institutions that enable individuals to learn how to become critically engaged citizens are being eviscerated. If unchecked, neoliberal barbarism will strengthen its dominance over everyday life, and the transition into authoritarianism will quicken. The way out of this conundrum is not to be found in the use of data-gathering technologies or in an uncritical faith in the expansion of new digital and social media. Neither will it be discovered in a callous retreat from compassion and social responsibility, or in reliance on a depoliticizing instrumental rationality.

It is only a rebirth of historical memory that will enable the merging of dangerous thinking, critical knowledge, and subversive action into a movement capable of reviving the dream of a future in which the practice of radical democratization prevails. Memory work is dangerous, particularly to those defenders of tyranny such as Cheney, Kristol, Rice, and other warmongers for whom the politics of forgetting is crucial to their own legitimation. When such antipublic intellectuals have returned to the national spotlight in order to revel in history's erasure, it is time to make trouble and to hope, as Herbert Marcuse once stated, that "the horizon of history is still open."[51]

4

Militarism's Killing Fields

From Afghanistan to Ferguson

⊷

> If this practice [of totalitarianism] is compared with that of tyranny, it
> seems as if a way had been found to set the desert itself in motion, to let
> loose a sand storm that could cover all parts of the inhabited earth. The
> conditions under which we exist today in the field of politics are indeed
> threatened by these devastating sandstorms.
>
> —*Hannah Arendt*

Militarism is like a lethal virus that wipes out historical memory, if not any
sense of moral and social responsibility. In the United States and many other
countries, at the present moment, it is no longer one strain of ideology that
permeates these societies; it is a general condition that gives meaning to
almost all aspects of life. Incapable of thinking beyond military solutions
to social problems, militarism absolves individuals and governments, if not
the general public, of the horror produced by the weapons it builds and the
violence it produces; moreover, just as it erases the memory of civilian deaths
in Hiroshima and Nagasaki, it suggests that the hundreds of children killed
in Iraq, Gaza, Afghanistan, and other war zones can be defended as a military
necessity. Militarized societies are comfortable with enemy/friend distinctions. They invite extreme nationalistic passions and are inclined to let loose
on others the forces of unlimited destruction, suffering, and murderous rage.

The apostles of militarism offer jobs to the public that engage in the production of organized violence; they preach war as a cleansing solution, while
they sanitize language of any meaning, erasing the suffering, misery, and

horror inflicted by their drone missiles, jets, Apache helicopters, and bombs. They recruit the poor into a war machine and a culture of violence and then abandon them when they return home. The biggest victims of war are those who are most vulnerable, such as children, the elderly, and the sick. Today, leaders ranging from Benjamin Netanyahu to Barack Obama reside over massive machineries of death, suffering, and destruction, all the while engaging in the slaughter of hundreds of children. As David Theo Goldberg points out, such actions are "predicated on accepting that there is some self-defending legitimacy to killing almost at random women, children, and men, even the unborn simply to be rid of them in the name of 'hunting out the terrorists.'"[1]

Yet the effects and social costs of war, rarely acknowledged, also include those sent to fight wars. As Bernie Sanders observes, the cost of war is not entirely measured by the wasted

hundreds of billions of dollars we spend on planes, tanks, missiles and guns ... [or] the 6,800 service members who have died in Iraq and Afghanistan. The cost of war is caring for the spouses and children who have to rebuild their lives after the loss of their loved ones. It's about hundreds of thousands of men and women coming home from war with post-traumatic stress disorder and traumatic brain injury, many of them having difficulty keeping jobs in order to pay their bills. It's about high divorce rates. It's about the terrible tragedy of veterans committing suicide.[2]

All that has to be invoked to justify the cost in resources and human lives are the words "collateral damage" or "military necessity" and the death-laden actions produced by the new militarists disappear into the ethically eviscerated vocabulary of authoritarian double-speak. War is no longer a source of alarm, but pride, and it has become an organizing principle of many societies. Informed by a kind of primitive tribalism, militarism enshrines a deadly type of masculinity that mythologizes violence and mimics the very terrorism it claims to be fighting. Militarism and war have changed not only the nature of the political order but also the nature and character of American life.

When children are killed by Israeli shells while playing on a beach or finding shelter in schools in Gaza, or for just living in the bombed-out rubble caused by militarized hysteria, the horror and sheer brutality of the murderous act is wiped away by the crude argument that such needless slaughter is a military requirement to destroy terrorists. Nor is much said about the millions of children killed "from American wars and sponsored conflicts in 37 countries since the Second World War."[3] The group Reprieve reports that US drone strikes killed twenty-eight people for every individual specifically targeted, and that of the forty-one targets reported killed in Yemen and Pakistan, more than a thousand nontarget civilians were killed. In addition, the CIA alone in its attempts to kill al-Qaeda leader Ayman al-Zawahiri has killed seventy-six children.[4] There is no defense for killing children, regardless of whether it is done by the Israeli state, the United States, Hamas, or anyone else. We live in a time in which political illiteracy and moral tranquilization work in tandem to produce the authoritarian subject, willing to participate in their own oppression and the oppression of others. Thus, the silence over filling our prisons with poor people of color, treating desperate immigrant children as if they were vermin, and allowing elected officials to replace reason with forms of militant religious fundamentalism.

What kind of moral arrangements does a society give up when there is no outrage over the fact that the United States supplies billions of dollars in armaments to other countries and thus is complicit in the killing of young children and others through acts of state terrorism? When coupled with an unchecked ethos of individualism, consumerism, and materialism with its toxic registers of racism and inequality, it is not difficult to imagine that young people who are no longer considered a social investment are increasingly subject to the same kind of violence at home that is produced by militarism abroad. The war abroad finds its counterpart in a militarized racism and neoliberal society that increasingly resorts to its own forms of domestic terrorism. Local police have become paramilitarized forces and no longer abide by the motto to serve and protect. Instead, for many black neighborhoods the police are more feared by the community than local gangs, armed with surplus weaponry from the battlefields of Iraq and Afghanistan and having turned many cities inhabited by people of color into war zones.

The United States may be fighting terrorists abroad, but it is attacking communities of color at home. Truth is now a casualty of violence and the very idea of politics is "backed up by the monopoly of violence."[5] The United States is a country that no longer questions itself and is largely driven by a mad quest for power and profits. One consequence of this intensity of violence and power is the replacement of the authoritarian state by the totalitarian market. State sovereignty has been replaced by corporate sovereignty, producing a new form of authoritarianism in the United States in which economics dominates and drives politics, producing a neoliberal militarized culture of misery, cruelty, and ruthlessness.[6] Peter Beilharz is correct in arguing that

> after all these years fighting those totalitarianisms delivered by the state, . . . we now face a discursive monopoly of claims to value, where only the market counts, and other kinds of value are for losers. . . . None of which is to say that humans have no place any longer in this world; the question, rather, is what kind of room for manoeuver they, we, have, and whether this is really the only, best possible way for us to live.[7]

Ghettoes that have been turned into war zones clearly have very little room to maneuver in the face of growing racist state terrorism. The tear gas that hung in the air for over a week in Ferguson, Missouri, has a long legacy of state repression that extends from Watts, Detroit, Harlem, and Oakland, to numerous other cities. Dissent, resistance, and popular uprisings are now fodder for a military machine and culture that has been growing in the United States for decades. Militarization and a military definition of life and culture have become normalized, a new common sense for a nation at war with minorities of class, color, ethnicity, and age. Not only has militarization produced and celebrated an aggressive and warriorlike mode of masculinity, it has imposed a surveillance state, devalued democratic citizenship, and subordinated a "concern for the common good to the paramount value of military effectiveness."[8] As Andrew Bacevich observes, "Americans have come to define the nation's strength and well-being in terms of military prepared-ness, military action, and the fostering of (or nostalgia for) military ideals."[9] The United States has moved from a culture of militarism, which was limited to the values associated with the military, to a more pervasive culture of militarization, which refers to what Catherine Lutz calls "the simultaneously material and discursive nature of military dominance" with its belief in force and violence as a dominant mediating and structuring force, creating what "C. Wright Mills called a 'military definition of reality.'"[10] This is a military metaphysics that not only produces material violence but also produces a military culture rooted in blind obedience, aggression, conformity, and warlike values. Chris Hedges describes this culture well. He writes:

> Repetitive rote learning and an insistence on blind obedience—similar to the approach used to train a dog—work on the battlefield. The military exerts nearly total control over the lives of its members. Its long-established hierarchy ensures that those who embrace the approved modes of behavior rise and those who do not are belittled, insulted and hazed. Many of the marks of civilian life are stripped away. Personal modes of dress, hairstyle, speech and behavior are heavily regulated. Individuality is physically and then psychologically crushed. Aggressiveness is rewarded. Compassion is demeaned. Violence is the favorite form of communication. These qualities are an asset in war; they are a disaster in civil society.[11]

We have seen a most vivid and disastrous expression of these values in the spate of violence recently waged against black youth in many urban cities. Social problems are now translated into military problems, just as behavior associated with problems such as burdensome debt and homelessness are now criminalized. The killing of an unarmed eighteen-year-old African American, Michael Brown, in Ferguson, Missouri, on August 9, 2014, by a white police officer has made visible how a form of toxic, racist, military metaphysics now dominates American life. His subsequent demonization by the media only confirms its entrance into the public consciousness as a form of vicious entertainment. The police have been turned into soldiers who view the neighborhoods in which they operate as war zones. Outfitted with full riot gear, submachine guns, grenade launchers, assault rifles, night vision equipment, armored vehicles, body armor, and other lethal weapons, their mission is to assume battle-ready behavior.[12] As Glenn Greenwald observes, "This has resulted in a domestic police force that looks, thinks, and acts more like an invading and occupying military than a community-based force to protect the public."[13] Is it any wonder that violence, rather than painstaking, neighborhood police work and community outreach and engagement, becomes the norm for dealing with alleged "criminals," especially at a time when more and more behaviors are being criminalized? Randy Balko has stated that the militarization of the police has isolated them from the communities in which they work, and as such they often treat the people they interact with in those neighborhoods as wartime combatants.[14] Of course, Ferguson made clear that police departments are now defined increasingly by a form of militarization in which violence rather than negotiation, insight, and thoughtfulness are brought to bear when confronting often young, unarmed black men. This should not be surprising in a country in which neighborhoods largely inhabited by blacks are considered war zones by the police, zones of disposability where extreme violence can be brought to bear with impunity. David Theo Goldberg offers the following insightful commentary on the expanding racialized militarized state:

> Ferguson revealed both the rapidly expanding program of militarizing urban control across the country and the coherent Pentagon program to pass along to police departments at almost no cost to local budgets some of its technologies of weaponized violence and control. Perhaps this was all too predictable in the wake of declarations of war on most every major social condition since the 1960s as well as the dramatic expansion of local securitization in the wake of 9/11 and the massive proliferation of intrusive data collection about the personal across America in the past few years. But Ferguson let us know very visibly that we have supplemented the carceral state of the 1980s and 1990s with the securitized state of late.[15]

The militarization of local police forces has a long history in the United States, beginning in response to the drug wars of the 1980s and the war on crime policies instituted by the Clinton administration, and amplified after the terrorist attack of 9/11.[16] Under the auspices of the National Defense Authorization Act and the military-transfer program created in the 1990s, "police departments … are adding more firepower and military gear than ever," even though violent crime has drastically plummeted since the early 1990s.[17] Consequently, not only have police departments been transformed into military units, taking on the appearance of SWAT teams now deployed to conduct even routine practices such as carrying out raids on unlicensed barbershops, and raiding night clubs in violation of liquor inspections, they have also become part of both a huge security industry "expected to grow to $31 billion by 2014" and a public and state spending program that amounts to "$75 billion a year on national security."[18] In 2013, SWAT teams in the United States conducted more than 80,000 raids, with "80 percent . . . linked to search warrants to investigate potential criminal suspects, not for high-stakes 'hostage, barricade, or active shooter scenarios.'"[19]

The militarization of American society is fueled by a Department of Defense program labeled 1033, which "has provided $4.3 billion in free military equipment to local police."[20] At the same time, states have "received at least $34 billion in federal grants to purchase military grade supplies in the decade after 9/11. . . . Even in remote cities like Fargo, North Dakota, rated one of the safest cities in America, police officers have traveled with military style assault rifles in their patrol cars."[21] What the arming of America testifies to is not simply the militarizing of the police but a process of militarization defined by Michael Geyer as the "contradictory and tense social process in which civil society organizes itself for the production of violence."[22] This speaks to a much broader threat to American society than the arming of the police.

In light of the ongoing militarization of American society, I want to introduce a caveat. I think it is a mistake simply to focus on the militarization of the police and their racist actions in addressing the killing of Michael Brown, Eric Garner, and Tamir Rice. What we are witnessing in this brutal killing and mobilization of state violence is symptomatic of the neoliberal racist punishing state emerging all over the world, with its encroaching machinery of social death. The neoliberal killing machine is on the march globally. The spectacle of neoliberal misery is too great to deny anymore, and the only mode of control left by corporate-controlled societies is violence—but a violence that is waged against the new precariat, such as immigrant children, protesting youth, the unemployed, and black youth. In the case of Michael Brown, it should be clear that his death cannot be reduced to an isolated incident in a town in which whites are overwhelmingly in power. In fact, as Kevin Johnson, Meghan Hoyer, and Bred Heath, point out in *USA Today*:

> Nearly two times a week in the United States, a white police officer killed a black person during a seven-year period [extending from 2005 to] 2012. . . . The shooting of a black teenager in Ferguson, MO., last Saturday was not an isolated event in American policing. Eighteen percent of the blacks killed during those seven years were under age 21, compared to 8.7 percent of whites.[23]

The racist, symbolic, and capacious violence now waged by the neoliberal state has become so widespread that it permeates the news, media, social networks, and online sources so as to become normalized rather than a source of alarm. And if such violence is not normalized, it is suppressed. Militarism goes hand in hand with a kind of hypermasculinity that often breeds monstrous deeds in those who take pride in their armed machismo. For example, when the press talks about the militarization of the police, little is said about the kind of violence and police brutality in which women are sexually assaulted, young people are endlessly subject to racial profiling, and black youth are endlessly harassed by the police. For many poor black youth, the police are not seen as a source of protection but as a repressive, dangerous occupying force. Surely, this type of domestic violence is as crucial to recognize as the ongoing militarization of local police departments. For instance, there are an increasing number of stories by young black women emerging in which they were assaulted and raped by police officers, and when they tried to report the crime they found themselves in a Kafkaesque world in which they were charged with a crime. Mariame Kaba, a Chicago-based organizer and educator, published a harrowing story of assault by a cop shared by a young black woman that is worth repeating.[24] The young black victim stated:

> I was walking to the bus when a police officer called out and said, "Hey you come here girl with all of that ass." I ignored the comment unaware of where it was coming from until he pulled up on the curb to block my path in his undercover cop car. He jumps out and yells, "Didn't you hear me calling you girl?" I replied by simply saying no, my name isn't aye girl with all that ass. He got really mad and slapped me saying that I was very disrespectful and do I know who he is and what he can do to me?[25]

The cop not only ended up sexually assaulting her, but the young woman, incongruously, ended "up getting arrested and jailed when she tried to report him."[26] This is not merely an example of criminal violence on the part of the police, it is symptomatic of a kind of lawlessness in which the servants of the powerful believe they can act with impunity. Is it any wonder that "black youth report the highest rate of harassment by the police (54.4 percent), nearly twice the rates of other young people?"[27] These acts of domestic terrorism are a direct result of the increasing rise of the punishing state in America and the unwillingness of the financial elite to invest any resources in solving the growing inequities that mark all aspects of society and range from a lack of resources for schools to the failure to invest in decaying infrastructures. State violence may have become the new metaphysic dominating everyday life, but the specter of authoritarianism is the larger issue that breeds and supports it, all of which speaks to a society that is breaking apart and undoing every vestige of justice, freedom, and equality necessary for a vibrant democratic society.

Yet, to the degree that neoliberal ideology is in disarray, it becomes more and more obsessed with security and expanding the punishing state. This suggests at one level that neoliberal states can no longer justify and legitimate their exercise of ruthless power and its effects under casino capitalism. Instead, the state no longer attempts to produce consensus but to reproduce a culture of fear.[28] But rather than responding with palliative reforms, the neoliberal state appears to be obsessed with security and politically indifferent and ethically frozen in light of the human suffering, exploitation, misery, and culture of mercilessness it produces. Part of this is due to the way in which global corporate power is now separated from the politics of the nation-state. As Zygmunt Bauman and Leonidas Donskis observe:

> The advanced separation aimed at divorce between power (the ability to see things done) and politics (the capacity to decide what things are to be done), has resulted in the ludicrous and degrading, all too manifest incapacity of nation-state politics to perform its function. . . . Power and politics live and move in separation from each other and their divorce lurks round the corner. On the one hand, there is power, safely roaming the global expanses, free from political control and at liberty to select its own targets; on the other, there is politics, squeezed and robbed of all or nearly all of its power, muscles and teeth.[29]

Yet, given the fact that corporate power now floats above and beyond national boundaries, the financial elite can dispense with political concessions in order to pursue their toxic agendas. Moreover, as Slavoj Žižek argues, "Worldwide capitalism can no longer sustain or tolerate ... global equality. It is just too much."[30] Moreover, in the face of massive inequality, increasing poverty, the rise of the punishing state, and the attack on all public spheres, neoliberalism cannot any longer pass itself off as synonymous with democracy. The capitalist elite, whether they are hedge fund managers, the new billionaires from Silicon Valley, or the heads of banks and corporations, are no longer interested in ideology as their chief mode of legitimation. Force is now the arbiter of their power and ability to maintain control over the commanding institutions of American society. Finally, I think it is fair to say that they are too arrogant and indifferent to how the public feels.

Neoliberal capitalism has nothing to do with democracy, and this has become more and more evident among people, especially youth all over the globe. As Žižek has observed, "The link between democracy and capitalism has been broken."[31] The important question of justice has been subordinated to the violence of unreason, to a market logic that divorces itself from social costs, and a ruling elite that has an allegiance to nothing but profit and will do anything to protect their interests. This is why I think it is dreadfully wrong just to talk about the militarization of local police forces without recognizing that the metaphor of "war zone" is apt for a global politics in which the social state and public spheres have been replaced by the machinery of finance, the militarization of entire societies (not just the police), and the widespread use of punishment that extends from the prison to the schools to the streets. Some have rightly argued that these tactics have been going on in the black community for a long time and that they are not new.[32] This is certainly true, but the reach and scope of intimidation and the nature of the violence that now marks such racist domestic terrorism needs to be updated. Police violence certainly has been going on for some time, but what is new is that the intensity of violence and the level of military-style machinery of death being employed is much more sophisticated and deadly. For instance, as Kevin Zeese and Margaret Flowers point out, the militarization of the police in the United States is a recent phenomenon that dates back to 1971. They write:

> The militarization of police is a more recent phenomenon [and marks] the rapid rise of Police Paramilitary Units (PPU's, informally SWAT teams) which are modeled after special operations teams in the military. PPU's did not exist anywhere until 1971 when Los Angeles, under the leadership of the infamous police chief Daryl Gates, formed the first one and used it for demolishing homes with tanks equipped with battering rams. By 2000, there were 30,000 police SWAT teams [and] by the late 1990s, 89 percent of police departments in cities of over 50,000 had PPUs, almost double the mid-80s figure; and in smaller towns of between 25,000 and 50,000 by 2007, 80 percent had a PPU quadrupling from 20 percent in the mid-80s. [Moreover,] SWAT teams were active with 45,000 deployments in 2007 compared to 3,000 in the early 80s. The most common use ... was for serving drug search warrants where they were used 80 percent of the time, but they were also increasingly used for patrolling neighborhoods.[33]

At the same time, the impact of the rapid militarization of local police forces on poor black communities is nothing short of terrifying and symptomatic of the violence that takes place in advanced genocidal states. Adam Hudson points out that "police officers, security guards, or self-appointed vigilantes extrajudicially killed at least 313 African-Americans in 2012. . . . This means a black person was killed by a security officer every 28 hours [and goes on to note] that it's possible that the real number could be much higher."

Glenn Greenwald is right in arguing that "abusive policing, police militarization is overwhelmingly and disproportionately directed at minorities and poor communities, ensuring that the problem largely festers in the dark"; it also "degrades the mentality of police forces in virtually every negative way and subjects their target communities to rampant brutality and unaccountable abuse" while posing "grave and direct dangers to basic political liberties, including rights of free speech, press and assembly."[34]

The emergence of the warrior cop and that of the surveillance state go hand in hand and are indicative not only of state-sanctioned racism but also of the rise of the authoritarian state and the dismantling of civil liberties. Brutality mixed with attacks on freedom, dissent, and peaceful protest recall memories of past brutal regimes such as the dictatorships in Latin America in the 1970s and 1980s. The events in Ferguson speak to a history of representation in both the United States and abroad that Americans have chosen to forget at their own risk. In spite of his generally right-wing political views, Rand Paul got it right in arguing that when you couple this militarization of law enforcement with an erosion of civil liberties and due process that allows the police to become judge and jury—national security letters, no-knock searches, broad general warrants, pre-conviction forfeiture—we begin to have a very serious problem on our hands. Given these developments, it is almost impossible for many Americans not to feel like their government is targeting them. Given the racial disparities in our criminal justice system, it is impossible for African-Americans not to feel like their government is particularly targeting them.[35]

What he does not name is the problem, which is a society marked "by a dangerous and unprecedented confluence of our democratic institutions and the military."[36] As Danielle M. LaSusa observes, the United States is a society that is not simply on the precipice of authoritarianism, but has fallen over the edge into what Hannah Arendt once called "dark times."[37] Under the regime of neoliberalism, the circle of those considered disposable and subject to state violence is now expanding. The heavy hand of the state is not only racist; it is also part of an authoritarian mode of governance willing to do violence to anyone who threatens neoliberal capitalism, white Christian fundamentalism, and the power of the military-industrial-academic-surveillance state. America's embrace of murderous weapons to be used on enemies abroad has taken a new turn and now will be used on those considered disposable at home. As the police become more militarized, the weapons of death become more sophisticated and the legacy of killing civilians becomes both an element of domestic as well as foreign policy. Amid the growing intensity of state terrorism, violence becomes the DNA of a society that refuses to deal with larger structural issues, such as massive inequality in wealth and power and a government that now unapologetically serves the rich and powerful corporate interests and makes violence the organizing principle of governance.[38]

The worldwide response to what is happening in Ferguson sheds a light on the racist and militarized nature of American society so as to make its claim to democracy seem both hypocritical and politically insipid. At the same time, such protests make visible what Goya called the sleep of reason, a lapse in witnessing, attentiveness, and the failure of conscience, which lies at the heart of neoliberalism's ongoing attempt to depoliticize the American public. Political life has come alive once again in America, moving away from its withdrawal into consumer fantasies and privatized obsessions. The time has come to recognize that Ferguson is not only about the violence and consolidation of white power and racism in one town; it is also symptomatic of white power and the deep-seated legacy of racism in the country as a whole, which goes along with what America has become under the intensifying politics of market fundamentalism, militarism, and disposability. Ferguson prompts us to rethink the meaning of politics and to begin to think not about reform but a major restructuring of our values, institutions, and notions of what a real democracy might look like. We need to live in a country in which we are alarmed rather than entertained by violence. It is time for Americans to unite around our shared fate as stakeholders in a radical democracy, rather than being united around our shared fears and the toxic glue of state terrorism and everyday violence. It is time to express a sense of moral outrage and engage in organized struggles to oppose and transform a society that, as Susan Sontag has observed, "dissolves politics into pathology."[39]

The militarists come from various political parties and are hooked into a market-driven logic that disdains thinking about social costs or the despair they create. They are unadulterated agents of cruelty, and their power serves a corrupt form of casino capitalism that breathes and breeds the ideology and policies of the military-industrial-surveillance complex. In the United States, trillions are spent on wars that were based on and initiated with lies. Equally egregious is the fact that the "federal government ... directs roughly $1 trillion every year into the United States military, depriving virtually everything else of needed resources."[40] At the same time, social services are cut, schools abandoned, infrastructures ignored so that the military can build 2,400 F35 Joint Strike Fighter jets at the cost of nearly $400 billion, as well as F-22 Raptor stealth fighter jets that cost $400 million each—both are pieces of junk plagued by mechanical failures and a sober witness to US unwillingness to use the money of war and violence to build a decent, democratic society in which vulnerability and care become the watchwords rather than violence and war.[41] The United States puts people in debtor prisons for not paying their bills but refuses to prosecute bankers and hedge fund managers who swindle the public out of billions while making miserable the lives of the people they swindled. Moreover, it is difficult to fathom a country that could provide every student in the United States with free tuition for a community college or four-year public university for the mere cost of $62 billion, a fraction of what is spent on wars, weapons production, and the military.[42] In fact, if the Pentagon's $526 billion budget for 2014 were trimmed by 12 percent, that would cover the cost of providing free tuition for students.[43]

The wretched killing of children in cities throughout the United States, Afghanistan, Syria, and Iraq is part of a larger problem, one that haunts the modern period, which is the rise of neoliberal totalitarianism—by which I mean an economic and cultural system that is sutured in its allegiance to money, profit, power, inequality, greed, militarism, the punishing state, and self-interests. The new global capital societies such as the United States have replaced the social contract with a defense contract. Zombie politics now rules as the living dead function as parasites on their respective societies, engulfing them with the fog of war, corruption, death, and an egregious lack of moral responsibility.[44] One egregious example was provided in 1996 by Madeleine Albright, former secretary of state. Asked by Leslie Stahl in an interview on CBS's *Sixty Minutes* whether the blockade of Iraq was worth the death of 500,000 children, she replied, "I think this is a very hard choice, but the price—we think is worth it."[45] Little has changed since that infamous plunge into what Joseph Conrad called in *Heart of Darkness*: "The horror! the horror!" The horror continues with the resurrection of the most recent death-dealing American politicians who gave us the Iraqi War. We are in the age of disposability whose reach and violence are spreading almost unchecked. The signposts are clear as we witness the evisceration and machinery of violence and disposability being waged against populations such as immigrants, Palestinians, low-income youths, poor minorities of color, or those who contest the authority of authoritarian states.

Like George Romero's zombies, Dick Cheney, John Bolton, and Bill Kristol are brought back to life in the mainstream media, and their sordid views proliferate like a lethal virus out of control. But pointing to the new forms of zombie politics awash in the United States and other countries is not enough. The question that must be raised is: What is it in the United States that produces an inattentiveness to moral outrage, dissent, and mass mobilizations? The failure of conscience and the willingness to stand up against the new authoritarians, whether in Israel, England, France, Greece, or the United States, promote a flirtation with modes of irrationality that lie at the heart of the triumph of everyday aggression over the slightest semblance of justice. Under such circumstances, war and the overidentification with militarism produces a new kind of national psychosis and collective pathology. We live in the age of killing machines, parading under the virus of exceptionalism and empire.[46]

We are in the midst of something different in the current historical moment. Democracy is losing its appeal, fascists are gaining in popularity around the globe, and millions of men, women, and children are now considered excess, disposable, because they are dehumanized, considered other, or fall outside of the blessings of a rabid consumerist society. The new breed of politicians unleashed by the Reagan revolution display disdain for the government, except when it benefits the rich and celebrates individual solutions to larger public issues, rendering individuals vulnerable, powerless, anxious, and disillusioned. Technology rather than ethics and compassion now provides the answers to society's problems.[47] Data has replaced words, ethics, and the hard work, as Marx once observed, of teaching everyone to be able to engage in a "ruthless criticism of everything."

The current crisis surrounding Syria, Iraq, Afghanistan, and the looting of the public treasury by the rich and financial elite speak to a crisis of individual, social, and historical agency. Democratic governance is no longer part of the vocabulary of the militarists because the latter would suggest an understanding of the morally rightful use of power, rule, representation, justice, and equality. The death-dealing zone of ethical tranquillization called Silicon Valley now provides the new model of consumer-tech obsessed citizens—largely illiterate, privatized, overly specialized, asocial beings so depoliticized that it becomes difficult for them even to talk on the phone with another person, never mind having actual, corporeal, thinking relationships with others. It also models a society that has no memory, ethics, sense of justice, or of the future.

Militarism is a new form of illiteracy and psychosis, symptomatic of the failure of civic courage because it demands obedience and punishes people who are critical, capable of questioning authority, and are willing to address important social issues. Edward Snowden and other courageous whistleblowers are considered traitors because they revealed the massive violation of civil liberties by the government and the existence of an authoritarian surveillance society in which the state and corporations fuse in their attempts to squelch dissent and freedom. Bill Gates is considered a hero, though he may be the most powerful force in the United States destroying public education and a grotesque symbol of massive inequality. Illiterate militarists and warmongering pundits such as senators John McCain, Lindsay Graham, Anne Coulter, Rush Limbaugh, and most of the Republican Party are given endless airtime even though their discourse is immersed in the blight of militarism, war, and state violence.

President Obama is defended by liberals in spite of his shredding of civil liberties and his unparalleled and unconscionable support of the financial crooks that caused the great recession in 2007. What Obama has made clear is that liberalism is now the new conservatism and that the two-party system is completely in the hands of the rich, corporations, and financial services. The reach of violence and death is everywhere, permeating the culture like an endless sandstorm that destroys everything it touches. Major articles and even a movie appear in the militarized state praising Ivy League schools, though they produce the criminogenic environments that gave us the intellectual villains that produced the slaughter in Vietnam, Iraq, and the endless forms of foreign and domestic terrorism that now reside in many of the advanced societies of the world. Mainstream media under corporate control has become simply an advertisement for US domestic and foreign policy, and has evolved into a mix of *Pravda* and *Entertainment Tonight*. Some would say we live in troubled times, and that is only partly true, because the times in which we live are more than troubled; they are close to coming to an end as the logic of the bomb expresses itself in devastating attacks on innocent civilians, crowded cities, defenseless children, and the ecological destruction of the planet.

Everything we have learned from the dominant ideologies, vocabularies, values, and social relations must be reexamined, discarded when necessary, and in its place we need a new political language, a new understanding of governance locally and globally. We need to resurrect a radical notion of what we all have in common, the common good and public values, and think hard about what work has to be done not just to survive but also to thrive in a democratically inspired world. Time has overcome us, outpaced our capacities to slow down and think critically and act courageously. This does not suggest that we need to change the world, a cliché used by Gates and other Silicon Valley, Wall Street agents of conformity. What it does suggest is a notion of social, economic, and political change inspired by a vision of a democracy to come, a society in which it is reprehensible even to consider using torture, killing children as a military necessity, and destroying social benefits to increase the wealth of corporations, hedge fund managers, and bankers who are soulless and a powerful threat to democracy and the planet. It is time to identify the people, institutions, social relations, values, and power relations that constitute the new authoritarianism and to hold them accountable.

It is also time to remember the suffering caused by militarists in the past, and it is time to remember the struggles waged by working people, women, young people, and others who dared to believe that another kind of vision, another kind of future is possible. We don't have much time left. Resistance is no longer a luxury; it is a necessity. This is why what is happening in Ferguson is so important to fighting militarism and the neoliberal system that supports it. Ferguson points to some nefarious truths about our past and present. But the public response points in another more hopeful direction. What Ferguson has told us is that the political and moral imagination is still alive, thirsting for justice, and unwilling to let the dark clouds of authoritarianism put the lights out for good. But for that to happen we must move from moral outrage to collective struggles as part of a wider effort to dismantle the mass incarceration society, the surveillance state, and the military-industrial-academic complex.[48] How many more low-income children, poor minorities of color, immigrants, and others have to die before the struggle deepens? What will it take to combat militarism as a problem that has national and global implications?

5
ISIS and the Spectacle of Terrorism
Resisting Mainstream Workstations of Fear[1]

↩

The use of the new digital technologies and social media by ISIS has drawn a great deal of attention by the dominant media not only because the extremists have used them as a form of visual terrorism to graphically portray the beheadings of captured Americans and British civilians, but also because of its alleged sophistication as a marketing tool. Examining ISIS's propaganda machine within a neoliberal frame of reference that responds to the latter in the language of the market does more than depoliticize the use of the media as a spectacle of terrorism; it also suggests that the new media's most important role lies in creating a brand, establishing a presence on Twitter, and producing a buzz among those individuals sympathetic to its violent ideological vision. For instance, Dinah Alobeid, a spokesperson for the social analytics company Brandwatch, told VICE News:

> Everyone needs a social media campaign today, even political movements in the Middle East it seems. The type of highly focused marketing and social media community building as exhibited by ISIS is something that brands strive for to get their message across. . . . Taking out the political and human rights implications of this situation, ISIS has a keen sense of how to attract their target demographics, keep them engaged, and spread their messaging and news via social to highly interested individuals. ISIS' strength lies in the recognizability of its brand, the reach of its network, and its capacity to boost its Twitter presence through a combination of carefully crafted "official" messages, as well as the buzz and volume of fans sharing content across the globe.[2]

David Carr, a media and culture writer for the *New York Times,* provides a more astute and complex analysis of the use of the new media by ISIS in pointing to its use of sophisticated means of production such as "good cameras, technically proficient operators and editors who have access to all the best tools" while making clear that the "true aim [of the videos] is to spread dread and terror."[3] Not only does he comment on the sophistication of the wardrobe selection in the beheading videos of James Foley and Steven Sotloff, he also goes to great lengths to explain what actually takes place in these videos, and seems particularly fascinated by the fact that the actual beheadings are not shown so as to "achieve maximum impact."[4] Carr's commentary then takes an odd turn when he compares the beheading to a scene near the end of Season 1 in the popular television series *Game of Thrones.* He writes:

> The act is shocking regardless of the context. Remember near the end of Season 1 of "Game of Thrones," when Eddard Stark, a main character, was poised to lose his head? We expected an arrow to come in from stage right to save him, but it did not and the blade fell swiftly. The audacity of the scene was something people talked about for weeks afterward, and the show's unflinching violence has been a core element of its escalating popularity.[5]

What is disturbing in this comparison is that the context of real-life violence is placed on an equal plane with the simulacrum of brutality, and thus their distinctive spaces in the political imagination become indistinguishable. What Carr participates in is a flattening of the spectacle of violence with real-life violence and as a result has no way of understanding how one feeds the other, particularly in a society wedded to violence as both a spectacle and as a legitimate form of state policy. Violence as a mode of entertainment becomes as equal a currency of shock as the violence waged by fundamentalists who believe that violence is the only tool for engaging social and political problems. Moreover, Carr seems to suggest that violence is only disturbing when Muslim fundamentalists produce what he terms their "medieval message" through the modern apparatuses of the digital media. What is missing in this account is a critical understanding of how modern oppressive governments use diverse media to produce violence as both a mode of entertainment and a way of legitimizing not only a culture of fear but also the military-industrial-surveillance state.

Power disappears in these analyses as the social media is stripped of its diverse sites and complex usages, defined largely in terms of its presence as either a marketing campaign, a space of technological innovation, or as a site of aestheticized medieval violence. The emphasis on spectacularized effects covers up too much and refuses to acknowledge that as the link between the media and power becomes more integrated, the visual theater of terrorism mimics the politics of the "official" war on terrorism and cannot simply be reduced to a tool for alleged terrorist acts committed by enemies of the United States. Violence not only becomes performative, functioning as a kind of representational politics linked to the death drive, but it is also packaged so as to mimic the unbridled monopolization of pleasure now associated with extreme and sensational images of brutality and cruelty. Moreover, representational shocks and outrages are now presented as either legitimate sources of entertainment or as part of a survival-of-the-fittest ethic endemic to neoliberal spectacles of misery, all of which are used by the major cultural apparatuses to flood the culture in spectacularized images of violence and graphic displays of terrorism. It should come as no surprise that when mainstream media report on the bombing of ISIS targets in Syria and Iraq they weaken the substance of politics by accompanying their comments and digital screenings with images of the actual bombings captured as if the viewer were looking at a video game rather than a brutalizing act of military aggression. The black-and-white grainy images draw the viewer into a video-produced simulacra in which the spectacle of the blast eliminates questions about who might have been killed in such attacks, why they are taking place, or whether they are legal. In this instance, entertainment collapses into an aesthetic of effects and in doing so dampens any concerns about causes, history, or the mapping of the complexity of reasons that lead to conflicts, especially in the Middle East.

Echoing the discourse of the "official" war on terrorism, the violence of extremist groups such as ISIS is produced almost exclusively within the vocabulary of moral absolutes pitting good against evil. Ironically, this is a binary discourse that mirrors a similar vocabulary used in the interest of the national security-surveillance state and the corporate-sponsored war machines of battle-ready domestic and global forces of repression.[6] What is clear is that the spectacle of terrorism trades in moral absolutes whether it makes such claims in the name of religion or human rights. This friend/enemy distinction wipes out any sense of uncertainty, need for thoughtful debate, and reason itself. Whether it is George W. Bush's now infamous claim that "You are either with us or against us,"[7] or ISIS's insistence that their enemies are infidels for whom there will be no mercy, this is a repressive binary logic that devalues democratic, reasoned debate in favor of feeding an apocalyptic desire for destruction and death. Hence, it is all the more troubling to read a September 29, 2014, op-ed in the *New York Times* by Roger Cohen titled "Here There Is No Why: For ISIS, Slaughter Is an End in Itself."[8] In referring to the US war against ISIS, Cohen states bluntly that "presented with the counter-human, the human must fight back." This is a dangerous binary because it closes down questions of history, politics, power, justice, and the ethical imagination while legitimating violence, revenge, and militarism through the language of an unchecked moralism. Demonizing other human beings makes it less difficult to commit crimes that otherwise are not only illegal but unthinkable. Surely, fighting "the inhuman" does not justify the indiscriminate killing of Syrian civilians by drones and high-tech fighter jets, among other dastardly crimes? Nor should it erase serious questions about the historical and political conditions that created ISIS in the first place. The neat and unethical distinction between those considered human and those labeled as inhuman overlooks the fact that such binarisms miss the fact that such distinctions often bleed into each destroying this wretched, unreflective rhetoric and demands a much more complicated understanding of the acts of barbarism that are currently sweeping over the globe.

Just as the necessity of fighting terror has become the central rationale for war by the Obama administration and other governments, a visual culture of shock and awe has become ubiquitous by the intensified and expanding presence of the Internet and twenty-four-hour cable news shows devoted to representations of the horrific violence associated with terrorism—ranging from images of bombing raids in Syria to the countervailing imagery of grotesque killings of hostages by ISIS fundamentalists. The visual theater of terrorism aestheticizes politics, celebrates a sacralization of politics as war, and stylizes raw violence as it is integrated into audio-visual spectacles that shock and massage the mind and emotions with the theatricality of power and a steady regimen of fear, extreme violence, and the drumbeat of a hypercharged masculinity.[9] If the media are to be believed, every aspect of life, as Brian Massumi has argued, increasingly appears as "a workstation in the mass production line of fear."[10] It gets worse. It is not unreasonable to assume that if the sheer brutality and barbarism of ISIS did not exist, it would have to be invented by the United States. ISIS not only symbolizes rightfully an extreme form of fundamentalist barbarism, but also offers the United States a new enemy that fits right into its need to legitimate its own culture and apparatuses of fear, spectacle of terrorism, and machinery of militarism, regardless of its disingenuous appeal to human rights.

As the US war machine increases the intensity of its bombing of Muslim fundamentalists and political extremists in various parts of the world, but especially in Syria and Iraq at the present moment, the official "workstations" of CNN and other news outlets engage in a kind of grotesque production of moral panics in their appeal to fear, insecurity, and imminent danger. Violence is not something to be condemned but to be appropriated as a productive source for higher Nielson ratings and more advertising revenue. The television and news reports read like scripts that have been written by ghostwriters from the defense department and the National Rifle Association. Violence, coupled with a disingenuous appeal to human rights, becomes both the only register by which to understand the conflicts in which the United States is engaged and to be used for solving the problems it evokes as a necessity for military action. The history, interests, and power relations behind such military actions, violations of international law, and global aggression that function almost exclusively in the service of violence, war, and global domination are eviscerated from any official government reporting or the staged performances of the dominant media. Armed struggle feeds the call for more weapons to be sold across the globe, more guns to be used at home, the ever-expanding militarization of all aspects of social life, and the production of desires, identities, and modes of subjectivity conducive to living in a state of permanent war.[11] ISIS represents only one part, though highly extreme, of the machinery of social and civil death that now drives and thrives on the spectacle of terrorism.

The spectacle of neoliberal terrorism, violence, and misery has become one of the major organizing principles of everyday life. Hence, it is all the more imperative for progressives and others to examine the centrality of a wide range of old and new media apparatuses as powerful political and pedagogical forces that shape the spectacle of terrorism. What is especially necessary is for educators, critics, journalists, and other cultural workers to provide a thorough analysis of how such ideological workstations redefine the very nature of politics itself.[12] The pressing nature of such a task is crucial because the spectacle of terrorism is unlike anything Americans have faced in the past—with its enshrinement of hyper-real violence, its unadulterated appeal to fear, diverse forms of resistance to state power, and its elevation of the digital, aural, and visual to a prominent feature of social and political power.[13]

The use of the new corporate-controlled media and technologies now propelling the spectacle of terrorism constitutes a distinct influence in their ability to undermine the radical imagination through a celebration of violence and an equally powerful disdain for all democratic values, making it all the more crucial to remember, as Hannah Tennant-Moore points out, punishment thrives on and is energized by fear.[14] While it is important to acknowledge that the spectacle of terrorism has played a significant role in propelling the United States into what Hannah Arendt once called "dark times," at the same time it is also crucial to remind ourselves, as Catherine Clement has noted, that "every culture has an imaginary zone for what it excludes, and it is that zone that we must remember today."[15] And what has been excluded in this instance is the role alternative forms of the new media have played in producing a new language and notion of solidarity, in which matters of justice and equality can be understood as part of a new historical moment in which politics and power as presently conceived no longer rule uncontested and are subject to repeated challenges and modes of resistance. Needless to say, the current neoliberal order will not loosen its grip on the machineries of war, inequality, finance, and disposability without a fight, and if any mode of collective resistance is to be successful, what is needed on the part of progressives and others is a new understanding of the relationship between culture and power on the one hand, and politics and pedagogy on the other.

The spectacle of terrorism not only requires a new conception of politics, pedagogy, strategy, and society; it also raises significant questions about the new media and its centrality to democracy.[16] In the United States and many other countries, the corporate media is under the control of a savage form of neoliberalism that decries the ethical imagination, human rights, and the fundamental elements of a democratic society. One consequence is that as image-based technologies have redefined the relationship between the ethical, political, and aesthetic, they are largely used to service the soft war of consumerism and the hard war of militarism.[17] This is an all-embracing form of domination in which the symbolic and the material forces of repression reinforce each other.

Yet, terrorism, consumerism, and the increasing privatization of everyday life are not the only elements that drive the new media technologies. The spectacle of terrorism and the conditions that have produced it neither sound the death knell of democracy, nor do they ensure that the new media are only on the side of domination. What they do point to is a need to rethink democracy as an antidote and form of resistance to the elevation of terror as a mode of neoliberal militarization and entertainment.[18] And key to this challenge is how the new media might be used to serve the practice of freedom, social change, and new modes of communication in the interest of solidarity and justice. For instance, how might we imagine the relations between culture and politics based on social relations that enable individuals and social groups to rethink the crucial nature of pedagogy, agency, and social responsibility in a media-saturated global sphere? How can we begin to address these new technologies and social media within a democratic cultural politics that challenges religious fundamentalism, neoliberal ideology, militarism, and the cult of entertainment? Such a project is collective by nature and requires a politics that is in the process of being invented, one that has to be attentive to the new realities of power, global social movements, and the promise of a planetary democracy. At stake here is a pedagogical and political ritual that necessitates new forms of knowledge and skills in order to critically understand the new visual and visualizing technologies and their attendant image-based pedagogies and cultural practices—not simply as new modes of communication, but as structural forces and pedagogical tools capable of expanding critical citizenship, animating public life, and extending democratic public spheres.

It would be a mistake to simply align the new media exclusively with the forces of domination and commercialism, or what Allen Feldman calls "total spectrum violence."[19] Instead, what has to be stressed is the complex and layered role of the new media within the larger political, social, and communicative landscape. It is too easy either to overly romanticize the new image-based technologies or to simply dismiss them as new sources of oppressive control. Even within the spectacle of terrorism, there are hints of structural forces and elements of resistance that could be used for emancipatory rather than oppressive purposes. Both the now shattering spectacle of the September 11 bombings and the more recent beheading videos produced by ISIS communicate far more than grisly acts of terror and atrocity. They also "point to ... a new structural feature of the international state system: that the historical monopoly of the means of destruction by the state is now at risk."[20] Destruction and violence have become decentered, infused with possibilities for new and more global forms of public pedagogy that are inventive, inspiring, and energizing.

Power now resides as much in the production of images as it does in the traditional machineries of violence colonized by the state. At the same time, terrorist spectacles illustrate how important it is to speak to the very forces that undermine them—that is, to engage in struggles to defend democracy and reclaim the social from the death-dealing necropolitics of state-sanctioned and stateless terrorists.[21] The danger and seduction offered by the spectacle of terrorism is that it thrives on new configurations of emotive and pedagogical violence that constitute subjects who, rather than being alarmed by violence, seek out more extreme spectacles of violence as a way to ramp up the collective desire for instant pleasure and the need to feel something, anything. The cultural and pedagogical "workstations" that produce this latest form of ideological monstrosity undermine any sense of justice, social responsibility, and compassion for others and must be addressed as part of the struggle against the spectacle of terrorism.

With its recognition of the image as a key force of social power, the spectacle of terrorism makes clear that culture deploys power and is now constituted by a plurality of sites of domination and resistance, offering up not simply ideological machineries of death but also new ways for progressives, not only terrorists—old and new—to conceptualize how the media might be used to create alternative public spheres and to provide democratic platforms for marginalized voices and radical imaginaries, to nurture the development of new forms of solidarity and modes of critique that rattle, upset, and critique the spectacle. This is evident in the emergence of new media such as Truthout, CounterPunch, and RiseUpTimes.org, as well as in the development of pirate radio, alternative film productions, new interactive forms of communication, phones with video cameras being used as "cop watching devices," and Twitter being employed to organize demonstrations and diverse modes of collective resistance.

Theorists such as Jürgen Habermas and Jacques Derrida are right in suggesting that the new electronic technologies and media publics "remove restrictions on the horizon of possible communications"[22] and, in doing so, suggest new possibilities for engaging the media as a democratic force both for critique and for positive intervention and change. We see evidence of such possibilities in the ways the new technologies or social media—whether they be cell phones, the Internet, or Twitter—have exposed the everyday violence of the police, the military, and the state in ways that a few decades ago would have been impossible. The Orwellian nightmare of being watched has been modified into a form of resistance as the foot soldiers of the Orwellian state now find themselves in the eye of surveillance conducted by bystanders, concerned citizens, and even by politicians calling for the police, for instance, to wear miniature video cameras. The spectacle of terrorism, if examined closely, provides some resources for rethinking how the political is connected to particular understandings of the social; how distinctive modes of address are used to marshal specific identities, memories, and histories; and how certain pedagogical practices are employed to mobilize a range of affective investments around images of trauma and suffering.

We live in a historical moment in which fear has become the primary pedagogical weapon of the new digital authoritarianism, whether on the part of the state or free-floating extremist groups. Fear redefines security as a legitimation for a military metaphysics that limits the reach of agency, empties out the social by creating armies of frightened, atomized individuals, and elevates an inflated and limited notion of security as the only basis for governance. The convergence of politics, power, subjectivity, and the new technologies demands that progressives ask hard questions about not only how to imagine the basic elements and long-term institutions of a radical democracy but also what it would mean to expand the reach of democratic values by placing limits on markets and the drive for efficiency, profits, and privatization. Let's be clear that placing limits on markets is not a call for reform; it is a call for completely transforming capitalism into a form of democratic socialism.

Equally important, the debate over the spectacle of terrorism must be part of a larger dialogue about the defense of public goods, substantive equality, and the redistribution of power and wealth downward to the people rather than upward to the 1 percent. In addition, such a debate must address the rising tide of militarism, racism, and economic injustice. The debate over terrorism cannot be isolated from a larger, comprehensive understanding of the diverse threats to democracy taking place under the regime of neoliberalism.

This is especially important at a time when democracy is being endlessly invoked as a justification for the culture of fear and the expansion of the national-security state. It is impossible to take up the new media and its use as an extension of war and violence without addressing these issues, because what is at stake here is not simply how such technologies are changing the political, emotive, and pedagogical landscape of American life but how they need to be analyzed against the recognition that any viable democracy requires informed citizens with access to information that enables them to reject the concept of passive citizenry. This is not merely a concern with how technologies can be mastered, what they communicate, or how they are used, but, most important, how they interface with matters of politics, power, inequality, and justice. At issue here is how the new technologies might be used to undercut their legitimating role in the production of a culture of vindictiveness and violence in order to resurrect the concept of an expansive social contract that views economic equality and difference as inseparable from political democracy.

Democracy implies an experience in which power is shared; dialogue is connected to involvement in the public sphere; competency is linked to intervention; and education enables a public to expand the new technologies, capacities, and social forms that inform public life. None of these issues can be separated from the current mobilization and needed debate about the spectacle of terrorism in the service of extremists or state power. Central to a rethinking of the spectacle of terrorism is the issue of pedagogy, both as a structural formation and as a moral and political practice. Pedagogy is now primarily public, no longer restricted to traditional sites of learning such as the school, family, or place of worship. Diverse material contexts and institutional forces, such as conservative foundations in the United States, fund new sites for the dissemination of knowledge, ranging from radio, cable, and television stations to high-speed Internet connections offering magazine and newspaper sites that are workstations in the production of the spectacle of terrorism and violence.[23] Think tanks vie with pirate radio stations, alternative online zines, and blogs.

These diverse pedagogical sites also organize "personal and public structures of attention" within specific circuits of power as part of their attempt to reach distinct audiences.[24] The combination of new technologies and diverse modes of circulation and interaction is mediated, in turn, through various interpretative communities that both situate texts and confer meanings in ways that cannot be specified in advance. As I have suggested throughout this chapter, domination is never completely on the side of power, and this suggests rightly that meanings are received, but never guaranteed, and posit an important terrain of struggle. And, while public pedagogy is the outgrowth of new public technologies,[25] the particular forms and ideologies it produces are almost always open to interpretation and resistance.

The current spectacle of terrorism suggests the need for educators and others to develop pedagogical practices that encourage a form of attentiveness that enable audiences to engage in a dialogue with the stories told by spectacles of terrorism.[26] A pedagogy of moral witnessing must inform the necessity for a formative culture in which power is made visible and held accountable while also producing the conditions for a more robust form of critical and engaged agency. Such a pedagogy would reject the anti-intellectualism, the fear of critical dialogue, and the general indifference to the stories of others that are embedded in the pedagogy of the spectacle. In addressing what kind of pedagogical work is performed by the spectacle of terrorism, audiences would analyze, first, how their own gaze might be aligned with the insidious modes and bodies of power that participate in images of destruction, and, second, what is at stake in their attraction, expanding upon the highly individuated response solicited by the spectacle. The experience of the spectacle must be collectivized through pedagogical practices that assert its social articulations—that is, articulations of "remembering" how it is intimately connected to historical struggles over power and mediates among different stories, contexts, and relations that can address a public rather than a merely private sensibility. The spectacle of terrorism currently resonates with the entrenched spirit of Social Darwinism, endemic to neoliberalism and the contemporary racial backlash. This entrenchment paralyzes critical agency through the regressive retreat into privatized worries and fears and powerfully undermines all notions of dialogue, critical engagement, and historical remembrance.

Against a pedagogy of closure, there is the need for a pedagogy that values a culture of questioning, views critical agency as a condition of public life, and rejects voyeurism in favor of the search for justice that is inextricably linked to how we understand our relationship to others within a democratic global public sphere. Such a pedagogy must reject the dystopian, anti-intellectual, and often racist vision at work in the spectacle of terrorism and, in doing so, provide a language of both criticism and hope as a condition for rethinking the possibilities of the future and the promise of global democracy itself. At the same time, it must struggle against the concentration of power in the hands of the few who now use the instruments that promote the spectacle of terrorism as an oppressive ideological and pedagogical tool. The struggle over the spectacle of terrorism is both symbolic and material, ideological and economic.

Finally, any viable pedagogical struggle against the spectacle of terrorism must work diligently to rescue the promise of a radical democracy from the clutches of religious, market, educational, and militaristic evangelicals who have hijacked a once-rich social imagination, reducing the politics of a radical democracy to the rabid discourses of economic, religious, and political fundamentalism, particularly as they are expressed in the conceits of neoliberal individualism, the utterly sectarian impulses of religious extremists, and the authoritarian values of a newly energized militarism. Although the spectacle of terrorism connects directly to affairs of state through the power of the corporate-controlled media, any politics that matters will have to engage both the screen culture of the image and those underlying related material relations of power and institutions on local, national, and global levels that deploy information technologies. Under the shadow of a growing authoritarianism, the spectacle of terrorism gives meaning to the social primarily through the modalities of xenophobia, violence, war, and death and, in doing so, makes fear the condition of unity and surrendering dissent and freedom the condition of agency. Any effective challenge to the spectacle of terrorism must embrace those strategies and movements willing to raise "democracy and politics to the global level at which capital seeks and enjoys its freedom from human ideas of decency and justice."[27] Integrating a global perspective and reclaiming the social as part of a broader radical democratic imagination means drawing attention to the realities of power and authority and locating across multiple and diverse spaces and borders what Edward Said calls "the energy of resistance ... to all totalizing political movements and institutions and systems of thought."[28]

What might it mean to address the spectacle of terrorism as part of a broader attempt to make the pedagogical more political by developing social relations grounded in a sense of power, history, memory, justice, ethics, and hope, all of which would be seen as central to connecting the new media to global democratic struggles? The spectacle of terrorism has developed a singular and successful form of public pedagogy and control, in part, because of the atrophy of public discourse. The central challenge here is to develop new forms of consciousness and solidarity in order not only to address the conditions of authoritarianism and various fundamentalisms, which increasingly generate a culture of fear and insecurity, but also to provide new ways of dealing with and defusing the experiences of fear, threat, and terror. Ideas matter, and changing consciousness is fundamental to any viable form of individual and collective resistance. Such a challenge points to the necessity of providing the public with an expanded vision and a productive sense of the common good, a new language for what it means to translate private considerations into public concerns, and a deeply felt concern with how power can work in both the symbolic and material realms to produce vocabularies of critique and possibility in the service of a substantive and inclusive global democracy. The essence of politics is as much about pedagogy and changing the way people think and act as it is about the use of the repressive state apparatuses. James Baldwin's notion that education is a paradox in that "as one begins to become conscious one begins to examine the society in which he is being educated" may be far more revolutionary than he imagined and far more necessary than is currently understood by the American public.[29]

6
Organized Forgetting
Memory and the Politics of Hope

⟡

Henry A. Giroux Interviewed by Victoria Harper

VICTORIA HARPER: *How has the violence of organized forgetting and the attack on memory impacted American culture and society?*

HENRY GIROUX: We live in a historical moment when memory if not critical thought itself is either under attack or is being devalued and undermined by a number of forces in American society. Historical memory has become dangerous today because it offers the promise of lost legacies of resistance, moments in history when the social contract was taken seriously (however impaired), and when a variety of social movements emerged that called for a rethinking of what democracy meant and how it might be defined in the interest of economic and social justice. Including violence and organized forgetting into the title of my latest book was meant to signal how mainstream politics devalues reason, dissent, and critique and the formative culture and institutions that support these crucial moments of thinking, agency, and collective struggle necessary for a democracy. It also registers how dominant regimes of power have resorted to a culture of fear, state repression, and the militarization of large parts of the society in order to enforce a state of terror, conformity, and privatization. Violence signals the state's complicity in creating a culture that is utterly commodified and privatized, one in which the obligations of citizenship are reduced to pursuing narrow individual interests and the demands of consumerism. How we define ourselves as Americans has a deeply historical

73

character, and to the degree that this history is impoverished, any viable notion of agency, justice, education, and democracy is devalued.

Fear, privatization, and depoliticization are the organizing principles of American society at the current moment and as such the defunding of critical public spheres such as schools is matched by forms of state repression that link education to purely instrumental interests, at least for most young people. The social and political cleansing of history, memory, and thought itself is in essence a part of a larger attack on dissent, critical thinking, engaged agency, and collective struggles. Purging dissent and public memory not only promotes among young people retreat from the public realm, it also empties out politics. As the public collapses into the private, injustices are viewed as a nuisance that interfere with private interests. Believing in a cause gives way to the quest to get ahead, while matters of social and civic responsibility disappear in a self-absorbed culture of narcissism, narrow individualism, and privatization.

What we are discovering is how the attack on history, witnessing, and critique breeds antidemocratic horrors including what my colleague David L. Clark terms "the wars against thought, and the flirtations with irrationality that lie at the heart of the triumph of every-day aggression, the withering of political life, and the withdrawal into private obsessions." This may be one reason why we are seeing such an upsurge of violence against black youth, college protesters, and those who have been part of the now quiet Occupy movement. Young people have become the chief object of oppression and punitive social policies because they represent the most promising group for reclaiming memory as a central political issue and using elements of the past to rethink a future very different from the one we now occupy. This may be one reason why the state is attempting to depoliticize young people through the onslaught of a consumer culture, the burden of extreme debt, and other social policies and survivalist pedagogies that lower their expectations while keeping them too busy to be able to address the political and social issues that underlie what it means to be young in a suspect society.

V. H.: *What do you mean by the disimagination machine?*

H. G.: Borrowing from and modifying Georges Didi-Huberman's use of the term "disimagination machine," I argue that the politics of disimagination refers to images, institutions, discourses, and other modes of representation that undermine the capacity of individuals to bear witness to a different and critical sense of remembering, agency, ethics, and collective resistance. The "disimagination machine" is both a set of cultural apparatuses extending from schools and mainstream media to the new sites of screen culture, social media, and a public pedagogy that functions primarily to weaken the ability of individuals to think critically, imagine the unimaginable, and engage in thoughtful and critical dialogue. Put simply, for them to become critically informed citizens of the world. The concept of the disimagination

74

machine signals a new and powerful moment in how authority depoliticizes, privatizes, and infantilizes Americans. It narrows the expanding circle of moral conscience, undercuts the radical imagination, and imposes on society the regressive morality of neoliberalism. The machinery of disimagination does not constitute a new form of social control that relies on colonizing subjectivity through the use of education in various sites to shape the identities, desires, values, modes of identification, and subjectivities of Americans in the interest of social control as much as it suggests more intensive and reconfigured attempts, aided by the new digital technologies, to generate a culture of mass forgetfulness, obedience, and conformity.

As all aspects of American life are transformed into a war zone, the state aggressively employs the mechanics and practices of a disimagination machine coupled with state terrorism. For instance, public schools are being privatized and militarized while higher education is being turned into a training ground for all but the elite in order to service corporate interests and power. At the same time, the cultural apparatuses of the mainstream media disavow critical issues by producing news and modes of popular culture that constitute an echo chamber for dominant class and financial interests along with the production of a celebrity culture and spectacles of violence that trivialize everything they touch. The United States appears trapped in a war psychosis as it wages wars at home and abroad, all the while treating violence as entertainment or the first response in its nurturing of a culture of fear. Moreover, these structural and symbolic mechanisms function increasingly in a digital world in which communication exhibits little respect for contemplation, critical dialogue, or informed judgment. Speed and an overabundance of information replace the time to think, just as being alone in privatized orbits of digitized technospheres constitutes a derailed notion of community. In the broader society, entertainment is the new mode of education, with its delivery of instant stimulation, excitement, gratification, and escape from the world of social and political responsibility while broader notions of education harness people's subjectivities to the narrow values of a market-driven society. In school, pedagogies of repression wage war on the critical and imaginative capacities of students. Under such circumstances, the disimagination machine represents a constellation of symbolic and institutional forces that attempt to shut down the possibility of critical thought and social agency. The disimagination machine combines Orwell's notion of state terror through a culture of fear, violence, and surveillance with, as Bill Moyers puts it, Huxley's notion of "people genetically designed to be regimented into total social conformity and subservient to the group think of the one percent [who] could easily have walked right out of Huxley and straight into Roger Ailes's Fox News playbook or Rush Limbaugh's studio." There is more at stake here than limited political horizons, as David Graeber has suggested. What is also put up for grabs is the notion of subjectivity in a neoliberal age, along with its deracinated view of agency and struggle.

V. H.: *The concept of disposability plays a central role in your work. Can you explain what it means, why it is new, and how it tends to manifest itself?*

H. G.: Since the late 1970s, American society has been transformed in ways that point to the abandonment of liberal democracy and the welfare state, while social policies have been promulgated that egregiously serve the interests of global markets. Within this period of the upsurge of market dreamworlds and increased economic control, the liberal market gave way to a punitive form of casino capitalism, or as some call it, neoliberalism. In addition, the collective sense of ethical imagination and social responsibility toward those who are vulnerable or in need of care has been increasingly viewed as a scourge or pathology. One consequence is that within this new historical conjuncture, the practice of disposability expands to include more and more individuals and groups who have been considered redundant, consigned to zones of abandonment, surveillance, and mass incarceration. Disposability is no longer the exception but the norm. As the reach of disposability has broadened to include a range of groups extending from college youth and poor minorities to the unemployed and members of the middle class who have lost their homes in the financial crisis of 2007, a shift in the radicalness and reach of the machinery of disposability not only constitutes a new mode of authoritarian politics but also demands a new political vocabulary for understanding how the social contract has virtually disappeared while the mechanisms of expulsion, disposability, and state violence have become more integrated and menacing.

We live in a new era of neoliberal savagery. Life has become cheap, emptied of its integrity and worth and reduced to the metrics of profit and a ruthless form of market fundamentalism. America occupies a historical moment characterized by market genocide—a time in which entire populations are considered disposable, left on their own to barely survive or die. Refusing Medicaid expansion by right-wing politicians such as Rick Perry is only one example of the death march at the heart of the politics of disposability and the culture of hyper-punitiveness. Up to 17,000 will die a year because of the refusal of these medical services by right-wing politicians. Surely, it is not an exaggeration to view this as the product of a death-machine, a form of genocide that hides behind an appeal to free-market practices that are far from free or innocent.

Citizens are now reduced to data, potential terrorists, consumers, and commodities and as such inhabit identities in which they become increasingly, drawing on João Biehl's words, "unknowables, with no human rights and with no one accountable for their condition." Within this machinery of social death, not only does moral blindness prevail on the part of the financial elite, but the inner worlds of the oppressed are constantly being remade under the force of economic pressures and a culture of fear, while their lives resemble the walking dead—discarded individuals who remain invisible and unaccounted for in the dominant discourse of politics, rights, and civic morality. The discourse of disposability points to and makes visible expanding zones of exclusion and invisibility incorporating more and more individuals and groups that were once seen as crucial to sustaining public life.

As we have seen with the brutalizing racist killing of black youth, including the most recent deaths of Trayvon Martin, Michael Brown, and Tamir Rice, disposability targets specific individuals and social spaces as sites of danger, violence, humiliation, and terror. This is most evident in the rise of a brutal punishing-incarceration state that imposes its racial and class-based power on the dispossessed, the emergence of a surveillance state that spies on and suppresses dissenters, the emergence of vast cultural apparatuses that colonize subjectivity in the interests of the market, and a political class that is uninterested in political concessions and appears immune from control by nation-states.

The politics of disposability is central to my work because it makes clear the mechanisms of a more brutal form of authoritarianism driven by an age saturated in a culture of cruelty, punishment, and death, in which matters of violence, survival, and trauma infuse everyday life. Discarded by the corporate state, dispossessed of social provisions, and deprived of the economic, political, and social conditions that enable viable and critical modes of agency, expanding populations of Americans now find themselves inhabiting zones of abandonment. These zones of hardship and terminal exclusion constitute a hallmark signature and intensification of a neoliberal politics of disposability that is relentless in the material and symbolic violence it wages against the 99 percent for the benefit of the new financial elite. What has become clear is that capitalist expropriation, dispossession, and disinvestment have reached a point where life has become completely unbearable for more than half of the American public living in or near poverty. As I have said on the pages of *Truthout*, evidence of such zones of abandonment and terror can be seen in the war against immigrants, poor minorities, the homeless, young people living in debt, the long-term unemployed, workers, the declining middle class—all of whom have been pushed into invisible communities of control, harassment, security, and the governing-through-punishment complex.

V. H.: *The drift toward authoritarianism is a central theme that you take up in your work. How would you describe the new authoritarianism?*

H. G.: In analyzing the emergence of authoritarianism in the United States, I focus on the ways in which the commanding institutions in the United States have been taken over by powerful corporate interests, the financial elite, and right-wing extremists whose strangulating control over politics renders democracy corrupt and dysfunctional, producing what might be called a neoliberal spectacle of misery and a culture of cruelty. Social Darwinism is the value system that drives casino capitalism in the United States. It is an ethic dominated by a war-against-all ethos that celebrates a radical individualism, extreme forms of competitiveness, engages in a culture of harshness, and separates actions from moral considerations. It is a poisonous system of power, control, and fear that views politics as an extension of war. In essence, America has devolved into a society that not only violates civil liberties, wages a war against unions, schoolteachers, women, youth, and social activists but also has inhabited a sphere of militarism that increasingly resembles a form of domestic terrorism. Again, this is amplified in the presence of a giant and wasteful war machine and in the ongoing militarization of local police forces who now assume the mantle of robo-swat teams, more willing to reduce policing to forms of high-powered assaults than dialogue, negotiation, and thoughtful investigations. The police have been transformed into soldiers outfitted with submachine guns and full riot gear, and trained to treat young people, poor minorities, immigrants, Muslims, and others as the enemy. Not only has society become more militarized but everyone is now treated as a criminal or potential terrorist. The contours of the authoritarian state become highly visible in the way in which, as Chase Madar observes, a wide range of behaviors are now criminalized, and the way in which "police power has entered the DNA of social policy, turning just about every sphere of American life into a police matter."

The militarization of local police forces combined with the larger intensified barbaric expressions of racism, especially the rise of the mass incarceration state and the racist comments so freely uttered by right-wing politicians and right-wing media, fuel a deadly mix for black youth that normalizes the wanton killing of African Americans and reinforces the impunity with which it is done. Nurtured by what Karen Garcia calls a "lifetime of consumption of violence-as-entertainment," images of expanding war zones come to life vividly in cities such as Ferguson, Missouri, where surplus military weaponry is now used by the police against African American youth and others marginalized by race and class in ways that make visible how the wars abroad have come home, and how weapons of war when combined with a hypermasculinity of brooding, resentful, and confused white men lead to violence in the streets. It is hard to disagree with a growing consensus that what we are witnessing in the United States is the legacy of slavery and the criminalization of people of color reasserting itself in a society in which justice has been willingly and aggressively replaced by racial injustice. And it is precisely this militarization that informs my analysis about the growing dangers of authoritarianism in America. Racist killings, the loss of privacy, the rise of the surveillance state, the growing poverty and inequality, and the increasing corporatization of the commanding institutions of the United States point to something more than civil unrest, spying, racism, and other specific antidemocratic issues. What is truly at work here and unites all of these disparate issues is a growing threat of authoritarianism—or what might be otherwise called totalitarianism with elections.

This new mode of authoritarianism mimics a form of terrorism because it abstracts economics from ethics and social costs, makes a mockery of democracy, works to dismantle the welfare state, thrives on violence, undermines any public sphere not governed by market values, and transforms people into commodities. American society's rigid emphasis on unfettered individualism, competitiveness, and flexibility displaces compassion, sharing, and a concern for the welfare of others. In doing so, it dissolves crucial social bonds, weakens public trust, and undermines the profound nature of social responsibility and its ensuing concern for others. In removing individuals from broader social obligations, it not only tears up social solidarities, it also promotes a kind of individual and collective psychosis that is pathological in its disdain for public goods, community, social provisions, and public values. As Hannah Arendt argued, we live in a time of absolute meaninglessness, which is the foundation of absolute evil, all of which produces a monstrous form of politics. Of course, this monstrous politics is revealed not only in savage social policies and attacks on the poor, public servants, women, and young people but also in the inability of American society to react to the suffering of others. Put differently, the United States has dethroned any viable notion of politics committed to the promise of a sustainable democracy. We have given up on the notion of the common good, social justice, and equality, which has been replaced by the crude discourses of commerce and militarization.

The new authoritarianism represents a mix of a widespread culture of fear, privatization, and consumer fantasies, along with a systemic effort to dismantle the welfare state and increase the power of the corporate and financial elite. Ideologically, the new authoritarianism works hard to instrumentalize knowledge, disparage reason, thoughtfulness, complexity, and critical dialogue, and in doing so contributes to a culture of stupidity and cruelty in which the dominant ethic is organized around the discourse of war and a survival-of-the-fittest mentality. Market sovereignty has replaced political sovereignty as the state is almost entirely corporatized, representing the antithesis of democracy. The consequences of antidemocratic tendencies are everywhere in American society. Deregulation, privatization, atomization, and commodification now rule American institutions, turning over the commanding heights of power to megacorporations, the defense industry, and ideological fundamentalists. America is a hugely rich country marked by massive poverty, inequality in wealth and income, and a political system controlled by big money. Its cultural apparatuses are controlled by megacorporations, and its political system is now largely controlled by the apostles of finance and militarism. One consequence is the coupling of a market-induced form of depoliticization with a deep-rooted cynicism. In this instance, the seeds of authoritarianism can be found in the disappearance of politics—that is, in the elimination of the conditions that create civic agents who are thoughtful, critical, ethically responsible, and imbued with a spirit of civic courage. The latter are not conditions that are valued in a society in which a war is waged on women's reproductive rights, civil liberties, immigrants, voting rights, and health care, along with the gleeful promotion of widening inequalities in wealth and income. As Slavoj Žižek points out, the link between capitalism and democracy is broken, and in its place is the emergence of an America that is on the brink of a very dark historical period in which the winds of authoritarianism are posed to destroy all remnants of a claim to equality, justice, and democracy.

V. H.: *Why is hope so central to your writings and the politics itself?*

H. G.: Hope gets a bad rap across diverse ideological lines. This is especially true in an age of crippling cynicism, precarity, uncertainty, and mass-produced fear. Yet, educated hope matters because it points to the possibility of rethinking not only politics but also matters of agency, struggle, and the future itself. Hope is a crucial element for energizing the radical imagination, one that allows people to repudiate and see through the manufactured cynicism that so well serves the new authoritarianism with its myriad of political, religious, and cultural fundamentalisms. Yet, hope must be tempered by the complex reality of the times and viewed as a project and condition for providing a sense of collective agency, opposition, political imagination, and engaged participation. It must be rooted in acknowledging the reality and the power of the ideological and structural forces that provide the foundation for authoritarian regimes. Hope, in this instance, breaks through the normalization of common sense as well as those educative dimensions of dominant culture that are used to legitimate an oppressive society and the oppressive forces that shape everyday life.

Without hope, even in the most dire of times, there is no possibility for resistance, dissent, and struggle. Furthermore, agency is the condition of struggle, and hope is the prerequisite of all modes of critically engaged agency. Hope expands the space of the possible, and becomes a way of recognizing and naming the incomplete nature of the present while providing the foundation for informed action. Throughout my work, I connect the issue of educated hope to the need to imagine the public as a site of possibility, one that harbors a trace of what it means to defend those public spaces where dissent can be produced, public values asserted, dialogue made meaningful, and opposition can be developed against the view that critical thought is an act of stupidity or irrelevant. As I have argued in much of my work for many years, one cannot be on the side of democratic ideas, causes, and movements and at the same time surrender to the normalization of a dystopian vision. Authoritarianism does not just breed conformity and cynicism; it relies on the death of hope to reproduce its dominant ideologies and practices while depoliticizing young people and others who should care about the fate of democracy. There is no room for romanticizing hope in Disney-like fashion. One has to demand the impossible in order to recognize the limits of what we are told is only possible. Hope as a form of antihope is connected not simply to inventing the future as a repeat of the present, but also normalizing the machineries of violence and oppression. This means that there is no room for a kind of romanticized utopianism. Instead, one has to be motivated by a faith in the willingness of young people principally and others to fight for a future in which dignity, equality, and justice matter, and at the same time recognize the forces that are preventing such a struggle from taking place. More specifically, hope has to be fed by the need for education and collective action. As I have argued repeatedly, power is never completely on the side of domination, and resistance is not a luxury but a necessity. In the present historical moment, hope needs to be tied to a politics that takes education seriously—that is, a politics for which matters of consciousness and agency mutually inform each other as part of a broader struggle for justice, freedom, and equality. This means that hope moves from an abstraction to creating the foundation for moving people to address the issue of economic inequality, the racist system and mass incarceration state, the sordid inequality gap in wealth and income, and the politics of disposability while building social movements that address the totality of power and oppression. This means taking seriously what it means to change the way people think while developing a comprehensive notion of politics, vision, and struggle to match.

SECTION 2
The Savagery of Neoliberalism

7
Beyond Orwellian Nightmares and the Politics of the Deep State

❧

To be corrupted by totalitarianism, one does not have to live in a totalitarian country.

—*George Orwell*

Central to George Orwell's nightmarish vision of a totalitarian society was a government so powerful that it not only dominated all of the major institutions in a society but was also quite adept at making invisible its inner workings of power. This is what some have called a shadow government, deep state, dual state, or corporate state.[1] In the deep state, politics becomes the domain of the super-rich, the powerful few who run powerful financial services, big corporations, and the imperious elites of the defense industries and other components of the military-industrial complex. Corporate interests such as ExxonMobil and other fossil fuel companies, megabanks such as the Bank of America, and defense industries such as Boeing, General Dynamics, Northrop Grumman, and Lockheed Martin are powerful lobbying groups, and as such have control of the major seats of political power and the commanding institutions necessary to ensure that the deeply antidemocratic state rule in the interests of the few while exploiting and repressing the many.[2] What Orwell could not have imagined was the transformation of the totalitarian state into a new form of authoritarianism marked by what Peter Beilharz has called "the effective totalitarianism of the market."[3]

This was recently made clear by a Princeton University scientific study that analyzed policies passed by the US government from 1981 to 2002; it discovered that the vast majority of such policies had nothing to do with the needs and voiced interests of the American people. As the authors pointed out, "The preferences of the average American appear to have only a minuscule, near-zero, statistically non-significant impact upon public policy."[4] Put bluntly, the study made clear that the opinions of the public per se simply *do not count.* The study concluded that rather than being a democracy the United States had become an oligarchy where power is effectively wielded by "the rich, the well connected and the politically powerful, as well as particularly well placed individuals in institutions like banking and finance or the military."[5]

Bill Blunden adds to this description with a useful map of the interpenetrating elements and overlapping layers of interest that make up the deep state. He writes:

> The American Deep State, or what Colonel Fletcher Prouty called the Secret Team, is a structural layer of political intermediaries: non-governmental organizations (e.g. National Endowment for Democracy, Ford Foundation), lobbyists (e.g. Chamber of Commerce, AIPAC), media outlets (e.g. Time Warner, News Corp), dark money pits (e.g. Freedom Partners, NRA), and private sector contractors (e.g. Booz Allen, SAIC) that interface with official government organs (CIA, Department of Defense). This layer establishes a series of informal, often secret, backchannels and revolving doors through which profound sources of wealth and power outside of government can purchase influence. . . . The American Deep State is a fundamentally anti-democratic apparatus that caters to the agenda of heavily entrenched elites.[6]

This is a state in which people participate willingly in their own oppression often out of deep insecurity about their freedom and the future. This is a mode of governance in which individual and social agency are in crisis and begin to disappear in a society in which 99 percent of the public, especially young people, low-income groups, and minorities of class and color are considered disposable. The rulers of the deep state no longer care about the social contract and make no concessions in their ruthless pursuits of power and profits. One consequence is the creation of a state and society that no longer believe in social investments and are more than willing to condemn young people, often paralyzed by the precariousness and instability that haunts their lives and future, to a savage form of casino capitalism. Poverty, joblessness, low-wage work, and the threat of state-sanctioned violence produce among many Americans the ongoing fear of a life of perpetual misery and an ongoing struggle simply to survive. Insecurity coupled with a climate of fear and surveillance dampens dissent and promotes a kind of ethical tranquilization fed daily by the mobilization of endless moral panics, whether they reference immigrants flooding the American Southwest, ISIS thugs blowing up malls, or Ebola spreading through the homeland like a mad, out-of-control death-dealing super-pathogen. Such conditions more often than not produce withdrawal, insecurity, paranoia, and cynicism rather than rebellion among the American populace. Under such conditions, the call for collective rebellion appears more like a joke for nighttime comics than a serious rethinking of politics and an attempt to engage in collective actions fueled by the need to reclaim and struggle over the promises of a radical democracy.

Politics and power are now on the side of lawlessness, as is evident in the state's endless violations of civil liberties, freedom of speech, and constitutional rights, mostly done in the name of national security. Lawlessness wraps itself in government dictates such as the Patriot Act, the National Defense Authorization Act, Military Commissions, and a host of other legal illegalities. These would include the right of the president "to order the assassination of any citizen whom he considers allied with terrorists,"[7] use secret evidence to detain individuals indefinitely, develop a massive surveillance panopticon to monitor every communication used by citizens who have not committed a crime, employ state torture against those considered enemy combatants, and block the courts from prosecuting those officials who commit such heinous crimes.[8] The ruling corporate elites have made terror rational and fear the modus operandi of politics. Such conditions more often than not produce withdrawal, insecurity, paranoia, and cynicism rather than rebellion among the American populace.

Power in its most repressive forms is now deployed not only by the police and other forces of repression, such as the seventeen American intelligence agencies, but also through a predatory and commodified culture that turns violence into entertainment, foreign aggression into a video game, and domestic violence into a goose-stepping celebration of masculinity and the mad values of militarism. Under the neo-Darwinian ethos of survival of the fittest, the ultimate form of entertainment becomes the pain and humiliation of others, especially those considered disposable and powerless, who are no longer an object of compassion but of ridicule and amusement. This becomes clear in the endless stories we are now hearing about the near epidemic of young women being sexually assaulted at fraternity parties or by professional football players. The medieval turn to embracing forms of punishment that inflict pain on the psyches and the bodies of young people is part of a larger immersion of society in public spectacles of violence. The Deluzian control society[9] is now the ultimate form of entertainment in America, as the pain of others, especially those considered disposable and powerless, is no longer an object of compassion but one of ridicule and amusement. Pleasure loses its emancipatory possibilities and degenerates into a pathology in which misery is celebrated as a source of fun. High-octane violence and human suffering are now considered consumer entertainment products designed to raise the collective pleasure quotient.

The medieval turn to embracing forms of punishment that inflict pain on the psyches and the bodies of young people is part of a larger immersion of society in public spectacles of violence. This becomes clear in the visibility of extreme violence in popular culture extending from video games to Hollywood films such as *John Wick* (2014) and *The Equalizer* (2014), both of which offer one of the few spaces amid the vacuity of a consumer culture where Americans can feel anything anymore. Brute force and savage killing are replayed over and over in the culture and now function as part of an anti-immune system that turns the economy of genuine pleasure into a mode of sadism that saps democracy of any political substance and moral vitality, even as the body politic appears engaged in a process of cannibalizing its own young.

It is perhaps not far-fetched to imagine a reality TV show in which millions tune in to watch young kids being handcuffed, arrested, tried in the courts, and sent to juvenile detention centers. No society can make a claim to being a democracy as long as it defines itself through shared hatred and fears, rather than shared responsibilities. Needless to say, extreme violence is more than a spectacle for upping the pleasure quotient of those disengaged from politics; it is also part of a punishing machine that spends more on putting poor minorities in jail than educating them. As Michelle Alexander points out, "There are more African American adults under correctional control today—in prison or jail, on probation or parole—than were enslaved in 1850, a decade before the Civil War began."[10]

Meanwhile the real violence used by the state against poor minorities of color, women, immigrants, and low-income adults barely gets mentioned, except when it is so spectacularly visible that it cannot be ignored, as in the case of the shooting of Trayvon Martin, Michael Brown, or Eric Garner, who was choked to death by a New York City policeman after he was confronted for illegally selling untaxed cigarettes. Responding to the exoneration of the white policeman who killed Michael Brown, Robin Kelley situates the shooting within a broader context of state violence. He is worth quoting at length:

> State violence is always rendered invisible in a world where cops and soldiers are heroes, and what they do is always framed as "security," protection, and self-defense. . . . Whether we call it a war on drugs, or "Operation Ghetto Storm" as the Malcolm X Grassroots Movement dubs it, what we are dealing with is nothing less than permanent war waged by the state and its privatized allies on a mostly poor and marginalized Black and Brown working-class. Five centuries in the making, it stretches from slavery and imperialism to massive systematic criminalization. We see the effects on our children, in the laws that make it easier to prosecute juveniles as adults; in the deluge of zero tolerance policies (again a by-product of the war on drugs); in the startling fact that expulsions and suspensions have risen exponentially despite a significant decline in violent crime. Crisis, moral panics, neoliberal policies, racism fuel an expansive system

of human management based on incarceration, surveillance, containment, pacification, lethal occupation, and gross misrepresentation.[11]

The "deep state" empties politics of all vestiges of democratic rule while attempting, on the one hand, to make its machinery of power invisible and, on the other, to legitimate neoliberal ideology as a matter of common sense. The decisions that shape all aspects of the commanding institutions of society are made largely in private, behind closed doors by the anonymous financial elite, corporate CEOs, rich bankers, the unassailable leaders of the military-industrial complex, and other kingpins of the neoliberal state. At the same time, the cultural apparatuses of casino capitalism wage an aggressive pedagogical assault on reason, thoughtfulness, critical dialogue, and all vestiges of the public good. Valuable resources and wealth are extracted from the commons in order to maximize the profits of the rich while the public is treated to a range of distractions and diversions that extend from "military shock and awe overseas" to the banalities of a commodified culture industry and celebrity-obsessed culture that short-circuits thought and infantilizes everything it touches.

Underlying the rise of the authoritarian state and the forces that hide in the shadows is a hidden politics indebted to promoting the fog of historical and social amnesia. The new authoritarianism is strongly indebted to what Orwell once called a "protective stupidity" that corrupts political life and divests language of its critical content.[12] Neoliberal authoritarianism has changed the language of politics and everyday life through a poisonous public pedagogy that turns reason on its head and normalizes a culture of fear, war, and exploitation. Even as markets unravel and neoliberalism causes increased misery, "the broader political and social consensus remains in place," suggesting that the economic crisis needs to be matched by a similar crisis in consciousness, ideas, language, and values.[13]

As the claims and promises of a neoliberal utopia have been transformed into a Dickensian nightmare, the United States, and increasingly Canada, continue to succumb to the pathologies of political corruption, the redistribution of wealth upward into the hands of the 1 percent, the rise of the surveillance state, and the use of the criminal justice system as a way of dealing with social problems. At the same time, Orwell's dark fantasy of an authoritarian future continues without massive opposition as students, low-income, and poor minority youth are exposed to a low-intensity war in which they are held hostage to disciplinary measures in which they are subject to police violence and corporate and government modes of surveillance.

Such disciplinary practices are designed to punish young people whenever they exercise the right of nonviolent dissent, or they are targeted because they are minorities of class and color and considered a threat, as was recently evident in the killings by a white policemen of Michael Brown in

Ferguson, Missouri. Or, even more egregiously, the killing on November 22 of Tamir Rice, a twelve-year-old African American boy who was shot by a first-year policeman from a short distance after brandishing what turned out to be a BB gun.

With the rise of state violence and what John Feffer calls "participatory totalitarianism,"[14] the rich get more powerful just as the middle and working classes sink into economic and existential despair and young people are saddled with debts and the prospect of a future of low-skill jobs and a limited sense of dignity and hope. What all of this suggests is that the real crisis is not simply around the growing inequality in wealth and power accompanied by the more visible use of state violence and an arrogant display of hatred for both democracy and the disadvantaged, but also a dismantling of what Hannah Arendt called "the prime importance of the political."[15]

What is not so hidden about the tentacles of power that now hide behind the euphemism of democratic governance is the rise of a punishing state and its totalitarian paranoiac mind-set in which everyone is considered a potential terrorist or criminal. This mind-set has resulted in the government arming local police forces with discarded weapons from the battlefields of Iraq and Afghanistan, turning local police into high-tech SWAT teams.[16] How else to explain the increasing criminalization of social problems, from homelessness and failure to pay off student loans to trivial infractions by students such as doodling on a desk or violating a dress code in the public schools, all of which can land the public and young people in jail? The turn toward the punishing state is especially evident in the war on young people taking place in many schools, which now resemble prisons with their lockdown procedures, zero-tolerance policies, metal detectors, and the increasing presence of police. One instance of the increasing punishing culture of schooling is provided by Chase Madar. He writes: "Though it's a national phenomenon, Mississippi currently leads the way in turning school behavior into a police issue. The Hospitality State has imposed felony charges on schoolchildren for 'crimes' like throwing peanuts on a bus. Wearing the wrong color belt to school got one child handcuffed to a railing for several hours. All of this goes under the rubric of 'zero-tolerance' discipline, which turns out to be just another form of violence legally imported into schools."[17]

Underlying the carnage caused by neoliberal capitalism is a free-market ideology in which individuals are cut off from the common good along with any sense of compassion for the other.[18] Economic Darwinism individualizes the social by shredding social bonds that are not commodified and in doing so depoliticizes, atomizes, and infantilizes the broader public. All problems are now defined as a problem of faulty character and a deficient sense of individual responsibility. At the same time, freedom is reduced to consumerism and self-interest becomes the only guiding principle for living one's life. What is crucial to recognize is that the central issues of power and politics can lead to cynicism and despair if capitalism is not addressed as a system of social relations that diminishes—through its cultural politics, modes of commodification, and market pedagogies—the capacities and possibilities of individuals and groups to move beyond the vicissitudes of necessity and survival in order to fully participate in exercising some control over the myriad forces that shape their daily lives. If neoliberal authoritarianism is to be challenged and overcome, it is crucial that intellectuals, unions, workers, young people, and various social movements unite to reclaim democracy as a central element in fashioning a radical imagination that foregrounds the necessity for drastically altering the material and symbolic forces that hide behind a counterfeit claim to participatory democracy. This means imagining a radical democracy that can provide a living wage, decent health care, public works, and massive investments in education, child care, housing for the poor, along with a range of other crucial social provisions that can make a difference between living and dying for those who have been cast into the ranks of the disposable. This means at the very least recognizing that government has a responsibility to serve the public good rather than the financial and corporate interests of the rich and powerful who are driving America into the dark recesses of authoritarianism.

What we have in the United States today is fundamentally a new mode of politics, one wedded to a notion of power removed from accountability of any kind, and this poses a dangerous and calamitous threat to democracy itself, because such power is difficult to understand, analyze, and counter. The collapse of the public into the private, the depoliticization of the citizenry in the face of an egregious celebrity culture, and the disabling of education as a critical public sphere makes it easier for neoliberal capital with its hatred of democracy and celebration of the market to render its ideologies, values, and practices as a matter of common sense, removed from critical inquiry and dissent. As commentators as diverse as philosopher Slavoj Žižek and journalist Bill Moyers now remind us, neoliberal global capitalism is no longer compatible with democracy. That is, it is at odds with a substantive democracy in which the wealth, resources, and benefits of a social order are shared in an equitable and just manner. Democracy held up as an ideal and a promise means that society must continually strive to raise the bar of justice, equality, and freedom and that the self-reflection and struggles that enable all members of the community to participate in the decisions and institutions that shape their lives must be continually debated, safeguarded, and preserved at all costs.

With privatization comes a kind of collective amnesia about the role of government, the importance of the social contract, and the importance of public values. For instance, war, intelligence operations, prisons, schools, transportation systems, and a range of other operations once considered public have been outsourced or simply handed over to private contractors who are removed from any sense of civic and political accountability. The social contract and the institutions that give it meaning have been transformed into entitlements administered and colonized largely by the corporate interests and the financial elite. Policy is no longer being written by politicians accountable to the American public. Instead, policies concerning the defense budget, deregulation, health care, public transportation, job training programs, and a host of other crucial areas are now largely written by lobbyists who represent megacorporations. How else to explain the weak deregulation policies following the economic crisis of 2007, or the lack of a public option in Obama's health care policies? Or, for that matter, the more serious retreat from any viable notion of the political imagination that "requires long-term organizing—e.g., single-payer health care, universally free public higher education and public transportation, federal guarantees of housing and income security."[19] The liberal center has moved to the right on these issues, while the left has become largely absent and ineffective.

Democracy is not compatible with capitalism but is congruent with a version of democratic socialism in which the wealth, resources, and benefits of a social order are shared in an equitable and just manner. Democracy as a promise means that society can never be just enough and that the self-reflection and struggles that enable all members of the community to participate in the decisions and institutions that shape their lives must be continually debated, safeguarded, and preserved at all costs. The rebuilding of a radical democracy must be accompanied with placing a high priority on renewing the social contract, embracing the demands of the commons, encouraging social investments, and the regeneration of the social contract. These are only a few of the issues that should be a central goal for the development of a broad-based radical social movement. I want to emphasize that I am not suggesting that reviving the radical imagination as a call to reclaim a radical democracy be understood as simply a pragmatic adjustment of the institutions of liberal democracy or a return to the social democracy of the New Deal and Great Society.

On the contrary, any rethinking of the political can only be comprehended as part of a radical break from liberalism and formalistic electoral politics if there is to be any move toward a genuine democracy in which matters of equality, power, and justice are central to what can be called a radical democratic politics. Electoral politics have become incompatible with a true democracy because they remove citizens from the tools of political power, eliminate the public spheres necessary for producing critical agents, and undermine those visions that can imagine a true democracy outside of the reach of capitalism. Lorenzo Del Savio and Matteo Mameli point to the antidemocratic forces at work in undermining electoral forms of liberal democracy. They state:

> The electoral-representative institutions of contemporary democracies have been captured by oligarchies. Oligarchs are able to control electoral-representative structures through lobbying, the financing of electoral campaigns, the revolving

doors between elected posts and consultancy jobs for big firms, etc., and other mechanisms of this sort. The super-rich can direct the action of elected executives and parliaments and thereby determine the economic policies that affect (often negatively) the rest of the population. Arguably, in the last few decades, these policies have resulted in increasingly more efficient and subtle ways for the super-rich to extract resources from the planet and from common people.[20]

Challenging the politics of oligarchic capitalism necessitates a politics and pedagogy that not only expand critical awareness and promote critical modes of inquiry but also sustain public connections and promote strategies and organizations that create not simply ruptures such as massive demonstrations but real changes that are systemic and long standing. If such a politics is to make any difference, it must be worldly—that is, it must incorporate a critical public pedagogy and an understanding of cultural politics that not only contemplates social problems but also addresses the conditions for different modes of democratic political exchange while enabling new forms of agency, power, and collective struggle. Neoliberalism empties the ideas of civic courage, social responsibility, agency, and citizenship of their political substance and value. The collapse of the United States into neoliberal authoritarianism signals not simply a crisis of politics and democracy but also a crisis of ideas, values, and agency itself. Hence, calling for a revival of the educative nature of politics is more than simply a call to find ways to change consciousness; it is first and foremost an attempt to understand that education is at the center of a struggle over what kinds of agency will be created in the interest of legitimating the present and producing a particular kind of future. This is an imminently educative, moral, and political task, and it is only through such a recognition that initial steps can be taken to challenge the powerful ideological and affective spaces through which neoliberalism produces the desires, identities, and values that bind people to its forms of predatory governance.

The moral, political, and economic violence of neoliberalism must be made visible, its institutional structures dismantled, and the elite interests it serves exposed. The fog of historical, social, and political amnesia must be eliminated through the development of educational programs, pedagogical practices, ideological interventions, and public narratives that provide the critical and analytical tools to enable the public to analyze both underlying ideologies and institutions of neoliberal capitalism, as well as the intellectual and economic resources needed to provide meaningful alternatives to the corporate authoritarianism that passes itself off as an updated mode of democracy. Stanley Aronowitz, Adolph Reed, and Barbara Epstein, among others, have all argued recently that the left needs a broad-based political movement that can provide real alternatives to the established money and power of the deep state, but for that to happen the left has to develop narratives that capture the imagination of the public so that they can willingly invest in the struggle against the smokescreens used by contemporary versions of authoritarian rule. Chris Hedges has argued that totalitarian states survive in part through orchestrated forms of historical amnesia that not only misrepresent or eliminate any radical vestige of public memory but also are sustained through what he calls a "state induced stupidity."[21] He is certainly correct in claiming that the crisis in historical memory often leads to a failure to remember the struggles on the part of women, gays, workers, young people, minorities of color, and others to secure their freedoms, civil rights, and opportunity to learn how to govern rather than simply be governed by an oppressive state.

For Hedges, public memory is crucial for organizing what he calls massive demonstrations and prolonged acts of civil disobedience in order to challenge the authoritarian state. But the question remains regarding how a public largely indifferent to politics and paralyzed by the need to just survive while caught in a crippling cynicism can be moved from "an induced state of stupidity" to a political formation willing to engage in various modes of resistance extending from "mass protests to prolonged civil disobedience."[22] In part, Hedges argues that terrifying intellectual and moral paralysis produced by the ruling elite must be offset by the development of alternative public spheres in which the left can change the terms of the debate in American culture and politics. I think it is crucial that the struggle against neoliberalism focus on those forms of domination that pose a threat to those public spheres essential to developing the formative cultures that nourish modes of thinking, analysis, and social formations necessary for a radical democracy. At the very least, such spheres would include the mainstream and alternative media, public and higher education, and other cultural apparatuses such as the new social media.

In addition, the left has to do more than chart out the mechanisms through which neoliberal authoritarianism sustains itself. And for too many on the left this means simply understanding the economic determinants that drive neoliberal global capitalism. While this structural logic is important, it does not go far enough. As Stuart Hall has insisted: "There's no politics without identification. People have to invest something of themselves, something that they recognize is of them or speaks to their condition, and without that moment of recognition," any effort to change the way people inhabit social relations of domination will fail.[23] Pierre Bourdieu takes this logic further in arguing that the left has often failed to recognize "that the most important forms of domination are not only economic but also intellectual and pedagogical, and lie on the side of belief and persuasion."[24] He insists, rightly, that it is crucial for the left and other progressives to recognize that intellectuals bear an enormous responsibility for challenging this form of domination by developing tactics "that lie on the side of the symbolic and pedagogical dimensions of struggle."[25]

All calls for the left to revitalize itself so it can become a formidable force in American politics will fail if it does not take seriously the educative nature of politics. Stanley Aronowitz is one of the few people on the left who has taken matters of subjectivity, education, and politics seriously. Not only has he fully recognized that we are in a new historical moment in which a powerful relationship now exists among cultural institutions, political power, and everyday life, but he has also proposed a three-pronged program to address the new forms of domination, which includes reviving the radical imagination, launching a comprehensive education program, and opening a conversation about the creation of a new left political formation.[26] In the first instance, he argues for a revival of the radical imagination as part of a larger project "to reinvent democracy in the wake of the evidence that, at the national level, there is no democracy—if by 'democracy' we mean effective popular participation in the crucial decisions affecting the community. Democracy entails a challenge to private property in productive activities and large-scale enterprises."[27] Aronowitz refuses to accept minimalist notions of democracy in which elections become the measure of democratic participation. Far more crucial in his call for change is the development of a formative culture in which the American public can imagine forms of democratic self-management of what he calls "key economic, political, and social institutions."[28]

Second, he insists that the left needs to develop a comprehensive educational program that would include a range of pedagogical initiatives from developing a national online news channel to creating alternative schools for young people in the manner of the diverse workers' socialist schools that existed in the 1930s and 1940s. Third, he argues that the assault by neoliberalism is so widespread that the left needs to develop a comprehensive vision of politics that "does not rely on single issues."[29] Following Herbert Marcuse, he believes rightly that the "truth is in the whole" and that it is only through an understanding of the wider relations and connections of power that the left can overcome misplaced concreteness, isolated struggles, and modes of identity politics that become insular and self-sabotaging.

Particular injustices must be understood not only with respect to the conditions and contexts in which they develop but also in terms of their relationship to the larger social order. This means developing modes of analysis capable of connecting particular instances of struggle to more generalized notions of freedom; it suggests developing theoretical frameworks in which it becomes possible to translate private troubles into broader, more systemic conditions. At stake here is an attempt to develop a more general understanding of liberty, equality, and freedom, and to recognize the necessity for modes of analysis that connect the dots. This is a particularly important goal given that one reason why the left has been so fragmented politically is that it has failed to develop a wider political and ideological umbrella that enables it to connect a range of problems including extreme poverty, the assault on the environment, the emergence of the permanent warfare state, the abolition of voting rights, the assault on public servants, women's rights, and social provisions, and a range of other issues that when analyzed in isolation further erode the possibilities for a radical democracy. Neoliberalism stands for the death of democracy, and any movement that is going to successfully challenge this historically specific mode of authoritarianism will have to attack all of the dominating mechanisms of casino capitalism in both their symbolic and material economies. This suggests understanding how issues interconnect, mutually inform, and bleed into each other.

There is one caveat here that cannot be forgotten. The fight against neoliberalism and the related antidemocratic tendencies that inform it must not settle for reforming a system that is as broken as it is dangerous, if not pathological, in the violence and misery it produces. Any viable struggle must acknowledge that if the current modes of domination are to change, a newly developed emphasis must be placed on creating the formative culture that inspires and energizes a faith in the culture and systems of power relations and popular participation that would characterize a radical democracy. Such a struggle will not emerge out of demonstrations but out of a vision that is boldly democratic, organizations that are durable and long standing, and strategies that take seriously what it means to make politics meaningful in order to make it both critical and transformative. The new American authoritarianism has emptied democracy of any substantive meaning. The time has come to do more than reclaim and recover democracy's legacy of liberal traditions. While such a task is not unimportant, it does not go far enough. There is a real need for progressives and others to radicalize these traditions, offer new vocabularies and visions for change, and think beyond a future that is nothing more than a cheap imitation of the present. Radical democracy inspires fear in the ruling elite just as it must inspire and energize diverse groups to reclaim their moral and political agency in order to step into a future in which the current nightmare of American authoritarianism has faded into memory.

8
Neoliberalism and the Machinery of Disposability

Under the regime of neoliberalism, especially in the United States, war has become an extension of politics as almost all aspects of society have been transformed into a combat zone. Americans now live in a society in which almost everyone is spied on, considered a potential terrorist, and subject to a mode of state and corporate lawlessness in which the arrogance of power knows no limits. The state of exception has become normalized. Moreover, as society becomes increasingly militarized and political concessions become relics of a long abandoned welfare state hollowed out to serve the interests of global markets, the collective sense of ethical imagination and social responsibility toward those who are vulnerable or in need of care is now viewed as a scourge or pathology.

What has intensified in this new historical conjuncture is the practice of disposability in which more and more individuals and groups are now considered excess, consigned to zones of abandonment, surveillance, and incarceration. Moreover, this politics of excess and disappearance has been strengthened by a systemic depoliticization, conducted largely through new modes of surveillance and the smothering, if not all-embracing, market-driven pedagogical force of commodification and consumption. Citizens are now reduced to data, consumers, and commodities and as such inhabit identities in which they increasingly "become unknowables, with no human rights and with no one accountable for their condition."[1] Within this machinery of social death, not only does moral blindness prevail on the part of the financial elite, but the inner worlds of the oppressed are constantly being remade under the force of economic pressures and a culture of fear.

According to Joao Biehl, as the realpolitik of disposability "comes into sharp visibility, tradition, collective memory, and public spheres are organized as phantasmagoric scenes, [that] thrive on the 'energies of the dead,' who remain unaccounted for in numbers and law."[2]

Economists such as Robert Reich, Paul Krugman, and Doug Henwood have argued that we are in a new Gilded Age, one that mimics a time when robber barons and strikebreakers ruled, and the government and economy were controlled by a cabal that was rich, powerful, and ruthless.[3] And, of course, blacks, women, and the working class knew their place in a society controlled by the rich. What is often missing in these analyses is that what is new in the second Gilded Age is not just the moral sanctioning of greed, the corruption of politics by big money, and the ruthlessness of class power. What is unique is the rise of a brutal punishing-incarceration state that imposes its power on the dispossessed, the emergence of a surveillance state that spies on and suppresses dissenters, the rise of vast cultural apparatuses that colonize subjectivity in the interests of the market, and a political class that is uninterested in political concessions and appears immune from control by nation-states. The second Gilded Age is really a more brutal form of authoritarianism driven by what psychologist Robert Jay Lifton rightly calls a "death-saturated age" in which matters of violence, survival, and trauma now infuse everyday life.[4]

Discarded by the corporate state, dispossessed of social provisions, and deprived of the economic, political, and social conditions that enable viable and critical modes of agency, expanding populations of Americans now find themselves inhabiting zones of abandonment marked by deep inequalities in power, wealth, and income. Such zones are sites of rapid disinvestment, places marked by endless spectacles of violence, and supportive of the neoliberal logics of containment, commodification, surveillance, militarization, cruelty, and punishment. These zones of hardship and terminal exclusion constitute a hallmark signature and intensification of a neoliberal politics of disposability that is relentless in the material and symbolic violence it wages against the 99 percent for the benefit of the new financial elite. Borrowing from Hannah Arendt, one could say that capitalist expropriation, dispossession, and disinvestment has reached a point where life has become completely unbearable for over half of the American public living in or near poverty.[5] Evidence of such zones can be seen in the war against immigrants, poor minorities, the homeless, young people living in debt, the long-term unemployed, workers, the declining middle class, all of whom have been pushed into invisible communities of control, harassment, security, and the governing-through-punishment complex.

The promises of modernity regarding progress, freedom, and hope have not been eliminated; they have been reconfigured, stripped of their emancipatory potential and subordinated to the logic of a savage market instrumentality and individualization of the social. Dispossession and disinvestment have invalidated the promise of modernity and have turned progress into a curse for the marginalized and a blessing for the super–financial elite. Modernity has reneged on its promise to fulfill the social contract, however disingenuous or limited, especially with regard to young people. Long-term planning and the institutional structures that support it are now weakened, if not eliminated, by the urgencies of privatization, deregulation, flexibility, and short-term investments. Social bonds have given way under the collapse of social protections and the welfare state and are further weakened by the neoliberal insistence that there are only "individual solutions to socially produced problems."[6]

Neoliberalism's disposability machine is relentlessly engaged in the production of an unchecked notion of individualism that both dissolves social bonds and removes any viable notion of agency from the landscape of social responsibility and ethical considerations. Absorbed in privatized orbits of consumption, commodification, and display, Americans vicariously participate in the toxic pleasures of a mode of authoritarianism characterized by the reactionary presence of the corporate state, the concentration of power and money in the upper 1 percent of the population, the ongoing militarization of all aspects of society, and the relentless, aggressive depoliticization of the citizenry. In its current historical conjuncture, the authoritarian state is controlled by a handful of billionaires (for example, the Koch Brothers), their families (for example, the Waltons), and a select class of zombielike financial and corporate elite who now administer the commanding economic, political, and cultural institutions of American society.

Mechanisms of governance have been transformed into instruments of war. Violence has become the organizing force of a society driven by a toxic notion of privatization in which it becomes difficult for ideas to be lifted into the public realm. Under such circumstances, politics is eviscerated because it now supports a market-driven view of society that now supports the idea that "humanity consists entirely of isolated and atomized, self-interested individuals."[7] That is, society has come undone in terms of the social contract and in doing so has turned its back on most Americans whose lives and futures are no longer determined by social spaces that give them a voice and provide the conditions for autonomy, freedom, and equality. This violence against the social mimics not just the death of the radical imagination but also a notion of banality made famous by Hannah Arendt, who argued that at the root of totalitarianism was a kind of thoughtlessness, an inability to think, and a type of outrageous stupidity in which "there's simply the reluctance ever to imagine what the other person is experiencing."[8] Neoliberal societies destroy democratic values as politics is eviscerated in "the striking absence of citizenship and agency."[9] Under the war machine of neoliberalism, the conditions for critical agency have dissolved into the limited pleasures of instant gratification wrought through the use of technologies and consuming practices that dampen, if not obliterate, the very possibility of thinking itself. What is particularly distinctive about this historical conjuncture is the way in which young people, particularly low-income and poor minority youth, are increasingly denied any place in an already weakened social order and the degree to which they are no longer seen as central to how the United States defines its future.

The plight of disposable populations can be seen in the fact that millions of Americans are unemployed and are receiving no long-term benefits. Shockingly, the only source of assistance for one in fifty Americans "is nothing but a food stamp card."[10] Close to half of all Americans live on or beneath the poverty line, while "more than a million public school students are homeless in the United States; 57 percent of all children are in homes considered to be either low-income or impoverished, and half of all American children will be on food stamps at least once before they turn 18 years old."[11] At the same time, the four hundred richest Americans "have as much wealth as 154 million Americans combined, that's 50 percent of the entire country [while] the top economic 1 percent of the US population now has a record 40 percent of all wealth and more wealth than 90 percent of the population combined."[12] Within this system of power and disposability, the ethical grammars that draw our attention to the violence of such suffering disappear while dispossessed populations lose their dignity, bodies, and material goods to the machineries of disposability. The fear of losing everything, the horror of an engulfing and crippling precarity, the quest to merely survive, and the impending reality of social and civil death have become a way of life for the 99 percent in the United States. Under the politics of disposability, the grammars of suffering, cruelty, and punishment have replaced the value of compassion, social responsibility, and civic courage.

The severity of the consequences of this shift in modernity under neoliberalism among youth is evident in the fact that this is the first generation, as Zygmunt Bauman argues, in which the "plight of the outcast may stretch to embrace a whole generation."[13] He rightly argues that today's youth have been "cast in a condition of liminal drift, with no way of knowing whether it is transitory or permanent."[14] Youth no longer occupy the hope of a privileged place that was offered to previous generations. They now inhabit a neoliberal notion of temporality marked by a loss of faith in progress along with the emergence of apocalyptic narratives in which the future appears indeterminate, bleak, and insecure. Heightened expectations and progressive visions pale and are smashed next to the normalization of market-driven government policies that wipe out pensions, eliminate quality health care, raise college tuition, and produce a harsh world of joblessness, while giving millions to banks and the military. Students, in particular, now find themselves in a world in which heightened expectations have been replaced by dashed hopes and onerous debt.[15]

What has changed about an entire generation of young people includes not only neoliberal society's disinvestment in youth and the permanent fate of downward mobility but also the fact that youth live in a commercially carpet-bombed and commodified environment that is unlike anything experienced by previous generations. Nothing has prepared this generation for the inhospitable and savage new world of commodification, privatization, joblessness, frustrated hopes, surveillance, and stillborn projects.[16] The present generation has been born into a throwaway society of consumers in which both goods and young people are viewed increasingly as redundant and disposable, or they are merely valued as consumers and commodities. In this discourse, young people are not seen as troubled but viewed as a source of trouble; rather than viewed as being "at risk," they are the risk and subject to a range of punitive policies.

The structures of neoliberal modernity do more than disinvest in young people and commodify them; they also transform the protected space of childhood into a zone of disciplinary exclusion and cruelty, especially for those young people further marginalized by race and class who now inhabit a social landscape in which they are increasingly disparaged as flawed consumers. With no adequate role to play as consumers, many youth are now forced to inhabit "zones of terminal exclusion" extending from bad schools to bulging detention centers to prisons.[17] Youth have become a marker for a mode of disposability in which their fate is defined largely through the registers of a society that throws away resources, people, and goods. These are zones not only in which the needs of young people are ignored but where many young people, especially poor minority youth, are subjected to conditions of impoverishment and punishment that often criminalize their behavior—and in some cases result in killing them. For example, with the hollowing out of the social state and the rise of the punishing state, the circuits of state repression, surveillance, and disposability increasingly "link the fate of blacks, Latinos, Native Americans, poor whites, and Asian Americans" to a crime youth complex, which now serves as the default solution to major social problems.[18] Within these "zones of abandonment" and social death, poor minority and low-income youth are viewed as out of step, place, and time and defined largely as "pathologies feeding on the body politic," exiled to spheres of "terminal exclusion."[19]

As the welfare state is hollowed out, a culture of compassion is replaced by a culture of ruthlessness and atomization. Within the existing neoliberal historical conjuncture, there is a merging of violence and governance and the systemic disinvestment in and breakdown of institutions and public spheres that have provided the minimal conditions for democracy. A generalized fear now shapes American society—one that thrives on insecurity, dread of punishment, and a perception of constant lurking threats. Americans occupy a historical conjuncture in which everything that matters politically, ethically, and culturally is being erased—either ignored, turned into a commodity, or simply falsified.

In the United States, and many other countries, the state monopoly on the use of violence has not only intensified since the 1980s but is unashamedly sanctioned by the new extremists in power. Under the regime of neoliberalism, this new-found embrace of Social Darwinism and the culture of violence has been increasingly directed against young people, poor minorities, immigrants, and increasingly women. In Europe, refugees, who are the most vulnerable, are experiencing intensified levels of violence on the part of governments and right-wing thugs. Alexandra Politaki has made clear that European Union migration policies "are creating a culture of cruelty that is already establishing its own vocabulary. The word 'refugee' is rapidly going out of use, and 'illegal immigration' is in widespread use instead of 'migration without documents.' . . . Not only is the welfare state in retreat, but a hostile attitude towards vulnerable social groups is becoming prevalent."[20] In countries such as Greece, the right-wing Golden Dawn, one of Europe's most violent neo-Nazi forces, has regularly staged multiple violent attacks on immigrants, leftists, and gay people. The language used by such radical anti-immigrant groups in Europe and the United States shares a startling similarity in their attempts to demonize such groups.

Abandoned by the existing political system, young people are placing their bodies on the line, protesting peacefully across the globe while trying to produce a new language, politics, long-term institutions, and "community that manifests the values of equality and mutual respect that they see missing in a world that is structured by neoliberal principles."[21] Such movements are not simply about reclaiming space but also about producing new ideas, generating new conversations, and introducing a new political language. While there has been considerable coverage in the progressive media since 2001 given to the violence being waged against the movement protesters in Brazil, the United States, Greece, and elsewhere, it is important to situate such violence within a broader set of categories that not only makes possible a critical understanding of the underlying social, economic, and political forces at work in such assaults but also makes it possible to reflect critically on the distinctiveness of the current historical period in which they are taking place. For example, it is difficult to address such state-sponsored violence against young people without analyzing the devolution of the social state, the politics of disposability, and the corresponding rise of the warfare and punishing state.

The merging of the military-industrial-academic-cultural complex and unbridled corporate power points to the need for strategies that address what is specific about the current warfare state and the neoliberal project and how different interests, modes of power, social relations, public pedagogies, and economic configurations come together to shape its politics of domestic terrorism, cruelty, and zones of disposability. Such a conjuncture is invaluable politically in that it provides a theoretical opening for making the practices of the neoliberal revolution visible in order to organize resistance to its ideologies, policies, and modes of governance. It also points to the conceptual power of making clear that history remains an open horizon that cannot be dismissed through appeals to the end of history or end of ideology.[22] It is precisely through the indeterminate nature of history that resistance becomes possible and politics refuses any guarantees and remains open.

A number of neoliberal societies, including the United States, have become addicted to violence. War provides jobs, profits, political payoffs, research funds, and forms of political and economic power that reach into every aspect of society. As war becomes a mode of sovereignty and rule, it erodes the distinction between war and peace. Increasingly fed by a moral and political frenzy, warlike values produce and endorse shared fears as the primary register of social relations. Shared fears and the media-induced panics that feed them produce more than a culture of fear. Such hysteria also feeds the growing militarization of the police, who increasingly use their high-tech scanners, surveillance cameras, and toxic chemicals on anyone who engages in peaceful protests against the warfare and corporate state. Images abound in the mainstream media of such abuses.

As a mode of public pedagogy, a state of permanent war needs willing subjects to abide by its values, ideology, and narratives of fear and violence. Such legitimation is largely provided through a market-driven culture addicted to the production of consumerism, militarism, and organized violence, largely circulated through various registers of popular culture that extend from high fashion and Hollywood movies to the creation of violent video games and music concerts sponsored by the Pentagon. The market-driven spectacle of war demands a culture of conformity, quiet intellectuals, and a largely passive republic of consumers. But it also needs subjects who find intense pleasure in the spectacle of violence.

As the pleasure principle is unconstrained by a moral compass based on a respect for others, it is increasingly shaped by the need for intense excitement and a never-ending flood of heightened sensations. In this instance, unfamiliar violence such as extreme images of torture and death become banally familiar, while familiar violence that occurs daily is barely recognized and relegated to the realm of the unnoticed and unnoticeable. As an increasing volume of violence is pumped into the culture, yesterday's spine-chilling and nerve-wrenching violence loses its shock value. As the need for more intense images of violence accumulates, the moral indifference and desensitization to violence grows while matters of cruelty and suffering are offered up as fodder for sports, entertainment, news media, and other outlets for seeking pleasure.

Marked by a virulent notion of hardness and aggressive masculinity, a culture of violence has become commonplace in a society in which pain, humiliation, and abuse are condensed into digestible spectacles endlessly circulated through extreme sports, reality TV, video games, YouTube postings, and proliferating forms of the new and old media. But the ideology of hardness and the economy of pleasure it justifies are also present in the material relations of power that have intensified across the globe since the 1970s. Conservative and liberal politicians alike now spend millions waging wars around the globe, funding the largest military state in the world, providing huge tax benefits to the super-rich and major corporations, and all the while draining public coffers, increasing the scale of human poverty and misery, and eliminating all viable public spheres—whether they be the social state, public schools, public transportation, or any other aspect of a formative culture that addresses the needs of the common good. State violence, particularly the use of torture, abductions, and targeted assassinations, is now justified as part of a state of exception that has become normalized. A "political culture of hyper punitiveness" has become normalized and accelerates throughout the social order like a highly charged electric current. [23]

A symptomatic example of the way in which violence has saturated everyday life can be seen in the growing acceptance of criminalizing the behavior of young people in public schools. Transgressions that were normally handled by teachers, guidance counselors, and school administrators are now dealt with by the police and the criminal justice system. The consequences have been disastrous for young people. Not only do schools resemble the culture of prisons, but young children are being arrested and subjected to court appearances for behaviors that can only be termed as trivial. This is not merely barbarism parading as reform—it is also a blatant indicator of the degree to which sadism and the infatuation with violence have become normalized in a society that seems to take delight in dehumanizing itself.

As the social is devalued along with rationality, ethics, and any vestige of democracy, spectacles of war, violence, and brutality now merge into forms of collective pleasure that constitute an important and new symbiosis between visual pleasure, violence, and suffering. The control/punishing society is now the ultimate form of entertainment as the pain of others, especially those considered disposable and powerless, has become the subject not of compassion but of ridicule and amusement. High-octane violence and human suffering are now considered another form of entertainment designed to raise the collective pleasure quotient. Reveling in the suffering of others should no longer be reduced to a matter of individual pathology, but now registers a larger economy of pleasure across the broader culture and social landscape. My emphasis here is on the sadistic impulse and how it merges spectacles of violence and brutality with forms of collective pleasure that often lend support and sway public opinion in favor of social policies and "lawful" practices that create zones of abandonment for youth. No society can make a claim to being a democracy as long as it defines itself through shared fears rather than shared responsibilities, especially in regard to young people. Widespread violence now functions as part of an anti-immune system that turns the economy of genuine pleasure into a mode of sadism that creates the foundation for sapping democracy of any political substance and moral vitality that might counter a politics of disposability more generally.

The prevalence of violence throughout American society suggests the need for a politics that not only negates the established order and the proliferating zones of disappearance and dispossession of subjects rendered useless or burdensome but also imagines new radical visions in which the future diverges from the dark conditions of the present.[24] In this discourse, critique merges with a sense of realistic hope, and individual struggles merge into larger social movements.

At the heart of the oppression experienced by young people and others are ideologies, modes of governance, and policies that embrace a pathological individualism, a distorted notion of freedom, and a willingness both to employ state violence to suppress dissent and abandon those suffering from a collection of social problems ranging from dire poverty and joblessness to homelessness. In the end, these are stories about disposability in which growing numbers of young people are considered dispensable and a drain on the body politic, the economy, and the sensibilities of the rich and powerful. Rather than work for a more dignified life, most young people now work simply to survive—that is, if they can find work—in a survival-of-the-fittest society in which getting ahead and accumulating capital, especially for the ruling elite, is the only game in town. In the past, public values have been challenged and certain groups have been targeted as superfluous or redundant. What is distinctive, and particularly dangerous, about the politics of disposability is the way in which such antidemocratic practices have become normalized in the existing neoliberal order. A politics of inequality and ruthless power disparities is now matched by a culture of vindictiveness soaked in blood, humiliation, and misery. Private injuries are not only separated from public considerations by such narratives, but accounts of poverty and exclusion have become objects of scorn. Similarly, all noncommercial public spheres where such stories might get heard are viewed with contempt, a perfect supplement to the chilling indifference to the plight of the disadvantaged and disenfranchised.

As politics is disconnected from its ethical and material moorings, it becomes easier to punish and imprison young people than to educate them. From the inflated rhetoric of the political right to market-driven media peddling spectacles of violence, the influence of these criminogenic and death-saturated forces in everyday life is undermining our collective security by justifying cutbacks to social supports and restricting opportunities for democratic resistance. Saturating mainstream discourses with antipublic narratives, the neoliberal machinery of social death effectively weakens public supports and prevents the emergence of much-needed new ways of thinking and speaking about politics in the twenty-first century.

Before this dangerously authoritarian mind-set has a chance to take hold of our collective imagination and animate our social institutions, it is crucial that all Americans think critically and ethically about the coercive forces shaping US culture—and focus our energy on what can be done to change them. It will not be enough only to expose the falseness of the propaganda pumped out by the commanding neoliberal cultural apparatuses. We also need to create alternative narratives about what the promise of democracy might be for our children and ourselves. This demands a break from established political parties, the creation of alternative public spheres in which to produce democratic narratives and visions, and a notion of politics that is educative, one that takes seriously how people interpret and mediate the world, how they see themselves in relation to others, and what it might mean to imagine otherwise in order to act otherwise.

At stake here is more than a call for reform. The American public needs to organize around a revolutionary ideal that enables people to hold power, participate in the process of governing, and create public institutions and discourses capable of explaining and reversing chronic injustices and power relations evident everywhere in society. This is a revolution that not only calls for structural change, but for a transformation in the ways in which subjectivities are created, desires are produced, and agency itself is safeguarded as crucial to any viable notions of community and freedom. Democracy requires, at the very least, a type of education that fosters a working knowledge of citizenship and the development of individuals with the capacity to be self-reflective, passionate about the collective good, and able to defend the means by which ideas are translated into the worldly space of the public realm. It is not enough to wait for the Occupy movement to revitalize itself.[25] That is important but is too limited a call for change. Such a struggle is impossible without an alliance between unions, working people, students, youth, educators, feminists, environmentalists, and intellectuals. In particular, organized labor, students, educators, and youth have to provide the base of a broader organization and social movement designed to dismantle casino capitalism. Such an alliance has to be built around defending the common good, public values, economic and racial justice, and environmental sustainability. As Noam Chomsky has pointed out, the biggest threat to the Gilded Age autocrats is solidarity, and rightly so. The time has come for a surge of opposition in the name of democracy, one designed to save the planet from destruction and for a social order in which economic justice is matched with a reverence for care for the other. Politics becomes meaningless without a vision, a willingness to develop a radical collective imagination rooted in a formative culture that nourishes a vibrant sense of critique, civic courage, and sustained collective struggle. Any struggle that matters will have to reimagine and fight for a society in which it becomes possible once again to dream the project of a substantive democracy. This means, as Ulrich Beck has pointed out, looking for politics in new spaces and arenas outside of traditional elections, political parties, and "duly authorized agents."[26] It suggests developing public spaces outside of the regime of predatory corporatism and engaging in a type of counter-politics that shapes society from the bottom up.

9
Higher Education and the New Brutalism

⌖

Across the globe, a new historical conjuncture is emerging in which the attacks on higher education as a democratic institution and on dissident public voices in general—whether journalists, whistleblowers, or academics—are intensifying with sobering consequences. The attempts to punish prominent academics such as Ward Churchill and Steven Salaita and others are matched by an equally vicious assault on whistleblowers such as Chelsea Manning, Jeremy Hammond, Edward Snowden, as well as on journalists such as James Risen.[1] Under the aegis of the national surveillance-security-secrecy state, it becomes difficult to separate the war on whistleblowers and journalists from the war on higher education—the institutions responsible for safeguarding and sustaining critical theory and engaged citizenship.[2]

Marina Warner has rightly called these assaults on higher education "the new brutalism in academia."[3] It may be worse than she suggests. In fact, the right-wing defense of the neoliberal dismantling of the university as a site of critical inquiry in many countries is more brazen and arrogant than anything we have seen in the past, and its presence is now felt in a diverse number of repressive regimes. For instance, the authoritarian nature of neoliberalism and its threat to higher education as a democratic public sphere was on full display recently when the multimillionaire and Beijing-appointed leader of Hong Kong, Leung Chunying, told prodemocracy protesters that "allowing his successors to be chosen in open elections based on who won the greatest number of votes was unacceptable in part because it risked giving poorer residents a dominant voice in politics."[4] Offering an unyielding defense for China's authoritarian political system, he argued that any candidate that might succeed him "must be screened by a 'broadly representative' nominating committee, which would insulate Hong Kong's next chief executive from popular pressure to create social provisions and allow the government to implement more business-friendly policies to address economic" issues.[5] This is not just an attack on political liberty but also an attack on dissent, critical education, and public institutions that might exercise a democratizing influence on the nation. In this case the autonomy of institutions such as higher education is threatened as much by corporate interests as by the repressive policies and practices of the state.

The hidden notion of politics that fuels this market-driven ideology also informs a more Western-style form of neoliberalism in which the autonomy of democratizing institutions is under assault not only by the state but also by the ultrarich, bankers, hedge fund managers, and the corporate elite. In this case, corporate sovereignty has replaced traditional state modes of governance, and turned political power over to corporate elites who despise the common good. As the South African Nobel Prize winner in literature J. M. Coetzee, points out, the new power elite "reconceive of themselves as managers of national economies" who want to turn universities into training schools equipping young people with the skills required by a modern economy."[6] Viewed as a private investment rather than a public good, universities are now construed as spaces where students are valued as human capital, courses are determined by consumer demand, and governance is based on the Walmart model of labor relations. For Coetzee, this attack on higher education, which is not only ideological but also increasingly relies on the repressive, militaristic arm of the punishing state, is a response to the democratization and opening up of universities that reached a high point in the 1960s all across the globe. In the last forty years, the assault on the university as a center of critique and democratization has intensified, just as the reach of this assault has expanded to include intellectuals, campus protesters, an expanding number of minority students, and the critical formative cultures that provide the foundation for a substantive democracy.[7]

In the United States and England, in particular, the ideal of the university as vital public good no longer fits into a revamped discourse of progress, largely defined in terms of economic growth. Under the onslaught of a merciless and savage financialization of society that has spread since the 1980s, the concept of social progress has all but disappeared amid the ideological onslaught of a crude market-driven fundamentalism that promises instant gratification, consumption, and immediate financial gain. If dissident intellectuals were the subject of right-wing attacks in the past, the range and extent of the attack on higher education has widened and become more insidious. As Ellen Schrecker succinctly notes:

> Today the entire enterprise of higher education, not just its dissident professors, is under attack, both internally and externally. The financial challenges are obvious, as are the political ones. Less obvious, however, are the structural

changes that have transformed the very nature of American higher education. In reacting to the economic insecurities of the past forty years, the nation's colleges and universities have adopted corporate practices that degrade undergraduate instruction, marginalize faculty members, and threaten the very mission of the academy as an institution devoted to the common good.[8]

Memories of the university as a citadel of democratic learning have been replaced by a university eager to define itself largely as an adjunct of corporate power. Civic freedom has been reduced to the notion of consumption, education has been reduced to a form of training, and agency has been narrowed to the consumer logic of choice legitimated by a narrow belief in defining one's goals almost entirely around self-interests rather than shared responsibilities of democratic sociability.

Coetzee's defense of education provides an important referent for those of us who believe that the university is nothing if it is not a public trust and social good—that is, a critical institution infused with the promise of cultivating intellectual insight, the civic imagination, inquisitiveness, risk-taking, social responsibility, and the struggle for justice. Rather than defining the mission of the university in terms that mimic markets-based ideologies, modes of governance, and neoliberal policies, the questions that should be asked at this crucial time in American history concern how the mission of the university might be better understood with respect to both developing and safeguarding the interests of young people at a time of violence and war, the rise of a rampant anti-intellectualism, the emerging specter of authoritarianism, and the threat of nuclear and ecological devastation. What might it mean to define the university as a public good and democratic public sphere rather than as an institution that has aligned itself with market values and is more attentive to market fluctuations and investor interests than educating students to be critically engaged citizens? Or, as Zygmunt Bauman and Leonidas Donskis write: "How will we form the next generation of ... intellectuals and politicians if young people will never have an opportunity to experience what a non-vulgar, non-pragmatic, non-instrumentalized university is like?"[9]

With the advance of a savage form of casino capitalism and its dream-worlds of consumption, privatization, and deregulation, not only are democratic values and social protections at risk, but also the civic and formative cultures that make such values and protections intelligible and consequential to a sustainable democratic society. As public spheres, once enlivened by broad engagements with common concerns, are being transformed into "spectacular spaces of consumption" and financial looting, the flight from mutual obligations and social responsibilities strengthens and has resulted not only in a devaluing of public life and the common good but also in a crisis of the radical imagination, especially in terms of rethinking the purpose, meaning, and value of politics itself.[10] Moreover, not only have academic fields become financialized but so have time and space. Students now labor under time constraints marked by the speeding up of time to pay off debts, the choosing of spaces and spheres of labor that offer quick returns—all done in the name of an indentured form of citizenship predicated on consuming and going into debt. And the consequences far exceed the more volatile examples of the violence waged by police on student protesters. Another index of such a crisis, as Mike Davis points out, is that we live in an era in which there is a supersaturation of corruption, cruelty, and violence "that fails any longer to outrage or even interest."[11] Moral outrage has been replaced by the shouting and screaming that is symptomatic of talk radio and television shows whose purpose is to replace critical dialogue with a cartoonish spectacle in which evidence and argument dissolve in opinions expressed in deafening volume. This type of celebrated illiteracy finds its counterpart in university commencement speeches often delivered by business icons such as Bill Gates, or more problematically, celebrities who confirm the triumph of anti-intellectualism over thoughtfulness, social responsibility, and the ethical imagination. Rarely are students in such commencements exposed to writers, journalists, artists, and other cultural workers who believe in the public good, fight against injustices, and dare at the risk of their jobs, and sometimes their lives, to hold power accountable.

Needless to say, the crisis of higher education is about much more than a crisis of funding, an assault on dissent, the emergence of a deep-seated anti-intellectualism, or its service to the financial elite; it is also about a crisis of memory, agency, and politics. What Mike Davis is suggesting is that politics has been emptied out of its political, moral, and ethical registers—stripped down to a machine of social and political death for whom the cultivation of the critical and radical imagination is a hindrance. Commerce is the heartbeat of social relations, and the only mode of governance that matters is one that mimics Wall Street.

We live in the age of a new brutalism marked not simply by an indifference to multiple social problems but also defined by a kind of mad delight in the spectacle and exercise of violence and cruelty. America is sullied by a brutalism that is perfectly consistent with a new kind of barbaric power, one that puts millions of people in prison, subjects an entire generation to a form of indentured citizenship, and strips people of the material and symbolic resources they need to exercise their capacity to live with dignity and justice. Academics who speak out against corruption and injustice are often censored and sometimes lose their jobs, proving that dissent has become a dangerous activity. At the same time, the Obama administration criminalizes public servants who expose unethical behavior, the violation of civil liberties, and corruption. One egregious and symptomatic case reported by Morris Berman took place in 2011 when "environmental activist Tim DeChristopher was sentenced to two years in prison for his repeated declaration that environmental protection required civil, i.e., nonviolent disobedience."[12] As Berman points out, one wonders if the judge that sentenced DeChristopher to prison "would also have put Rosa Parks and Mahatma Gandhi in jail, had he been around in their lifetimes."[13] If democratic political life is emptied out by the rise of the national security apparatus, the increasing criminalization of dissent, and the ongoing militarization of everyday life, it is equally devalued and threatened by modes of public pedagogy, circulating in Fox News, for example, that trade in lies, ignorance, and a full-fledged attack on reason and critical thought.

In this instance, the new barbarism produces and sanctions a civic illiteracy and retrograde consumer consciousness in which students are taught to mimic the economic success of alleged "brands" such as the reality TV star Kim Kardashian. Her celebrity is promoted around a kind of idiocy, as exemplified in the publicity surrounding the publication of her new book, *Selfish*, the unique selling feature of which is that it contains 2,000 selfies. The challenge for higher education in this debacle goes beyond refusing to produce modes of agency that embrace this kind of deadly anti-intellectualism and rabid individualism, but to enable students to critically interrogate what stands for public engagement, and how this debased mode of being in the world gains prominence in the public sphere. More importantly, what obligation does a university have to teach students to judge the character of their society not by the lives of celebrities, new technologies, or the endless production of needless consumer goods, but by its intellect, reason, compassion for the poor, social investment in young people, and its willingness to provide economic support and social provisions for all, including those marginalized by race, class, gender, and sexual orientation? How we treat those considered vulnerable says much more about the state of a democratic society and the institutions that support it than how we treat the rich, celebrities, and those who either trivialize democracy or intentionally undermine it for their own benefit. There is no way to escape the relationship between education and power, pedagogy and social justice, knowledge and the production of the ethical and civic imagination. These neoliberal agendas have sought ways to mystify and undermine these connections.

As the corporatization of higher education intensifies, there is little talk in this view of higher education about the history and value of shared governance between faculty and administrators, nor of educating students as critical citizens rather than potential employees of Walmart. There are few attempts to affirm faculty as scholars and public intellectuals who have a measure of autonomy and power. Instead, faculty members are defined less as intellectuals than as technicians and grant writers, or they are punished for raising their voices against various injustices. Students fare no better in this debased form of education and are treated as either clients, consumers, or as restless children in need of high-energy entertainment—as was made clear in the 2012 Penn State scandal and the ever-increasing football scandals at major universities, where testosterone-fueled entertainment is given a higher priority than substantive teaching and learning—to say nothing of student safety and protection. Precious resources are now wasted by universities intent on building football stadiums, student dorms that mimic resort hotels, and other amenities that signal the Disneyification of higher education for students and the Walmartification of labor relations for faculty. For instance, High Point University seeks to attract students with "its first-run movie theater, ever-present ice cream trucks, a steakhouse, outdoor hot tubs, and dorms with plasma-screen TVs."[14] Such modes of education do not foster a sense of organized responsibility fundamental to a democracy. Instead, they encourage what might be called a sense of organized irresponsibility—a practice that underlies the economic Darwinism and civic corruption at the heart of a debased politics of consumption, finance, and privatization. When one combines the university as a Disneyfied entertainment center with labor practices that degrade and exploit faculty, the result is what Terry Eagleton has recently called the "death of universities as centers of critique."[15]

Governance under higher education is being stripped of any viable democratic vision. In the United States, college presidents pride themselves on defining their role almost entirely in a vocabulary that mimics the language of Wall Street and hedge fund managers. With few exceptions, they are praised as fund raisers but rarely acknowledged for the quality of their ideas. Moreover, trustees have not only assumed more power in higher education, but are largely drawn from the ranks of business, and yet, as in the Steven Salaita case, are making judgments about faculty that they are unqualified to make.

For those of us who believe that education is more than an extension of the business world marked by a new brutalism, it is crucial to address a number of issues that connect the university to the larger society while stressing the educative nature of politics as part of a broader effort to create a critical culture, supportive institutions, and a collective movement that supports the connection between critique and action and redefines agency in the service of the practice of freedom and justice. Let me mention just a few.

First, educators can address and make clear the relationship between the attack on the social state and the transformation of higher education into an adjunct of corporate power. The attack on higher education cannot be understood outside of the attack on the welfare state, social provisions, public servants, and democratic public spheres. Nor can it be understood outside of the production of the neoliberal subject, one who is atomized, unable to connect private issues to larger public considerations, and is taught to believe in a form of radical individualism that enables a fast withdrawal from the public sphere and the claims of economic and social justice. Clearly, in any democratic society, education should be viewed as a right, not an entitlement. This suggests a reordering of state and federal priorities to make that happen. Much-needed revenue can be raised by putting into play even a limited number of reform policies in which, for instance, the upper 10 percent and corporations would be forced to pay a fair share of their taxes; a tax could also be placed on trade transactions; and tax loopholes for the wealthy would be eliminated. It is well known that the low tax rate given to corporations is a major scandal. For instance, and this is only one egregious example, the Bank of America paid no taxes in 2010 and "got $1.9 billion tax refund from the IRS, even though it made $4.4 billion in profits."[16]

In addition, academics can join with students, public schoolteachers, unions, and others to bring attention to wasteful military spending that if eliminated could provide the funds for a free public higher education for every qualified young person in the country. Brown University's Watson Institute for International Studies has done extensive research on military spending and the costs of war and states that as a result of the Iraq War alone "American taxpayers will ultimately spend roughly $2.2 trillion on the war, but because the U.S. government borrowed to finance the conflict, interest payments through the year 2053 [mean] that the total bill could reach nearly $4 trillion."[17] While there is growing public concern over rising tuition rates along with the crushing debt students are incurring, there is little public outrage from academics over the billions of dollars wasted on a massive and wasteful military budget and arms industry. As Rabbi Michael Lerner of *Tikkun* has pointed out, democracy needs a Marshall Plan in which funding is sufficient to make all levels of education free, while also providing enough social support to eliminate poverty, hunger, inadequate health care, and the destruction of the environment.[18] There is nothing utopian about the demand to redirect money away from the military, powerful corporations, and the upper 1 percent.

Second, addressing these tasks demands a sustained critique of the transformation of a market economy into a market society along with a clear analysis of the damage it has caused, both at home and abroad. Power, particularly the power of the largest corporations, has become more unaccountable, and "the subtlety of illegitimate power makes it hard to identify."[19] The greatest threat posed by authoritarian politics is that it makes power invisible and hence defines itself in universal and commonsense terms, as if it is beyond critique and dissent. Moreover, disposability has become the new measure of a savage form of casino capitalism in which the only value that matters is exchange value. Compassion, social responsibility, and justice are relegated to the dustbin of an older modernity that now is viewed as either quaint or a grim reminder of a socialist past. This suggests, as Angela Davis, Michelle Alexander, and others have argued, that there is a need for academics and young people to become part of a broader social movement aimed at dismantling the repressive institutions that make up the punishing state. The most egregious example of which is the prison-industrial complex, which drains billions of dollars in funds to put people in jail when such resources could be used to fund public and higher education. As Ferguson makes painfully clear, the police have become militarized, armed with weapons from the battlefields of Iraq and Afghanistan.[20] The US prison system locks up more people than that of any other country in the world, and the vast majority of them are people of color.[21] Moreover, public schools are increasingly modeled after prisons and are implementing policies in which children are arrested for throwing peanuts at a school bus or violating a dress code.[22] The punishing state is a dire threat to both public and higher education and democracy itself. The American public does not need more prisons; it needs more schools; accessible, low-cost health services; and a living wage for all workers. This type of analysis suggests that progressives and others need a more comprehensive understanding of how politics and power are interrelated, of how different registers of oppression mutually inform each other and can be better understood in terms of their connections and deeply historical and social relations.

Third, academics, artists, journalists, and other young people need to connect the rise of subaltern, part-time labor—or what we might call the Walmart model of wealth and labor relations—in both the university and the larger society to the massive inequality in wealth and income that now corrupts every aspect of American politics and society. No democracy can survive the kind of inequality in which "the 400 richest people ... have as much wealth as 154 million Americans combined, that's 50 percent of the entire country [while] the top economic 1 percent of the U.S. population now has a record 40 percent of all wealth and more wealth than 90 percent of the population combined."[23] Senator Bernie Sanders provides a startling statistical map of the massive inequality at work in the United States. In a speech to the US Senate, he states:

Today ... the top 1 percent owns 38 percent of the financial wealth of America, 38 percent. And I wonder how many Americans know how much the bottom 60 percent own. They want people to think about it. Top 1 percent own 38 percent of the wealth. What do the bottom 60 percent own? The answer is all of 2.3 percent. Top 1 percent owns 38 percent of the financial wealth. The bottom 60 percent owns 2.3 percent. Madam President, there is one family in this country, the Walton family, the owners of Wal-Mart, who are now worth as a family $148 billion. That is more wealth than the bottom 40 percent of American society. One family owns more wealth than the bottom 40 percent of American society.... That's distribution of wealth. That's what we own. In terms of income, what we made last year, the latest information that we have in terms of distribution of income is that from 2009–2012, 95 percent of all new income earned in this country went to the top 1 percent. Have you all got that? 95 percent of all new income went to the top 1 percent, which tells us that when we talk about economic growth, which is 2 percent, 3 percent, 4 percent, whatever it is, that really doesn't mean all that much because almost all of the new income generated in that growth has gone to the very, very, very wealthiest people in this country.[24]

Democracy in the United States has been hijacked by a free-floating class of ultrarich and corporate powerbrokers and transformed into an oligarchy in which a small group of individuals now wield power with impunity.[25] As I have mentioned previously, this is the conclusion of a recent Princeton University study, and at the risk of being charged with hyperbole, the report may be much too moderate in its conclusions.

Fourth, academics need to fight for the rights of students to get a free education, be given a formidable and critical education not dominated by corporate values, and to have a say in the shaping of their education and what it means to expand and deepen the practice of freedom and democracy. In many countries, such as Germany, France, Denmark, Cuba, and Brazil, postsecondary education is free because these countries view education not as a private right but as a public good. Yet, in some of the most advanced countries in the world, such as the United States and Canada, young people, especially from low-income groups, are being systemically excluded from access to higher education, and, in part, this is because they are left out of the social contract and the discourse of democracy. They are the new disposables who lack jobs, a decent education, hope, and any semblance of a life better than that of their parents. They are a reminder of how finance capital has abandoned any viable vision of a better future for young people. Youth have become a liability in the world of high finance, a world that refuses to view them as important social investments. And the consequences are terrifying. As Jennifer M. Silva points out in her insightful book, *Coming up Short,* coming of age for young people "is not just being delayed but fundamentally dismantled by drastic economic restructure, profound cultural transformations, and deepening social inequality."[26] The futures of young people are being refigured or reimagined in ways that both punish and depoliticize them. Silva writes that many young people are turning away from politics, focusing instead on the purely personal and emotional vocabularies of self-help and emotional self-management. As she puts it:

This emerging working-class adult self is characterized by low expectations of work, wariness toward romantic commitment, widespread distrust of social institutions, profound isolation from others, and an overriding focus on their emotions and psychic health. . . . [They] are working hard to remake dignity and meaning out of emotional self-management and willful psychic transformation.[27]

Finally, though far from complete, there is a need to oppose the ongoing shift in power relations between faculty and the managerial class. Too many faculty are now removed from the governing structure of higher education and as a result have been abandoned to the misery of impoverished wages, excessive classes, no health care, and few, if any, social benefits. As political scientist Benjamin Ginsburg points out, administrators and their staffs now outnumber full-time faculty, accounting for two-thirds of the increase in higher education costs in the past twenty years. This is shameful and is not merely an education issue but a deeply political matter, one that must address how neoliberal ideology and policy have imposed on higher education an antidemocratic governing structure.

We may live in the shadow of the authoritarian corporate state, but the future is still open. The time has come to develop a political language in which civic values and social responsibility—and the institutions, tactics, and long-term commitments that support them—become central to invigorating and fortifying a new era of civic engagement, a renewed sense of social agency, and an impassioned international social movement with the vision, organization, and set of strategies capable of challenging the neoliberal nightmare that now haunts the globe and empties out the meaning of politics and democracy.

10
The Poison of Neoliberal Miseducation
Higher Education as Dead Zones of the Imagination

᪤

Academics who function as critical public intellectuals have always posed a threat to authoritarian states and corporate entities, just as the institutions in which they worked were viewed as a threat to authoritarian powers. There is little doubt in the current historical moment that the ideal, however flawed, of the university as a democratic public sphere is truly dangerous to the apostles of casino capitalism, who deride any notion of education that challenges the neoliberal assumption that higher education should be predicated on a business model, people should be treated as consumers, and capital as the only subject of history. At a time when the economic crisis and the increasing corporatization of the university are not matched by a crisis of ideas among the general public, market fundamentalists around the globe have gone on the offensive, doing everything they can to strip education of its civic purposes and to prevent individuals from translating personal troubles into broader social issues.

For most critics of neoliberalism, this attack is primarily an economic one, characterized by a massive defunding of higher education, the attempt to eliminate tenure, and the transformation of higher education into an institution driven by the demands of commerce, one in which the only value that matters is exchange value. But the crisis in higher education is not only economic, resulting largely from defunding and deficit reduction policies. As Gene Nichol has pointed out, universities are at risk, at least in the United States, because of a "conservative-led campaign to end higher education's democratizing influence on the nation."[1] This suggests that the attack on higher education is not because it is failing but because it defines its mission as public. The consequences of such increasing attacks on higher education have resulted not only in the ongoing corporatization of the university but also a full-fledged attack on academic labor, students, and an attempt to eviscerate the radical civic imagination.

This is evident as universities turn toward corporate management models and increasingly use and exploit cheap faculty labor, while expanding the ranks of their managerial class. Modeled after a savage neoliberal value system in which wealth and power are redistributed upward, a market-oriented class of managers have largely taken over the governing structures of most institutions of higher education in the United States. As Debra Leigh Scott points out, "Administrators now outnumber faculty on every campus across the country."[2] But there is more at stake here than metrics. Benjamin Ginsberg views this shift in governance as the rise of what he calls ominously "the all administrative university," noting that it does not bode well for any notion of higher education as a democratic public sphere.[3]

Many colleges and universities are drawing more and more upon adjunct and nontenured faculty—whose ranks now constitute 1 million out of 1.5 million faculty—many of whom occupy the status of indentured servants who are overworked, lack benefits, receive little or no administrative support, and are paid salaries that increasingly qualify them for food stamps.[4] Students increasingly fare no better in sharing the status of a subaltern class beholden to neoliberal policies and values, and largely treated as consumers for whom education has become little more than a service. Too many students are buried under huge debts that have become a major source of celebration by the collection industry because it allows them to cash in on their misfortune. Similarly, debt has become a form of subjectivity, a normalized form of servitude that imposes a truncated notion of agency in which debt controls one's life and one's entire time is now subject to the debtor-creditor relationship.[5] Under the regime of neoliberal education, misery breeds a combination of contempt and source of profits for the banks and other financial industries. Jerry Aston, a member of that industry, wrote in a column after witnessing a protest rally by students criticizing their mounting debt, that he "couldn't believe the accumulated wealth they represent—for our industry."[6] And, of course, this type of economic injustice is taking place in an economy in which rich plutocrats such as the infamous union-busting Koch brothers each saw "their investments grow by $6 billion in one year, which amounts to three million dollars per hour based on a 40-hour 'work' week."[7] One astounding figure of greed and concentrated power is revealed in the fact that in 2012, the Koch brothers "made enough money in one second to feed one homeless woman for an entire year."[8] Workers, students, youth, and the poor are all considered expendable in this neoliberal global economy. Yet the one institution, education, that offers the opportunities for students to challenge these antidemocratic tendencies is under attack in ways that are unparalleled, at least in terms of the scope and intensity of the assault by the corporate elite and other economic fundamentalists.

Casino capitalism does more than infuse market values into every aspect of higher education; it also wages a full-fledged assault on public goods, democratic public spheres, and the role of education in creating an informed and enlightened citizenry. When former presidential candidate and senator Rick Santorum argued that intellectuals were not wanted in the Republican Party, he was articulating what has become common sense in a society wedded to narrow instrumentalist values, ignorance as a political tool, and a deep-seated fear of civic literacy and a broad-based endorsement of the commons. Critical thinking and a literate public have become dangerous to those who want to celebrate orthodoxy over dialogue, emotion over reason, and ideological certainty over thoughtfulness.[9] Hannah Arendt's warning that "it was not stupidity but a curious, quite authentic inability to think"[10] at the heart of authoritarian regimes is now embraced as a fundamental tenet of right-wing politicians and pundits and increasingly has become a matter of common sense for the entertainment industry and the dominant media, all primary modes of an education industry that produces consumers, smothers the country in the empty fog of celebrity culture, and denounces democracy as tantamount to the enemy of free-market fundamentalism. How else to explain the willingness of so many people today to give up every vestige of privacy to the social media, the government, and anyone else interested in collecting data for the most despicable and antidemocratic purposes. Self-interest does more than embrace a new culture of narcissism; it empties out any viable notion of the social, compassionate, and the ethical imagination.

Right-wing appeals to austerity provide the rationale for slash-and-burn policies intended to deprive government-financed social and educational programs of the funds needed to enable them to work, if not survive. Along with health care, public transportation, Medicare, food stamp programs for low-income children, and a host of other social protections, higher education is being defunded as part of a larger scheme to dismantle and privatize all public services, goods, and spheres. The passion for public values has given way to the ruthless quest for profits and the elevation of self-interests over the common good. The educational goal of expanding the capacity for critical thought and the outer limits of the imagination have given way to the instrumental desert of a mind-deadening audit culture. But there is more at work here than the march toward privatization and the never-ending search for profits at any cost; there is also the issue of wasteful spending on a bloated war machine, the refusal to tax fairly the rich and corporations, the draining of public funds for the US military presence in Iraq and Afghanistan, and the ongoing consolidation of class power in the hands of the 1 percent.

The deficit argument and the austerity policies advocated in its name is a form of class warfare designed largely for the state to be able to redirect revenue in support of the commanding institutions of the corporate-military-industrial complex and away from funding higher education and other crucial public services. The extent of the budget reduction assault is such that, in 2012, "states reduced their education budgets by $12.7 billion."[11] Liberals and conservatives justify such cuts by pointing to declining revenues brought in by the state, but what is missing from this argument is that one major reason for the decline is right-wing policies and legislation that lowers the taxes of the rich and major corporations. Of course, the burden of such reductions falls upon poor minority and other low-income students, who will not be able to afford the tuition increases that will compensate for the loss of state funding. As the political state is replaced by the corporate state, tuition rises, the ranks of the poor expand, more social problems are criminalized, and the punishing state blooms as a default register for potential dissent. What has become clear in light of such assaults is that many universities and colleges have become unapologetic accomplices to corporate interests, values, and power, and in doing so increasingly regard social problems as either irrelevant or make them invisible.[12] The transformation of higher education both in the United States and abroad is evident in a number of registers. These include: decreased support for programs of study that are not business oriented; reduced funds for research that does not increase profit; the replacement of shared forms of governance with rigid business management models; the lessening of financial support for academic fields that promote critical thinking rather than an entrepreneurial culture; the ongoing exploitation of faculty labor; and the use of purchasing power as the vital measure of a student's identity, worth, and access to higher education.[13] In addition, many universities are now occupied by security forces whose central message is that dissent and protest, however peaceful, will be squelched through violence. Leftover weapons from the battlefields of Iraq and Afghanistan have found a home on many college campuses, which increasingly look as if they have become potential war zones. These weapons stand as a grim reminder that they could be used against all those students who question authority, imagine a more democratic role for the university, and connect learning to social change.

Universities are increasingly becoming dead zones of the imagination, managed by a class of swelling bureaucrats, inhabited by faculty who constitute a new class of indentured, if not sometimes willing, technicians, and students who are demeaned as customers and saddled with crippling debts. Not all faculty and students fit into this description. Some raise their voices in protest, while others enjoy the benefits of being accomplices to power, and others get lost in the orbits of privatized interests or academic specialization. The university is a site of struggle and beset by many contradictions, but I don't believe it is an exaggeration to say that higher education since the late 1970s has been hijacked by a mix of political and economic fundamentalist forces that have worked hard to empty higher education of what it means to truly educate young people to be knowledgeable, critical, thoughtful, and sensitive to the plight of others and the larger society.

Most important, higher education too often informs a deadening dystopian vision of corporate America and old-style authoritarian regimes that impose pedagogies of repression and disciplined conformity associated with societies that have lost any sense of ethical responsibility and respect for equality, public values, and justice. The democratic imagination has been transformed into a data machine that marshals its inhabitants into the neoliberal dreamworld of babbling consumers and armies of exploitative labor whose ultimate goal is to accumulate capital and initiate faculty and students into the brave new surveillance/punishing state that merges Orwell's Big Brother with Huxley's mind-altering soma.

One consequence of this ongoing disinvestment in higher education is the expansion of a punishing state that increasingly criminalizes a range of social behaviors, wages war on the poor instead of poverty, militarizes local police forces, harasses poor minority youth, and spends more on prisons than on higher education. The punishing state produces fear and sustains itself on moral panics. Dissent gives way to widespread insecurity, uncertainty, and an obsession with personal safety.[14] Precarity has become an organizing principle of a social order so as to legitimate and expand the ranks of those considered disposable while destroying those public sites that give voice to the narratives of those marginalized by race, class, gender, sexuality, and ideology. Public places are now militarized, and those spaces once designed for dialogue, critique, informed exchange, and dissent are occupied by the police and other security forces who have become the most visible register of the surveillance-security state.

Political, moral, and social indifference is the result, in part, of a public that is increasingly constituted within an educational landscape that reduces thinking to a burden and celebrates civic illiteracy as foundational for negotiating a society in which moral disengagement and political corruption go hand in hand.[15] The assault on the university is symptomatic of the deep educational, economic, and political crisis facing the United States. It is but one lens through which to recognize that the future of democracy depends on achieving the educational and ethical standards of the society we inhabit.[16] This lapse of the US public into a political and moral coma is also induced, in part, by an ever-expanding, mass-mediated celebrity culture that trades in hype and sensation. It is also accentuated by a governmental apparatus that sanctions modes of training that undermine any viable notion of critical schooling and public pedagogy. While there is much being written about how unfair the left is to the Obama administration, what is often forgotten by these liberal critics is that Obama has aligned himself with educational practices and policies as instrumentalist and anti-intellectual as they are politically reactionary, and therein lies one viable reason for not supporting his initiatives and administration.[17] What liberals refuse to entertain is that the left is correct in attacking Obama for his cowardly retreat from a number of progressive issues and his dastardly undermining of civil liberties. In fact, they do not go far enough in their criticisms.

Often, even progressives miss that Obama's views on what type of formative educational culture is necessary to create critically engaged and socially responsible citizens are utterly reactionary and provide no space for the nurturance of a radically democratic imagination. Hence, while liberals point to some of Obama's progressive policies—often in a New Age discourse that betrays their own supine moralism—they fail to acknowledge that Obama's educational policies do nothing to contest, and are in fact aligned with, his weak-willed compromises and authoritarian policies. In other words, Obama's educational commitments undermine the creation of a formative culture capable of questioning authoritarian ideas, modes of governance, and reactionary policies. The question is not whether Obama's policies are slightly less repugnant than those of his right-wing detractors. On the contrary, it is about how educators and others should engage politics in a more robust and democratic way by imagining what it would mean to work collectively and with "slow impatience" for a new political order outside of the current moderate and extreme right-wing politics and the debased, uncritical educational apparatus that supports it.[18]

The transformation of higher education into an adjunct of corporate control conjures up the image of a sorcerer's apprentice, of an institution that has become delusional in its infatuation with neoliberal ideology, values, and modes of instrumental pedagogy. Universities now claim that they are providing a service and in doing so not only demean any substantive notion of governance, research, and teaching, but abstract education from any sense of civic responsibility. Neoliberal ideology and modes of governance represent a toxin that supplies a predatory class of zombies who produce dead zones of the imagination, spaces in which an audit culture triumphs over critical thinking, informed debate, decent working conditions, and a vision in which social bonds and civic responsibility are central to learning itself. Higher education reneged on enlightenment ideals and lost its sense of democratic mission, but it also increasingly offers no defense to the "totalitarianism that haunts the modern ideal of political emancipation."[19] Driven by an audit culture and increasingly oblivious to the demands of a democracy for an informed and critical citizenry, it now devours its children, disregards its faculty, and resembles an institution governed by myopic accountants who should be ashamed of what they are proud of. The university needs to be reclaimed as a crucial public sphere where administrators, faculty, and students can imagine what a free and substantive democracy might look like and what it means to make education relevant to such a crucial pedagogical and political task. Universities must press the claim for creating social bonds and public spheres in which democracy is viewed as a struggle over agency and new modes of communal relations that refuse to reduce social interaction to a form of social combat and Social Darwinism as the organizing principle of politics and everyday life. Any viable notion of a radical democracy needs critical and engaged agents capable of developing the disposition and capacities to resist repressive attacks on thinking, feeling, and desiring so they can create the conditions for them not only to shape ideological, economic, and political forces that govern their everyday lives, but also so they can imagine alternative futures and horizons of possibility.

II
Predatory Neoliberalism as a Global Force

⟜

Henry A. Giroux Interviewed by Michael Nevradakis for *Dialogos*

MICHAEL NEVRADAKIS: *Let's begin with a discussion about some topics you've spoken and written extensively about . . . neoliberalism and what you have described as "casino capitalism." How have these ideas taken hold politically and intellectually across the world in recent years?*

HENRY GIROUX: I think since the 1970s it's been the predominant ideology, certainly in Western Europe and North America. As is well known, it raised havoc in Latin America, especially in Argentina and Chile and other states. It first gained momentum in Chile as a result of the Chicago Boys. Milton Friedman and that group went down there and basically used the Pinochet regime as a type of Petri dish to produce a whole series of policies. But I think if we look at this very specifically, we're talking about a lot of things.

We're talking about an ideology marked by the selling off of public goods to private interests; the attack on social provisions; the rise of the corporate state organized around privatization, free trade, and deregulation; the celebration of self-interests over social needs; the claim that government is the problem if it gets in the way of profits for the megacorporations and financial services; the investing in prisons rather than schools; the modeling of education after the culture of business; the insistence that exchange values are the only values worthy of consideration, the celebration of profit-making as the essence of democracy coupled with the utterly reductionist notion that consumption is the only applicable form of citizenship. But even more than that, neoliberal ideology upholds the notion that the market serves as a model for structuring all social relations: not just the economy, but the governing of all of social life.

I think that as a mode of governance, it is really quite dreadful because it tends to produce identities, subjects, and ways of life driven by a kind of "survival of the fittest" ethic, grounded in the notion of the free, possessive individual and committed to the right of individual and ruling groups to accrue wealth removed from matters of ethics and social cost.

That's a key issue. I mean, this is a particular political and economic and social project that not only consolidates class power in the hands of the 1 percent but also operates off the assumption that economics can divorce itself from social costs, that it doesn't have to deal with matters of ethical and social responsibility, that these things get in the way. And I think the consequences of these policies across the globe have caused immense suffering, misery, and the spread of massive inequalities in wealth, power, and income. These massive dislocations have also produced serious mental health crises. We are witnessing a number of people who are committing suicide because they have lost their pensions, jobs, and dignity. We are witnessing a ruthless attack on the welfare state; we see the privatization of public services; the dismantling of the connection between private issues and public problems; the selling off of state functions, deregulation, and unchecked emphasis on self-interest; the refusal to tax the rich; and really the redistribution of wealth from the middle and working classes to the ruling class, the elite class, what the Occupy movement called the 1 percent. It really has created a very bleak emotional and economic landscape for the 99 percent of the population throughout the world.

M. N.: *And having mentioned this impact on the social state and the 99 percent, would you go as far as to say that these ideologies have been the direct cause of the economic crisis the world is presently experiencing?*

H. G.: Oh, absolutely. I think when you look at the crisis in 2007, what are you looking at? You're looking at the merging of unchecked financial power, a pathological notion of greed that implemented corrupt banking policies, deregulated the financial world and allowed the financial elite, the 1 percent, to pursue a series of policies, particularly the selling of junk bonds and the illegality of what we call subprime mortgages, to people who couldn't pay for them. This created a bubble and it exploded. This is directly related to the assumption that the market should drive all aspects of political, economic, and social life and that the ruling elite can exercise their ruthless power and financial tools in ways that defy accountability. And what we saw is that this experiment failed, and it not only failed, but it fueled an enormous amount of cruelty and hardship across the world. More important, the apostles of neoliberal logic emerged from the crisis not only entirely unapologetic about what they had done, but reinvented it, particularly by preventing any policies from being implemented that would have overturned this massively failed policy of deregulation.

It gets worse. In the aftermath of this sordid crisis produced by the banks and financial elite, we have also learned that the feudal politics of the rich was legitimated by the false notion that they were too big to fail, an irrational conceit that gave way to the notion that they were too big to jail, which is a more realistic measure of the criminogenic/zombie culture that nourishes casino capitalism.

M. N.: *Henry, to build on your last point, how has this growth in neoliberal thought and doctrine contributed, in your view, to a democratic deficit nowadays in Europe and the United States?*

H. G.: Democracy has really become two things for a whole range of antidemocratic politicians, anti-intellectuals, and the people who support these policies. Democracy basically is a word they use, but they empty it of any substance, and invert its meaning to justify the most antidemocratic practices and policies, meaning that it's a term that has nothing to do with questions of justice, nothing to do with questions of rights, nothing to do with questions of legality. Neoliberal democracy disdains democratic values and undermines any sense of civic responsibility for the other and in doing so weakens any viable sense of political and social responsibility. This mode of democracy privatizes any sense of hope and agency and in doing so it becomes a term of deception and diversion—a kind of counterfeit term that's used to justify a whole range of policies that actually are antidemocratic. It's oxymoronic. The other side of this is that the financial elites and oligarchs despise democracy, since they know that neoliberalism is the antithesis of real democracy because it feeds on inequality; it feeds on privilege, it feeds on massive divisiveness, and it revels in producing a theater of cruelty. All you have to do is look at the way it enshrines a kind of rabid individualism. It believes that privatization is the essence of all relationships. It works very hard to eliminate any investment in public values, in public trust and in doing so undermines politics as a necessary condition for engaged citizenship and democracy. It believes that democracy is something that doesn't work, and we hear and see this increasingly from the bankers, antipublic intellectuals, and other cheerleaders for neoliberal policies. What shocks me about neoliberalism in all of its forms is how utterly unapologetic it is about the misery it produces. And it is unapologetic not just in that it is indifferent to the violence it causes, but it also blames the very victims that suffer under these policies.

The vocabulary of neoliberalism posits a false notion of freedom, which it wraps in the mantle of individualism and choice, and in doing so reduces all problems to private issues, suggesting that whatever problems bear down on people, the only way to understand them is through the restrictive lens of individual responsibility, character, and self-resilience. In this instance, the discourse of character and personal responsibility becomes a smoke screen to prevent people from connecting private troubles with larger social and systemic considerations. Under neoliberalism, freedom and choice have been outsourced to the logic of privatization, out of reach of the political, social, economic, and cultural forces that give them meaning. For example, the notion of choice in this discourse exists free of constraints, as if matters of power, class, wealth, and having access to crucial social provisions have no bearing on the choices that people make. Choice as a political concept only becomes meaningful when understood with the network of constraints that inform it. Choice is not some free-floating capacity that enables individuals to make decisions and act on them; it is a condition based on material and symbolic forces that make some choices possible and others impossible to make.

This displacement of communal bonds, public values, and wider structural forces is really pathological and points to an utter disdain for communal relationships, an utter disdain for unions, for public servants, and the common good. In this instance, neoliberalism views anything to do with supporting the public good as something to be attacked, whether we are talking about public transit or public schools, because these things, according to the logic of the market, should be privatized. The only value public goods may have are as assets from which people can make money by selling them to private interests. They're not seen as institutions that somehow contribute to a formative culture that's essential for any viable democracy.

M. N.: *And having mentioned public education just now, a big issue in Greece, as well as in many other countries today, is the increasing privatization of education, and certainly this is something that has been promoted heavily during the crisis in many of these countries. How have neoliberalism and casino capitalism impacted the quality of education and also access to education?*

H. G.: That's a terrific question. Regarding the quality, it's dumbed down education to the point where it literally behaves in a way that's hard to fathom or understand. Education has become a site of policies that devalue learning, collapsing education into training, or they are viewed as potential sites for neoliberal modes of governance and in some cases to be privatized. The radical and critical imagination is under assault in most neoliberal societies because it poses a threat, as does the idea that the mission of education should have something to do with creating critically thoughtful, engaged young people who have a sense of their own agency and integrity and possibility to really believe they can make a difference in the world. Neoliberals believe that the curriculum should be organized around testing, creating passive students, and enforcing a pedagogy of repression. Most important, the attack on communal relationships is also an attack on democratic values and the public spaces that nourish them. These spaces are dangerous because they harbor the possibility of speaking the unspeakable, uttering critical thoughts, producing dissent, and creating critically engaged citizens.

What is at stake here is the notion that thinking is dangerous. It's a policy that suggests that education is not about creating critically informed young people. It's really about training for the workplace. It tends to promote a kind of political and ideological conformity; it's a depoliticizing process—and it's also oppressive, because it removes from education any sense of vision that suggests that education is really about constructing a future that doesn't repeat the worst dimensions of the present, that can see beyond the horizons of the alleged practical and possible. I think in that sense, this emphasis on rote memorization, this emphasis on testing, this emphasis on discipline is quite compatible with the fact that . . . many of these schools are being turned into military academies, particularly in Chicago. Much of public education has lost its mission as a democratic public sphere, and schools are being turned into factories of repression designed to kill the imagination and impose a deadly conformity upon students.

I think that what neoliberal reforms do is ignore all those basic problems that matter through which schools have to be understood in order to be reformed in the interest of creating critically engaged citizens. This suggests that any attempt at reforming schools has to be connected to the wider struggles over racism, inequality, poverty, militarization, and the rise of the punishing state. Kids can't learn if they're hungry. Kids can't learn if they find themselves in schools where there are no resources. Kids can't learn in classes that have forty students in them. You don't need to be a rocket scientist to figure this out. And I think that what you really need to figure out is that the right wing knows this. This is not just a kind of willful ignorance. Schools are not being defunded because the state and federal governments don't have the money. They are being defunded because the right wing wants them to fail. The funds are available, but they are being redirected into the military-industrial complex, into policies that lower taxes for the rich, and into the exorbitant salaries of the financial elite. This is a very systemic policy to make sure that if education is going to matter, it's going to matter for the elite. It's not going to matter for everybody else, in the sense of offering the best possible resources and capabilities that it can offer.

M. N.: *So would you go as far as saying that education, and particularly higher education today, actually reinforces neoliberal doctrine inside the classroom?*

H. G.: I don't think there's any question about this. You can pick up the paper every day and read the idiocy that comes out of the mouths of these administrators, whether you're talking about Texas or Arizona or Florida. The university is being corporatized in a way that we've never seen before. And we know what that means; we know what the conditions are that are producing this. What is particularly disturbing is how alleged reforms such as the Common Core standards—which decontextualize teaching and learning by claiming that the larger conditions that place all kinds of constraints on public schools, teaching, and how students learn—do not matter. This is a very privatizing and commerce-driven form of education that depoliticizes as it decontextualizes the most important aspects of schooling and pedagogy. How can we talk about learning without talking about the machinery of inequality that drives how schools are financed, the right-wing policies that are implementing the fundamentalist modes of learning such as creationism, or the deskilling of teachers by suggesting that their only role is to teach to the test? This is truly a pedagogy of repression and ironically is being championed not just by conservatives, the billionaires club, but also by some progressives.

At one level you have right-wing governors who view themselves as the servants of corporate rich, and are all too willing to view all social relations in strictly commercial terms. This dastardly political worldview is reinforced by democrats who should be viewed not simply as another branch of the business party but as members of the deceitful club that might be called "Republicans lite." What both parties share is a love affair with a capitalist society structured in massive inequalities in wealth and power, a strong belief in military expansion abroad, the intensification of militarization at home, and the ruthless ongoing shift in power from the working and middle classes to the 1 percent. We see glimpses of their shared ideology in their mutual embrace of military hardware such as the F-35 strike fighter jet, which will not fly in the rain and costs about $200 million apiece. Politicians today are mostly groupies of the rich and powerful who are all too willing to dish out billions for the warfare state but very little to provide every young person in the United States with a quality education and decent way of life. As Imara Jones has pointed out, the $4.4 trillion already spent on the wars in Iraq and Afghanistan could finance a free college education for every person in America for the next ten years.

I mean, the military budget is bloated; it's the largest in the world; you can combine the next fifteen military budgets: they don't add up to the cost of America's military budget. So you have this misappropriation of money. It's not that we don't have the money for education, it's how we appropriate those funds. We don't appropriate them in the interest of young people. We don't appropriate them in the interest of education. We don't use our wealth to create a single-payer health system, or provide food for the needy. And so, as education is being defunded, what happens is that you have these business models now being incorporated at the university that call, for instance, administrators "CEOs." And by the way, as you know, they're the largest-rising group in education in the United States. Administrators now outnumber faculty, and they're draining huge amounts of resources away from students.

Secondly, of course, faculties have lost power. Thirdly, they're abolishing unions, dissent is being cracked down on in ways that are abominable and reminders of the McCarthy period. You have faculty who basically are being defined by the degree to which they can write grants. Subjects that don't lend themselves immediately to training are going to cost more for students in states like Texas. Texas went so far as to claim that it would lower tuition for those faculties and courses that lent themselves directly to business interests. Can you imagine? While raising the tuition for courses in the humanities and the liberal arts, which these right-wing governors claim contribute nothing to the economy. And of course students, on the other hand, are now seen as consumers or restless children who need to be entertained. They're not seen as important investments in the future, and particularly for a democratic future. They're just seen as slots, and that's why there's a big push in the universities for foreign students, because they're a cash cow. I think the university is in crisis, and it's in a terrible crisis over what's going on in terms of its inability to really take advantage of a mission that in the '50s and '60s, for all of its contradictions and all of its problems, at least had a sense that college was more than simply a job-training opportunity or that the university was more than an adjunct of the military-industrial complex.

M. N.: *Henry, building on what you said about the university being in crisis, how has this shift that has taken place impacted education specifically in the liberal arts and the humanities, and how has it impacted the job market for academics? There are many in Greece, for instance, who view an academic career overseas as a "way out" of the crisis in their country.*

H. G.: I think two things have happened. I think that the liberal arts and the humanities are being defined as useless. They don't correlate well with the notion of the university as a factory. They don't correlate well with the university as a place that really is less interested in teaching kids how to think critically than it is about teaching them how to be semiskilled workers. And it doesn't work well with the governing structure in the university that, in some fundamental ways, says, "Hey, look, power is basically in the hands of CEOs; it's a business culture; we'll tell you what to do."

While it is true that democratic visions and matters of critique and engaged analysis are not simply invested in humanities and the liberal arts, what is true is that the liberal arts and the humanities have a long history of supporting those ideals. Those ideals are not prized or in favor at this moment in higher education, except for the elite schools. Politicians from Arnie Duncan, the secretary of education, to a number of state politicians, education officials, and popular pundits scorn these ideals because they get in the way; they create problems for administrators who don't want critical faculty, who don't want students learning how to think, who want to build on the educational struggles that went on in the 1960s. Not only did you have students demanding all kinds of things, from more inclusive courses, eliminating racism, making schools more democratic, but they opened up schools—and this relates to your second question—these student struggles opened up schools in ways that allowed for the education of a variety of subordinate groups who were excluded from education—those others from the working class, low- and middle-income students, immigrants, poor minorities, and so it goes. See, for instance, the brilliant work by Chris Newfield on this issue. This utterly petrified the right. The fact that blacks, minorities of race and color, and immigrants could become educated was a terrifying assumption for many right wingers, to say the least.

I think what we see now, and you have to connect the dots here . . . remember, you have a Republican Party in the United States that is doing everything it can to violate the Voting Rights Act. It's trying to limit, as much as possible, the ability of black people to vote. Think about how that correlates so easily with making sure that tuitions are sky high in the schools, a policy that enables the evisceration from higher education of working-class people, poor minorities, people who are considered disposable, people who basically would never be able to afford college, unless they had adequate funds, adequate grants, adequate scholarships.

This is really not just about a predatory economic system trying to redistribute wealth from students to administrators to the military-industrial complex or the financial elite. It's also basically about a systemic policy of exclusion. So yes, I think there are questions of opportunity—as tuitions get raised to unbelievable heights, you have an endless range of students who can't get in because the tuition is too high, or you have students who will be saddled with debt for the rest of their lives in a way so that they would never even imagine going into public service, because it doesn't provide the salaries that the private market does. I think when you begin to put these dots together, you begin to see how crucial education is to the neoliberal project.

M. N.: *People in Greece oftentimes have this perception that the international media operates on a very objective and credible basis. . . . How do you see the media's role, however, in reinforcing this system of neoliberalism and casino capitalism?*

H. G.: I think it's silly, it borders on being silly if not utterly naive to assume that the media is somehow removed from questions of power. In the United States, the statistics are very clear. You have six major companies that control the media. The media is in the hands of corporate power. Whether we're talking about Fox News or any of these other right-wing groups, the Murdochs that control the media. . . . Where do you see left-wing analysis included in the mainstream media? Almost never. But if you look at the new media, if you look at alternative media, like the radio station I'm on right now, there are new spaces that are opening up and that's very encouraging, because it speaks to and encourages further cracks in the system that both limit the ability of the system, in light of these new technologies, to be able to wage the type of control that they have in the past, but also provide a space for more critical voices.

So in spite of that concentrated economic power in the media, which is far from objective and unbiased—the mainstream media for the most part is entirely tuned into reproducing a society that upholds massive class ineq-uities, racist policies, an attack on women's reproductive rights, and holds hostage the future of young people at any cost, and whether that means further policies designed to destroy both a free press and a country like Greece, or Spain, or Portugal, or Chile, or Argentina, they have no trouble with that; they don't think twice about it. These people are basically ideo-logical lackeys. They're in the service of the financial elite, and that's what they do, they do their job. But to claim that they're objective, that makes no sense to me.

M. N.: *From a political point of view, we've seen a rising tide of authoritarian-ism and official far-right parties making electoral gains in recent years in numerous countries. On the other hand, we've perhaps seen a failure of the left to respond to this new political climate. How would you characterize the response of the global left to this trend that we have been discussing?*

H. G.: I think there are three things missing from the left that need to be addressed. I think we need to be careful in assuming that the left has failed, as much as the left is learning as quickly as it possibly can about what it needs to do in light of policies that it's used in the past that don't basically work anymore, particularly when it comes to developing policies in a world in which power has become globalized. Three important issues can be mentioned.

First, I believe that the left has to become an international left. Power is now separated from politics, meaning that power is global and politics is local, so that local politics really has very little power; states really have very little power over corporate sovereignty anymore. They can't control it; it has an allegiance to no one; it floats above national boundaries. So we have to begin to think about ways to create movements, laws, policies that actually deal with this kind of global network of power. That's the first thing.

Secondly, I think the left has to take the question of education seriously. Education is not marginal to politics; it's central to politics! If we can't create the formative culture globally that allows people to understand that their interests are being trampled on, that they live in a political system that has been constructed by human beings and can be overturned by human be-ings, but also, a political, economic, and social system that has nothing to do with their needs, that basically exploits their needs, then people will not be moved to think critically and act collectively.

Thirdly, it seems to me that the left has got to get beyond demonstrations. I mean, it's got to come up with an international vision of what it wants to do, one that is flexible, so that it can work in association with a variety of groups. For this to happen, it needs a comprehensive vision that brings vari-ous groups together so that it can develop an organization that basically is going to have some clout, and in some cases that means it can be involved in local elections, and in some cases it can develop third parties, and in some cases it can work with NGOs. But it's got to take the question of power seriously. Power is not just a one-shot deal. It doesn't mean you demonstrate in the street with 200,000 people and then you walk away. It's got to become more systemic. We need more than what my friend Stanley Aronowitz calls "signpost politics," the politics of banners. Mass demonstrations for climate change, for instance, are encouraging because they draw attention to a crucial threat to the planet, and that's a pedagogical moment, but we have to go far beyond that. We need to create, ideologically, politically, educationally, international organizations that can begin to bring their weight to bear on this global politics that now controls basically state politics and nations all across the world. This means moving from education to confrontation; it means moving from critique to action; it means moving from recognizing a crisis to the practice of freedom, one driven by sustainable organizations, self-sustaining resources, and the collective will to act.

Reclaim the Radical Imagination

Politics beyond Hope

12

The Responsibility of Intellectuals in the Shadow of the Atomic Plague

Fighting Back against the Neoliberal Disimagination Machine

⟿

> Lacking the truth, [we] will however find *instants of truth*, and those instants are in fact all we have available to us to give some order to this chaos of horror.
>
> —*Hannah Arendt*[1]

Seventy years after the horror of Hiroshima, intellectuals negotiate a vastly changed cultural, political, and moral geography. Pondering what Hiroshima means for American history and consciousness proves as fraught an intellectual exercise as taking up this critical issue in the years and the decades that followed this staggering inhumanity, albeit for vastly different reasons. Now that we are living in a 24/7 screen culture hawking incessant apocalypse, how we understand Foucault's discerning observation that history is always a history of the present takes on a greater significance. This is especially true in light of the fact that historical memory is not simply being rewritten, but disappearing.[2] Once an emancipatory pedagogical and political project predicated on the right to study and engage the past critically, history has now receded into a depoliticizing culture of consumerism, a wholesale attack on science, the glorification of military ideals, an embrace of the punishing state, and a nostalgic invocation of World War II's birthing of "the greatest generation." Inscribed in insipid patriotic platitudes and decontextualized isolated facts, history under the reign of neoliberalism has been either cleansed of its most critical impulses and dangerous memories, or it has been reduced to a contrived narrative that sustains the fictions and ideologies of the rich and powerful. History has become not only a site of collective amnesia but also a tool appropriated under neoliberalism so as to transform "the past into a container full of colourful or colourless, appetizing or insipid bits, all floating with the same specific gravity."[3] Consequently, what intellectuals now have to say about Hiroshima and history in general is not of the slightest interest to nine-tenths of the American public. While writers of fiction might find such a generalized indifference to their craft freeing, even "inebriating," as Philip Roth has recently stated, "for the chroniclers of history it is a cry in the wilderness."[4]

At the same time, historical traces of Hiroshima remain present but forgotten in themes that capture the shift from the existential anxieties and dread of nuclear annihilation that racked the early 1950s to a contemporary fundamentalist despair embodied in collective uncertainty, a predilection for apocalyptic violence, a political economy of disposability, and an expanding culture of brutality that has fused with the entertainment industry. We've not produced a generation of war protestors or government agitators to be sure, but rather a generation of youth who no longer believe they have a future that will be any different from the present.[5] That instructive connections tying the past to the present are lost indicates not merely the emergence of a disimagination machine that wages an assault on historical memory, civic literacy, and civic agency. It also points to a historical shift in which the perpetual disappearance of that atomic moment signals a further deepening of our own national psychosis.

If, as Edward Glover once observed, "Hiroshima and Nagasaki had rendered actual the most extreme fantasies of world destruction encountered in the insane or in the nightmares of ordinary people," then the neoliberal disimagination machine has rendered such horrific reality a collective fantasy driven by spectacles of violence and the theater of entertainment.[6] The disimagination machine threatens democratic public life by devaluing social agency, historical memory, and critical consciousness; in doing so, it creates the conditions for people to be ethically compromised and politically infantilized. Returning to Hiroshima is necessary not only to break out of the moral cocoon that puts reason and memory to sleep but also to rediscover our imaginative capacities for civic literacy on behalf of the public good. Such remembrance enables us to see, as Robert Jay Lifton and Greg Mitchell have asserted, that "every small act of violence [today] has some connection with, if not sanction from, the violence of Hiroshima and Nagasaki."[7]

I

On Monday, August 6, 1945, the United States unleashed an atomic bomb on Hiroshima, killing 70,000 people instantly and another 70,000 within five years—an opening strike in a nuclear campaign that was also visited on Nagasaki in the days that followed.[8] In the immediate aftermath of the bombings, the incineration of mostly innocent civilians was buried in official US government pronouncements of victory. The atomic bomb was celebrated by those who argued that its use was responsible for concluding the war with Japan. Also applauded were the power of the bomb and the wonder of science in creating it, fueled especially by "the atmosphere of technological fanaticism" in which scientists had worked to create the most powerful weapon of destruction then known to the world.[9] Conventional justification for dropping the atomic bombs held that "it was the most expedient measure to securing Japan's surrender [and] that the bomb was used to shorten the agony of war and to save American lives."[10] Left out of that succinct legitimating narrative were the growing objections to the use of atomic weaponry put forth by a number of top military leaders and politicians, including General Dwight Eisenhower, who was then the supreme allied commander in Europe, former president Herbert Hoover, and General Douglas MacArthur—all of whom argued that dropping the atom bomb was not necessary to end the war.[11]

For a brief time, the atom bomb was celebrated as a kind of magic talisman entwining salvation and scientific inventiveness. It functioned to "simultaneously domesticate the unimaginable while charging the mundane surroundings of our everyday lives with a weight and sense of importance unmatched in modern times."[12] In spite of the initial celebration of the effects of the bomb and the orthodox defense that accompanied it, whatever positive value the bomb may have had among the American public, intellectuals, and popular media began to dissipate as more and more people became aware of the massive deaths, suffering, and misery it had caused.[13]

Kenzaburo Oe, the Nobel Prize winner for Literature, has noted that in spite of attempts to justify the bombing, "from the instant the atomic bomb exploded, it [soon] became the symbol of human evil, [embodying] the absolute evil of war."[14] What particularly troubled Oe was the scientific and intellectual support for its creation and the lobbying for its use despite an acute awareness that the exploded bomb would turn anything it hit into a "vast ugly death chamber."[15] Hiroshima designated the beginning of the nuclear era in which, as Oh Jung points out, "Combatants were engaged on a path toward total war in which technological advances, coupled with the increasing effectiveness of an air strategy, began to undermine the ethical view that civilians should not be targeted."[16] More pointedly, Hiroshima revealed a new stage in the merging of military actions and scientific methods, indeed a new era in which the technology of destruction could destroy the earth in roughly the time it takes to boil an egg. The bombing of Hiroshima extended a new industrially enabled kind of violence and warfare in which the distinction between soldiers and civilians disappeared and the indiscriminate bombing of civilians became normalized, even celebrated. The American government exhibited a "total embrace of the atom bomb" that signaled support for the first time of a "notion of unbounded annihilation [and] the totality of destruction."[17]

The destructive power of the bomb and its use on civilians also marked a turning point in American identity as the United States began to think of itself as a superpower, which as Robert Jay Lifton points out, refers to "a national mindset—put forward strongly by a tight-knit leadership group—that takes on a sense of omnipotence, of unique standing in the world that grants it the right to hold sway over all other nations."[18] The power of the scientific imagination and its murderous deployment gave birth simultaneously to the American disimagination machine with its capacity to rewrite history in order to render truth an irrelevant relic best forgotten.

What remains particularly ghastly about the rationale for dropping two atomic bombs was the attempt on the part of its defenders to construct a redemptive narrative through a perversion of humanistic sentiment by justifying mass slaughter in the name of saving lives and winning the war.[19] This was humanism under siege, surrendered to political expediency and transformed into its terrifying opposite—a grotesque Faustian rationalization leading to what Edmund Wilson called "plague and annihilation."[20] In part, Hiroshima represented the integration of a military metaphysics as a defining feature of US national identity—along with its poisonous and powerful investment in the cult of scientism, instrumental rationality, and technological fanaticism—and the simultaneous marginalization of scientific evidence and intellectual rigor, even reason itself. That Hiroshima was used to redefine America's "national mission and its utopian possibilities"[21] can be considered nothing less than what the late historian Howard Zinn called a "devastating commentary on our moral culture."[22] More pointedly, it serves as a grim commentary on our national sanity. In most cases, matters of morality and justice were dissolved into technical questions or a reductive chauvinism rooted in notions of governmentally massaged efficiency, scientific "expertise," and American exceptionalism. As Robert Jay Lifton and Greg Mitchell have stated, the atomic bomb was viewed as a symbol of the powerful destiny of postwar America rather than a "ruthless weapon of indiscriminate destruction" that conveniently put to rest painful questions concerning justice, morality, and ethical responsibility. They write:

> Our official narrative precluded anything suggesting atonement. Rather the bomb itself had to be "redeemed." As "a frightening manifestation of technological evil ... it needed to be reformed, transformed, managed, or turned into the vehicle of a promising future," [as historian M. Susan] Lindee argued. "It was necessary, somehow, to redeem the bomb." In other words, to avoid historical and moral responsibility, we acted immorally and claimed virtue. We sank deeper, that is, into moral inversion.[23]

This narrative of redemption was soon challenged by a number of historians who argued that the dropping of the atomic bomb had less to do with winning the war than with an attempt to deter the Soviet Union from expanding its empire into territory deemed essential to American interests.[24] Protecting America's superiority in a potential Soviet-American conflict was a decisive factor in dropping the bomb. In addition, the Truman administration needed to provide legitimation to Congress for the staggering sums of money spent on the Manhattan Project in developing the atomic weapons program and for procuring future funding necessary to continue military research long after the war ended.[25] Historian Howard Zinn asserted that the government's weak defense for the bombing of Hiroshima was knowingly false and tantamount to an act of terrorism. Zinn, always a public intellectual willing to hold power accountable, asked: "Can we … comprehend the killing of 200,000 people to make a point about American power?"[26] Other historians also attempted to challenge the official defense of Hiroshima by providing counterevidence that the Japanese were ready to surrender as a result of a number of factors, including the nonstop bombing of twenty-six cities before Hiroshima and Nagasaki were bombed, the success of the naval and military blockade of Japan, and the Soviet Union's entrance into the war on August 9.[27]

The narrative of redemption and the criticism it provoked are important for understanding both the role that intellectuals assumed at this historical moment by addressing what would be the beginning of the nuclear weapons era and how that critical role has faded at the beginning of the twenty-first century. Historical reflection on this tragic inception of the nuclear age reveals the decades-long dismantling of a culture's infrastructure of ideas and its growing intolerance for critical thought. It sheds light on the increasing pressures exerted on the media, universities, and responsible intellectuals either to face hostility and isolation by continuing to voice unpopular realities or to cede to comforting mythologies and support official narratives.

Within a short time after the dropping of the atomic bombs on Hiroshima and Nagasaki, John Hersey wrote a devastating description of the misery and suffering caused by nuclear warfare. Challenging abstract arguments that linked the bomb to considerations of technique, efficiency, and national honor, Hersey first published in *The New Yorker,* and later in a widely read book, an exhaustive and terrifying description of the suffering caused by the bomb to the people of Hiroshima. There is one haunting passage that not only illustrates the horrifying pain and suffering experienced by the burned and blinded victims but also offers a powerful metaphor for the moral blindness that overtook the perpetrators. He writes:

On his way back with the water, [Father Kleinsorge] got lost on a detour around a fallen tree, and as he looked for his way through the woods, he heard a voice ask from the underbrush, "Have you anything to drink?" He saw a uniform. Thinking there was just one soldier, he approached with the water. When he had penetrated the bushes, he saw there were about twenty men, they were all in exactly the same nightmarish state: their faces were wholly burned, their eye sockets were hollow, the fluid from their melted eyes had run down their cheeks. Their mouths were mere swollen, pus-covered wounds, which they could not bear to stretch enough to admit the spout of the teapot.[28]

The nightmarish image of fallen soldiers with hollow eye sockets and purulent, swollen mouths offers as well an image of the American military mind-set that speaks in bloated lies and refuses to see the moral witnessing necessary to keep alive for future generations the memory of the horror of nuclear weapons and the need to eliminate them. Hersey's graphic depiction of mass violence against civilians serves as a kind of mirrored doubling, referring at one level to nations blindly driven by militarism and hypernationalism. At another level, perpetrators of violence, like an inverted image of their victim's damaged bodies, display mutilated consciences, seizing upon a sense of their expressed victimization as a rationale to become blind to their own injustices.

Pearl Harbor enabled Americans to view themselves as victims but then, exhibiting a perverse form of mimicry, they became perpetrators who denied any responsibility or role in escalating the violence and injustice. Employing both a poisonous racism and weapons of mad violence against the Japanese people, the US government imagined Japan as the ultimate enemy and then pursued tactics that turned the American public into its own worst enemy by substituting military measures for its most cherished democratic principles. In a sense, this self-imposed blindness functioned as part of what Jacques Derrida once called a societal autoimmune response, one in which the body's immune system attacked its own bodily defenses.[29] Fortunately, this state of political and moral myopia did not envelop the whole nation, and a number of critics for the next fifty years denounced the dropping of the atomic bombs and the beginning of the nuclear age.

Responding to Hersey's article on the bombing of Hiroshima, Mary McCarthy argued that he had reduced the bombing to the same level of journalism used to report natural catastrophes such as "fires, floods, and earthquakes," and in doing so had turned a grotesque act of barbarism into "a human interest story" that diminished the bomb's significance and the role that "bombers, the scientists, the government," and others played in producing this monstrous act.[30] McCarthy expressed alarm that Hersey had "failed to consider why it was used, who was responsible, and whether it had been necessary."[31] McCarthy was only partly right. While it was true that Hersey did not tackle the larger political, cultural, and social conditions of the event's unfolding, his article provided one of the few detailed reports at the time of the horrors the bomb had inflicted; his report stoked a sense of trepidation about nuclear weapons along with a modicum of moral outrage over the decision to drop the bomb—positions to which most Americans had not yet given much consideration. Hersey was not alone. Wilfred Burchett, writing for the London *Daily Express*, was the first journalist to provide an independent account of the suffering, misery, and death that engulfed Hiroshima after the bomb was dropped on the city. For Burchett, the cataclysm and horror he witnessed firsthand resembled a vision of hell that he aptly termed "the Atomic Plague." He wrote:

> Hiroshima does not look like a bombed city. It looks as if a monster steamroller had passed over it and squashed it out of existence. I write these facts as dispassionately as I can in the hope that they will act as a warning to the world. In this first testing ground of the atomic bomb I have seen the most terrible and frightening desolation in four years of war. It makes a blitzed Pacific island seem like an Eden. The damage is far greater than photographs can show.[32]

In the end, in spite of such accounts, fear and moral outrage did little to put an end to the nuclear arms race, but it did prompt a number of intellectuals to enter into the public realm to condemn the bombing as well as the ongoing advance of a nuclear weapons program and the ever-present threat of global annihilation it posed.

A number of important questions emerge from the above analysis, but two issues in particular stand out for me with respect to the role that academics and public intellectuals have played in addressing the bombing of Hiroshima, the emergence of nuclear weapons on a global scale, and the continued danger posed by the existence and use of such weapons. The first question focuses on what has been learned from the bombings of Hiroshima and Nagasaki, and the second question concerns the disturbing issue of how the potential for violence on the scale witnessed at Hiroshima and Nagasaki has become normalized in the collective American psyche.

In the aftermath of the bombing of Hiroshima, there was a major debate not just about the emergence of the atomic age and the moral, economic, scientific, military, and political forces that gave rise to it, but also about the ways in which nuclear armament altered the nature of state power, gave rise to new forms of militarism, created environmental hazards, produced an emergent surveillance state, furthered the politics of state secrecy, and put into play a series of deadly diplomatic crises reinforced by the logic of brinkmanship and a belief in the totality of war.[33] Hiroshima not only unleashed immense misery, unimaginable suffering, and wanton death on Japanese civilians; it also gave rise to antidemocratic tendencies in the US government that put the health, safety, and liberty of the American people at risk. Shrouded in secrecy, the government machinery of death that produced the bomb did everything possible to cover up the most grotesque effects of the bombing of Hiroshima and Nagasaki, as well as the dangerous hazards it posed to the American people. Lifton and Mitchell argue convincingly that while the bomb's effects were concealed by the government in the immediate aftermath of the bombings, before long this secrecy evolved into a wholesale cover-up marked by government lies and, even more alarming, the falsification of information.[34] With respect to the horrors visited upon Hiroshima and Nagasaki, films taken by Japanese and American photographers were hidden for years from the American public for fear that they would create both a moral panic and a backlash against the funding for nuclear weapons.[35] For example, the Atomic Energy Commission lied about the extent and danger of radiation fallout, going so far as to mount a campaign claiming that "fallout does not constitute a serious hazard to any living thing outside the test site."[36] This act of falsification took place in spite of the fact that thousands of military personnel were exposed to high levels of radiation within and outside of the test sites.

In addition, the Atomic Energy Commission in conjunction with the Central Intelligence Agency, the departments of Defense and Veterans' Affairs, and other government collaborators engaged in a series of medical experiments designed to test the effects of different levels of radiation exposure on military personnel, medical patients, prisoners, and others in various sites. According to Lifton and Mitchell, these experiments took the shape of exposing people intentionally to "radiation releases or by placing military personnel at or near ground zero of bomb tests."[37] It gets worse. They also note that "from 1945 through 1947, bomb-grade plutonium injections were given to thirty-one patients" in a variety of hospitals and medical centers, and that all of these "experiments were shrouded in secrecy and, when deemed necessary, in lies. . . . The experiments were intended to show what type or amount of exposure would cause damage to normal, healthy people in a nuclear war."[38] Some of the lasting legacies of the birth of the atomic bomb also included the rise of plutonium dumps, environmental and health risks, the cult of expertise, and the subordination of the peaceful development of technology to a large-scale interest in using technology for the organized production of violence. Another notable development raised by many critics in the years following the launch of the atomic age was the rise of a government that sought power over its citizens through surveillance and secrecy, the repression of dissent, and the legitimation of a type of civic illiteracy that told Americans to leave "the gravest problems, military and social, completely in the hands of experts and political leaders who claimed to have them under control."[39] This tendency to subordinate criticism to the all-knowing power of experts who served the power elite was further intensified with the ongoing attempts by the Reagan administration and the Republican Party after 1980, and especially after the terrorist attack on 9/11, to both conflate criticism with treason and more generally to demean intellectuals, critical thinking, and, more importantly, intellectualism. Richard Hofstadter's warning about paranoia and anti-intellectualism in American life blossomed into a full-throttle plague after the 1980s.[40]

All of these antidemocratic tendencies unleashed by the atomic age came under scrutiny during the latter half of the twentieth century. The terror of a nuclear holocaust, an intense sense of alienation from the commanding institutions of power, and deep anxiety about the demise of the future spawned growing unrest, ideological dissent, and massive outbursts of resistance among students and intellectuals all over the globe from the 1960s until the beginning of the twenty-first century. Protesters called for the outlawing of militarism, nuclear production and stockpiling, and the nuclear propaganda machine. Literary writers extending from James Agee to Kurt Vonnegut, Jr., condemned the death-saturated machinery launched by the atomic age. Moreover, public intellectuals from Dwight Macdonald and Bertrand Russell to Helen Caldicott, Ronald Takaki, Noam Chomsky, and Howard Zinn fanned the flames of resistance to nuclear weapons as well as the development of nuclear technologies. Others, such as environmental activist George Monbiot, supported the nuclear industry but denounced the nuclear arms race. In doing so, he argued that "the anti-nuclear movement ... has misled the world about the impacts of radiation on human health [producing] claims ... ungrounded in science, unsupportable when challenged and wildly wrong [and] have done other people, and ourselves, a terrible disservice."[41]

Yet, in response to crises arising from nuclear technology—extending from the Three Mile Island accident in 1979 to the Chernobyl disaster of 1986 and the more recent Fukushima nuclear disaster of 2011—a myriad of social movements along with a number of mass demonstrations against nuclear power have developed and taken place all over the world.[42] When deep moral and political concerns over the legacy of Hiroshima seemed to be fading in the United States, the tragedy of 9/11 and the endlessly replayed images of the two planes crashing into the twin towers of the World Trade Center resurrected once again the frightening specter of what Colonel Paul Tibbets, Jr., the *Enola Gay*'s pilot, referred to as "that awful cloud ... boiling up, mushrooming, terrible and incredibly tall" after "Little Boy," a seven-hundred-pound uranium bomb, was released over Hiroshima. Following 9/11, however, collective anxieties were focused not on the atomic bombing of Hiroshima and its implications for a nuclear Armageddon but on the fear of terrorists using a nuclear weapon to wreak havoc on Americans. A decade later, that fear, however parochially framed, seems to have diminished, if not entirely disappeared, despite the fact that it enabled an aggressive attack on civil liberties throughout the culture and ceded more power to an egregious and dangerous surveillance state.

The world now confronts a reality in which nine states have nuclear weapons, and a number of them, such as North Korea, Pakistan, and India, have threatened to use them. James McCluskey points out that "the nine nuclear states have more than 10,000 nuclear weapons in their stockpiles [and] a single US nuclear warhead ... is 30 times more destructive than the bomb that wiped out Hiroshima."[43] Moreover, these weapons have "sufficient destructive power to incinerate every human being on the planet three times over, [and] there are more than 2,000 held on hair-trigger alert, already mounted on board their missiles and ready to be launched at a moment's notice."[44] These weapons are far more powerful and deadly than the atomic bomb, and the possibility that they might be used, even inadvertently, is greater. This threat becomes all the more real in light of a history of miscommunications, mismanagement, and technological malfunctions, suggesting both the fragility of such weapons and the dire stupidity of positions that defend their safety and value as a nuclear deterrent.[45] A 2014 report, *Too Close for Comfort—Cases of Near Nuclear Use and Options for Policy*, not only outlines a historical pattern of near misses in great detail but also makes terrifyingly clear that "the risk associated with nuclear weapons is high."[46] It is also worth noting that an enormous amount of money is wasted to maintain these weapons, develop more sophisticated nuclear missiles, and invest in ever more weapons laboratories. McCluskey estimates world funding for such weapons at $1 trillion per decade, while *Arms Control Today* "reported in 2012 that yearly funding for U.S. nuclear weapons activity was $31 billion."[47]

In the United States, the historical connection to Hiroshima is presently connected to a series of mushrooming forces of destruction, including a turn to instrumental reason over moral considerations, the normalization of violence in America, the militarization of local police forces, an attack on civil liberties, the rise of the surveillance state, a dangerous turn toward state secrecy under President Obama, the rise of the carceral state, and the elevation of war as a central organizing principle of society. Rather than stand in opposition to a potential nuclear disaster or the expansion of the arms industry, the United States places high up on the list of those nations that could fall prey to what Amy Goodman calls that "horrible moment when hubris, accident or inhumanity triggers the next nuclear attack."[48] Given the history of lies, deceptions, falsifications, and retreat into secrecy that characterizes the American government's suffocating embrace of the military-industrial-surveillance complex, it would be naive to assume that the US government can be trusted to act with good intentions when it comes to matters of domestic and foreign policy. State terrorism has increasingly become the DNA of American governance and politics.

II

Nuclear weapons are an obscenity. They are the very antithesis of humanity.
—*Desmond Tutu*

At the dawn of the twenty-first century and the seventieth anniversary of Hiroshima, it seems evident that the poisonous legacy of the atomic bomb poses a greater threat to humanity than ever before. This legacy appears to be increasingly infused with a celebration of militarism and an investment in technological fanaticism, both of which lay bare an utter disregard for the possibility of nuclear warfare and planetary obliteration. In spite of the fact that President Obama campaigned for a "nuclear-free world," the Obama administration is "engaging in extensive atomic rebuilding," suggesting that "the modernization of nuclear capabilities has become an end unto itself."[49] Not only is the Obama administration building and upgrading "eight major plants and laboratories employing more than 40,000 people," it has also "told the Pentagon to plan for 12 new missile submarines, up to 100 new bombers and 400 land-based missiles, either new or refurbished [with an] estimated total cost of the nuclear enterprise over the next three decades at roughly $900 billion to $1.1 trillion."[50]

Reflecting on the tragic historical events of 1945, American intellectuals offer nothing more than a tepid response to the birth of the atomic age, which cannot but signify a moral failure and political retreat tantamount to a callous indifference to human suffering. The threat of global nuclear annihilation appears to have dissolved into a domestication of the unimaginable.[51] America's intellectuals have lost sight of the horror, fear, anxieties, and sense of doom that gripped both the American public and its intellectuals during the second half of the twentieth century, in spite of the fact that such fears and anxieties—and the criticism and modes of resistance to nuclear technology that grew out of them—were not without reason and are even more relevant today.[52] If this threat is more dangerous and imminent today than in the past, how does one explain the retreat of intellectuals in the twenty-first century from addressing the memory of Hiroshima and the danger that such amped-up nuclear destructions pose to the world at this historical moment?

Jacques Derrida identified the possibility of a nuclear catastrophe as a "non-event," a likelihood beset by a paradox caught between "the necessity and the impossibility of thinking the event."[53] In an age in which wars have become indiscriminately murderous, intellectuals find themselves confronting forms of symbolic and material violence that produce an endless series of crises. Yet these crises have been reduced to Hollywood spectacles, just as the notion of crisis now gives way to a "disimagination machine" that divorces critically engaged modes of individual and collective agency from an understanding of the conditions that threaten human beings with apocalyptic disasters.[54] Instead of addressing the dark shadow of extinction that extends from Hiroshima to Fukushima, American intellectuals appear to have become quiet, tamed by the forces of privatization, commodification, and militarism while constantly being bombarded by the celebration of popular powerlessness.

As the widely circulated videos of the horrific decapitations of James Foley, Steven Sotloff, and others by Islamic extremists in 2014 made clear, terrorism in the age of mass media and communications technology attaches itself to the spectacle of violence so as to open up a new space in which global politics is shaped by the regressive morality of ideological fundamentalism, one that willfully exhibits its degeneration into a totalitarian pathology. As shocking as these atrocious events are, they offer no guarantees of moral outrage or political action because the substantive nature of crisis itself has become frail, subject to its colonization by a neoliberal "disimagination machine" that thrives on representational excess and surrender to the political cynicism of apocalyptic despair.

In contrast to the postwar reactions to the monstrous violence wrought by the atomic bomb on Hiroshima and Nagasaki, violence, torture, and human suffering are now framed outside of the realm of historical memory, readily dissolving into the nonstop production of Hollywood movies, media spectacles, and a screen culture that promises instant gratification. In a society in which our inner worlds are subject to the reign of the "death-haunted"[55] dictates of casino capitalism with its endless series of environmental, political, financial, and social cataclysms, the apocalypse has become a spectacle. Moreover, it is a spectacle that produces political infantilism and civic illiteracy, while thriving on a plethora of excessive violence. This is all done in the name of entertainment, which remains safely removed from the work of many academics—even though its messages are widely viewed and accepted as common sense by the American public—as if the public pedagogy produced by the merchants of desire and entertainment only exists in the realm of fiction and functions exclusively as a form of harmless amusement.[56]

Too many academics and other intellectuals now live under the shadow of a manufactured precarity and relentless catastrophe in the wake of endless disasters that have become an ongoing feature of everyday life. Massive hurricanes, tsunamis, earthquakes, floods, droughts, along with the rise of racism, mass violence, terrorism, xenophobia, nationalism, and an increase in war around the globe are ignored or explained away in forms of trivial analyses offered by the corporate media. Thus removed from any understanding of the conditions that produce catastrophic events, media coverage provides an endless cycle of material for consumption by what has become a culture that feeds on disaster and aesthetic depravity and that turns everything into a cheap form of entertainment or simply a crude spectacle. Lured by neoliberal dream-machines into their theater of cruelty, there is a tendency on the part of both intellectuals and the general public to become indifferent to even extreme forms of violence, preferring to flirt with irrationality and withdraw into private obsessions, all the while becoming complicit with the withering of political life.

Violence has become normalized even as the scale of destruction appears overwhelming and seems beyond the control of neoliberal societies such as the United States, where all social problems are increasingly understood through the reductive registers of individual character, responsibility, and atomized resilience. Under such circumstances, wider public and political concerns dissolve into personal dilemmas. In the absence of conceptual or practical means to address the conditions of our collective existence, growing fear feeds a crisis of meaning for many intellectuals. Any sustained critique that could motivate political action gives way to a sense of despair and flight from responsibility. The overwhelming array and scope of disaster appear beyond any hope of being addressed through the efforts of isolated individuals. As Michael Levine and William Taylor point out:

> People are left without the mental or physical abilities they need to cope. Government is absent or useless. We find ourselves in what amounts to what Naomi Zack ("Philosophy and Disaster"; Ethics for Disaster) describes as a Hobbesian second state of nature—where government is inoperative and chaos (moral, social, political, personal) reigns. . . . Genuine [crisis], for example war, undermines and dismantles the structures—material structures to be sure but also those of justice, human kindness, and affectivity—that give us the wherewithal to function and that are shown to be inimical to catastrophe as such. Disaster dispenses with civilization while catastrophe displaces it.[57]

The horrors of crises such as Hiroshima were met in the past by many intellectuals with moral outrage, criticism, and collective resistance, informed by a sense of hope for the future rooted in the power of the radical imagination. Today, such a culture of thoughtful reasoning and insightful analyses has been corroded under the flood of made-for-screen catastrophes that drown the moral conscience and muddy political reflection. Derrida's call for the necessity of action in the face of a crisis such as Hiroshima and the dawn of the nuclear age becomes difficult, if not impossible, to understand and act upon at the present time as the meaning of "crisis"—with its underlying appeal to critique and action—has now given way to a notion of catastrophe in which inconceivable disasters and terrors dissolve into what Susan Sontag called "the threat of unremitting banality."[58] As endless neoliberal spectacles of catastrophe move between the registers of transgressive excess and extreme violence, they exhaust their shock value and degenerate into escapist entertainment, while posing as a moral necessity.

Under such circumstances, many intellectuals are no longer dealing with crises, which in the past were often met by thoughtful, responsible, and organized responses to the challenges produced by calamitous events such as the bombing of Hiroshima. Such a state of ethical tranquilization and political paralysis induced by catastrophic spectacles is further reinforced by the widespread cynicism that has become the modus operandi of the neoliberal machinery of misery and precarity. Rather than lift people out of the rubble of disaster, catastrophes serve to "distract us from terrors . . . by an escape into the exotic dangerous situations which have last-minute happy endings."[59] As Mark Fisher points out, catastrophe speaks to a world that is falling apart and for which no intervention can be anticipated. Catastrophe becomes synonymous with a kind of senseless hope rooted in a faith that denies reason and cancels out action while resorting to "superstition and religion, the first resorts of the helpless, proliferate."[60] Catastrophe not only cancels out the future by simply reproducing the present, it also exhausts historical memory "because tradition counts for nothing when it is no longer contested and modified."[61]

Manufactured catastrophes—and with them a generalized sense of manufactured helplessness—now reign supreme in the new interregnum of late modernity, a kind of in-between space that serves to neutralize action, derail the challenges posed by real social and political problems such as the threat of nuclear annihilation, and substitute the escape into fantasy for any attempt to challenge the terrifying conditions that often accompany a serious crisis. Such retreats from reality blunt civic courage, dull the radical imagination, and dilute any sense of moral responsibility, plunging historical acts of violence such as Hiroshima into the abyss of political indifference, ethical insensitivity, and depoliticization. Catastrophe, as Brad Evans has observed, speaks to an era of late modernity marked by "a closing of the political."[62] Resignation and acceptance of catastrophe have taken root in the ground prepared by the neoliberal notion that "nothing can be done." If, as Zygmunt Bauman argues, crisis speaks to the need to address what exactly needs to be done,[63] then what has been lost in the age of catastrophe and its overwhelming sense of precarity and uncertainty is a properly political response in the face of a crisis.

In the aftermath of the bombing of Hiroshima, the question emerged as to what was to be done about such horror. Catastrophe, in contrast, tends to be so overpowering that the issue is no longer how might intellectuals address and rectify a crisis, but how do they endure and survive it. The horror of the atomic bomb once inspired the Beat Generation, a literature of resistance, film documentaries, and a plethora of thoughtful criticism. As Howard Zinn pointed out, today's images of violence and "the statistics of death and suffering that figures in the millions leave us numb, and nothing but the personal testimonies of individuals—even if they only faintly represent the reality—are capable of shaking us out of that numbness."[64] Such horror now survives as a script, not for confronting dark truths about human civilization, but for incorporating and embellishing as part of a Hollywood blockbuster.

Neoliberal regimes locked into the orbits of privatization, commodification, disposability, and militarization elevate extreme violence and its effects into a cultural and pedagogical spectacle. The spectacle in this sense is part of a pedagogical disimagination apparatus in which historical, individual, and social modes of agency degenerate, presenting a serious challenge to intellectuals regarding the very possibility of addressing diverse crises. Instead of responding to crises with the desire to correct a wrong and to reimagine a different future, all that appears to be left among many intellectuals, especially in the academy, is the desire merely to survive in the face of endless representations of state and nonstate violence and the ever-encroaching apocalypses produced by the neoliberal machinery of disposability. The mass public indifference to the nuclear arms race and the threat of human extinction; the use of state torture; the indiscriminate and mass killing of children; the rise of debtors' prisons; the war against women; the militarization of the totality of American society; and the state violence waged against nonviolent students protesters—is only a short list indicating how the looming shadows of apocalypse and experiences of actual suffering have moved out of the realm of political responsibility and moral sensibility into the black hole of a depoliticizing disimagination machine.

At the same time, mass violence has become individualized in that real-life violence in both screen culture and the corporate-controlled media is reduced to representations of suffering and tortured individuals rather than masses of people. Under such circumstances, mass violence such as what happened at Hiroshima becomes faceless and invisible, since only the individual body denotes a legitimate representation of suffering, violence, brutality, and death. This individualization of violence reinforces the logic of neoliberal misery and disposability construing the individual's plight as a matter of fate removed from larger structural forces as the normal and acceptable state of affairs. Mass deaths make it more difficult to strip away the humanity of the victims and the horror of the violence and are not easily forgotten. Today, the traces of both memory and moral responsibility become more difficult for intellectuals to address and grasp as crises are abstracted from the broader social, economic, and political conditions of their production.

As crisis gives way to catastrophe, the quest to merely survive now misdirects moral and political outrage toward forms of entertainment that in turn lull them into a moral coma. As violence becomes part of a disimagination machine, it becomes more difficult to conceive other kinds of social behavior, modes of mediation, and types of collective resistance, let alone a more just and democratic future. Hence, the spectacle of the catastrophe signals a society in which a collective sense of despair merges with the notion of a future that is no longer worth fighting for. The lesson to be drawn here, however tentative, is that under the reign of neoliberalism, the roles and responsibilities of the intellectual are being devalued, reduced to a stance marked by a flight from moral and political responsibility, infused by an indifference to the unpleasant necessities of mass violence, and safely tamed within public spheres such as higher education that have given themselves over to a crude instrumental rationality and endorsement of market-based values, practices, and policies.[65]

Many Americans now inhabit modes of time and space in which violence and the logic of disposability mutually reinforce each other. For example, the unarmed African American youth, Michael Brown, standing with his hands raised, was not only shot and killed by a white policeman in Ferguson, Missouri, but his body was left in the street for four hours—this eerily reminiscent of the treatment given the low-income, largely African American inhabitants of New Orleans whose bodies, rendered worthless and undeserving of compassion, were also left in the streets after Hurricane Katrina swept through the city.

The logic of disposability has a long history in the United States and has spurned a number of resistance movements and a plethora of dissent among intellectuals. Unfortunately, times have changed for the worst. In the case of the shooting of Michael Brown, there was an enormous expression of outrage by many poor minorities of color and some white progressives, yet too little was heard from American intellectuals and academics. In the absence of such an outcry, public attitudes are reinforced in their acceptance of the neoliberal notion that disposable populations and individuals are the new living dead—legitimately made invisible and rightly relegated to zones of terminal exclusion and impoverishment. Such silence reinforces the notion that the disposable are by their own actions the unknowable, invisible, and powerless marginalized by class and race and living in ghettoes that serve as dumping grounds largely patrolled by armies of police dressed like soldiers inspecting a war zone.

The disposable people inhabiting these sites, or what João Biehl calls "zones of social abandonment,"[66] constitute a new form of underclass, an expanding group of the American population that extends from poor urban minorities to a collapsing middle class to the millions incarcerated by the punishing state to an entire generation of young people whose lives have been short-circuited by a rogue financial class that has robbed them of a future and who now live in a constant state of uncertainty and precarity.[67] Made voiceless, and hence powerless, the subjectivity of the dispossessed becomes not just the locus of politics, but part of the machinery of social and political death. The logic of disposability has become all-encompassing in American society, extending its tentacles outward from the neighborhoods of the poor and destitute to the middle-class confines of the suburbs and outlying rural communities. The power and reach of neoliberal misery and disposability have created a new culture of hopelessness and conformity among many intellectuals who are themselves feeling always on the brink of being thrust into the ranks of the disposable. Increasingly, they appear too afraid of losing their jobs or of a fate even worse—such as incarceration—if they speak out against the violence that is now embedded in the DNA of American society. In the face of a state government that hardly shies away from surveillance, punishment, and mass incarceration—and in these respects appears far more harsh and powerful than the one that dropped the bomb on Hiroshima—many intellectuals fear for their futures, and in some cases their lives.[68] Abandoning all efforts to advocate for change and embracing the survivalist mode peddled by the neoliberal social order and a 24/7 nonstop consumerist culture, intellectuals retreat from dangerous memories, making it easier for the logic of disposability to become the norm rather than the exception.

As consumerism becomes the only obligation of citizenship and expression of agency left, the pleasure of passive spectatorship along with a sterile careerism blunt for many intellectuals any sense of political engagement and the need to address crucial social problems. At the same time, the machinery of commodification rolls on in its efforts to promote a cleansing of historical memory, removing any trace of social and political irresponsibility, if not willful indifference, for which past and current generations might be held accountable.[69] Any thoughts of challenging mass violence and apocalyptic crisis are now left to the superheroes that populate comics, video games, and Hollywood films, all of which testify to the ways in which the dominant cultural apparatuses of our time depoliticize intellectuals by rendering, as David Graeber points out, "any thought of changing the world seem [like] an idle fantasy."[70] The apocalypse has come home, and it has become a video game and reality TV show, effectively dethroning the political while smothering the never-ending task of history to enable moral witnessing and a critique of the horrors that give rise to what seems like an endless series of crises. The disimagination machine, especially regarding the nightmare of Hiroshima and Nagasaki, which ushered in the nuclear age, now controls all the commanding institutions that once preserved history, and serves largely to erase memory. As Tom Engelhardt observes:

> Seventy years later, the apocalypse is us. Yet in the United States, the only nuclear bomb you're likely to read about is Iran's (even though that country possesses no such weapon). For a serious discussion of the U.S. nuclear arsenal, those more than 4,800 increasingly ill-kept weapons that could incinerate several Earth-sized planets, you need to look not to the country's major newspapers or news programs.[71]

Yet there is more at stake here than the erasure of historical memory among American intellectuals. Across the whole culture, the machinery of entertainment and its various cultural apparatuses advance the celebration of what might be called an aesthetics of catastrophe that merges spectacles of violence, war, and brutality into forms of collective pleasure that constitute an important and new symbiosis among visual gratification, violence, and suffering. The aesthetics of catastrophe revels in images of human suffering that are subordinated to the formal properties of beauty, design, and taste—thus serving in the main to "bleach out a moral response to what is shown."[72] For Susan Sontag and many other critical theorists, the aesthetics of catastrophe reveals itself when it takes as its object the misery of others, murderous displays of torture, mutilated bodies, and intense suffering while simultaneously erasing the names, histories, and voices of the victims of such brutal and horrible acts. Paul Virilio, in a meditation on the extermination of bodies and the environment from Hiroshima and Auschwitz to Chernobyl, refers to this depraved form of art as an "aesthetics of disappearance that would come to characterize the whole fin-de-siècle" of the twentieth century.[73]

The spectacles of intense violence, hypermasculinity, celebrity culture, and extreme sports fit neatly into a culture that celebrates the devastation wreaked by unchecked market forces and embraces a survival-of-the-fittest ethic. Conformity and forgetting increasingly give way to a heightened mode of cruelty that is pleasure-driven and infuses not only the video game and Hollywood film industries but also the military-industrial-surveillance complex. Tied to forms of consumption and sensations that delight in images of suffering, the depravity of catastrophe functions to anaesthetize the entire culture ethically and politically, prompting passivity or even joy in the midst of violence, suffering, and injustice. Embodied in the form of reality TV shows, video games, and escapist entertainment, neoliberal public pedagogy now suppresses concrete memories of the suffering and horror associated with war and events such as the bombing of Hiroshima. This marriage of pleasure and depravity should not be seen as the province of individual pathology or evil; to the contrary, it functions largely to produce a collective subject through an economy of affect and meaning that traps people in their own narcissistic desires and callous self-interests, while promoting an endless spectacle of catastrophes. Drawing upon the work of Robert Jay Lifton and Greg Mitchell, I would argue that the aesthetics of catastrophe works in tandem with casino capitalism so as to produce a kind of "psychic numbing" both for intellectuals and the American public. Psychic numbing manifests itself most clearly in the total disregard, if not disdain, voiced in response to the suffering of others on the part of powerful conservative elite, antipublic intellectuals, mainstream politicians, and the financial ruling classes. This is a notion of catastrophe in which unrestrained self-interest and ruthless competiveness become the only intellectual and ethical values that matter.[74]

Surely, it is possible to reinvigorate society in which there is a collective understanding that the problems people suffer individually should only be understood within a wider set of economic, social, and political considerations. There is no other choice, as a social order that has become a breeding ground for violence against those considered excess, disposable, and other is set on a course for self-destruction.[75] As material and symbolic forms of violence merge with the sadistic discourse of hate radio and right-wing politicians, a new and more intense culture of spitefulness emerges that targets increasing numbers of people for disposal rather than compassion, trust, and empathy. Humane interventions and public values wane, while the celebration of warlike values, militarism, a friend/enemy divide, and even the killing of children as we have seen in Gaza, is sanctioned by the ruthless logic of military necessity.[76]

We now live in a time of administered lawlessness that not only fabricates legal illegalities but also suggests that any impending crisis *demands* lawlessness and preemptive violence, which, while defining itself as an exception, becomes normalized as an expected facet of everyday behavior—if not also a source of cheap sensationalism and entertainment. Lawlessness is not only justified as a military imperative; it becomes part of the workings of corrupt politics and financial power. How else to explain that President Obama refused to prosecute the CIA operatives who illegally tortured people under the Bush-Cheney administration?[77] Or the fact that the "Director of National Intelligence James Clapper perjured himself on camera with little or no fallout"?[78] Another example of lawlessness is clear in the case of "the CEO of JPMorgan who presided over various scams that resulted in $20 billion worth of fines and, for his trouble, he was awarded a 74 percent raise," rather than being prosecuted and put in jail.[79] Then there is the egregious example of banking giant HSBC, "which admitted to laundering $850 million for a pair of Central and South American drug cartels," and, once again, nobody went to jail.[80]

Inundated by apocalyptic catastrophes and their spectacularization, we seem to shrug off the reign of corrupt financiers and politicians who operate outside of the law. As Lifton and Mitchell have argued, we also fail to see the plight of those living in our midst as we "become increasingly insensitive to violence and suffering around us, to killing in general, but also to poverty and homelessness."[81] This echoes the sentiments of Zygmunt Bauman and Leonidas Donskis, who insist that "violence shown every day ceases to provoke amazement, or disgust. It, as it were, grows on you. At the same time, it stays unreal—it still seems it cannot happen to us."[82] It gets worse. Rather than being alarmed, for example, over the defense industry, which "embodies the primeval archetype of unencumbered raw violence,"[83] growing numbers of intellectuals mimic through their silence, if not tacit support, an American public that seeks out more spectacular bloodshed as a way to ramp up the pleasure quotient and fulfill a collective desire for instant gratification and the need to feel something, anything. How else to explain the muteness of intellectuals regarding the legislation now being passed in a number of states that will require teachers to carry weapons in their classrooms and allow people to take weapons into bars, thus clearly promoting a toxic gun culture that gives rise to, among other things, vigilante and militia groups patrolling the borders of the Southwest hunting for illegal immigrants?[84] How else to understand the silence in the face of an endless spate of violence against black urban youth in the past decade, which until recently has been barely reported in the media except in terms that describe it as routine policing rather than as acts of exceptional and unacceptable brutality?[85] As Antonio Thomas points out, according to the 2010 National Police Misconduct Statistics and Reporting Project, within a timeframe of sixteen months there were

> 5,986 reports of police brutality that are reported resulting in 382 deaths, [of which] a great majority of these individuals have been black men and women. But due to the amount of fear that police uses to terrorize the black community … most victims of police brutality do not report it to the proper authorities for fear of retaliation from a police force who has sworn to serve and protect them. What is wors[e] is that out of those 5,986 reports only 33 percent went through conviction, [of those convicted] only 64 percent has received a prison sentence and on an average the police only serve a maximum of 14 months.[86]

How is it that intellectuals have so little to say publicly about the overt racism in law enforcement, not to mention the way the media downplay the shootings of poor minority youth in the nation's cities strictly as homicides when time and again those responsible for the social order indicate that they would rather inflict violence on young people and punish them in jail than provide them with decent education, training, health care, and employment? As intellectuals surrender their civic courage and intellectual capacities to the dictates of a neoliberal regime, it becomes all the more difficult to recognize that a pervasive inattentiveness to the lessons of history will inevitably breed these kinds of horrors.

As the spectacle of neoliberal terrorism, violence, and misery becomes one of the major organizing principles of daily life, it is all the more imperative for intellectuals, educators, artists, parents, students, and others to examine the myriad of cultural apparatuses that currently represent not only powerful political and pedagogical forces in shaping a culture of fear and violence—invoked by state and nonstate groups to legitimate lawlessness—but also a new technology and pedagogical machinery for redefining the very nature of power itself. This is all the more crucial to recognize since the central elements of the spectacle of terrorism and the aesthetics of catastrophe are unlike anything intellectuals have faced in the past—given their enshrinement of hyper-real violence, unadulterated appeal to fear, resistance to state authority and the rule of law, and elevation of the visual image to a place of social, cultural, and political dominance. Given how such cultural apparatuses have the power to work pedagogically and politically to wage a war on communal relations, the social state, and the radical imagination, it is crucial to remember, as Hannah Tennant-Moore reminds us, that "fear loves nothing so much as punishment."[87]

The spreading orgy of global violence that characterizes the twenty-first century can be traced from at least the birth of the atomic age extending to the 9/11 attacks on the twin towers. This historical trajectory links the power of violent images with the culture of fear, constituting a new space that has opened up for intellectuals to engage the political as a pedagogical force and the spectacle as the new language of politics.[88] C. Wright Mills raised this issue in his analysis of the importance of what he called the pedagogical role of the cultural apparatuses in capitalist societies, as did Raymond Williams in his astute definition of what he called "permanent education." Williams wrote:

> What [permanent education] valuably stresses is the educational force of our whole social and cultural experience. It is therefore concerned, not only with continuing education, of a formal or informal kind, but with what the whole environment, its institutions and relationships, actively and profoundly teaches.[89]

The tangible effects of extreme violence are now made visible through the theatrical staging efforts of both state and nonstate terrorists. Shock videos such as the strangling of Eric Garner by a New York police officer are aired repeatedly on the nightly news right alongside references to beheading videos (though the actual act is never shown on mainstream media outlets). In these circumstances, such horrific violence is removed from any historical context and aired within the registers of a smothering disimagination machine of shock, hyperviolence, and an aesthetics of destruction, rendering almost impossible any serious analysis of such events. Dwight Macdonald once argued after the firebombing of Tokyo that liberal intellectuals "have grown callous to massacre," dismissing them as "totalitarian liberals."[90] One might argue that the tepidness of intellectuals has gotten worse in that they now find themselves living under a regime of neoliberalism in which virtually everyone is at risk of homelessness, facing a life of uncertainty and temporary jobs, and cut off from larger social issues. This is especially true for academics, given the current state of higher education in which the concept of the intellectual has been reduced to the status of a Walmart worker or technician. Professionalism has become corporatized, thus banishing the imperative for intellectuals to relate their academic interest and scholarship to larger social issues. Increasingly, broader political engagement is neglected in an attempt to survive in institutions that now resemble corporations governed by a business culture and that view students as customers whose education involves nothing more than job training.

Under the reign of the neoliberal dystopian dream machine, war, violence, and politics have taken on a new disturbing sense of urgency. As politics is constituted increasingly outside of the law, one of its first victims is any viable sense of the relationship between private troubles and larger public considerations. The public sphere withers into privatized orbits of desire and understanding, and not surprisingly the diverse realms of public life decay. American intellectuals now inhabit an amnesiac, if not psychopathic, society—one that under the reign of a depoliticizing neoliberalism appears to forget Hannah Arendt's warning that "humanity is never acquired in solitude."[91] For many intellectuals, the radical imagination has dissolved into a dystopian nightmare as marketplace values and the dictates of financialization define politics, the national zeitgeist, and the country's utopian possibilities. Charles Pierce is right in suggesting that many intellectuals along with the American public have allowed themselves "to become mired in the habits of oligarchy, as though no other politics is possible."[92]

When the struggle to survive is removed from the much-needed fight for justice, the results will be increasingly limited political horizons. In the United States, the specter of militarism, the ongoing pursuit of perpetual war, and commodification of just about everything have provided the conditions for the production of a new form of politics and a disimagination machine—which raises serious questions that intellectuals need to address. These include: How are fear and anxiety marketed; how is terrorism used to recruit people in support of authoritarian causes; how is the neoliberal theater of violence being produced in a vast array of pedagogical sites created by the old and new media; how does the state use mediated images of violence to justify its monopoly over the means of coercion; and how does the aesthetics of catastrophe manifest itself in an age of enormous injustices, deep insecurities, disembodied social relations, fragmented communities, and a growing militarization of everyday life? Totalitarian politics, militaristic violence, and a life-draining social atomization not only mutually inform each other, they have become the most important elements of power as mediating forces that shape identities, desires, and social relations. Given these circumstances, it is no wonder that the legacy of Hiroshima has dissolved into a neoliberal culture of violence, cruelty, and disposability.

The United States is in a new historical conjuncture defined largely by global neoliberal capitalism, in which the relationships among cultural institutions, political power, and everyday life have become central to how we understand politics and the work that it does.[93] At one level, the market has eroded the affective and symbolic bonds that create public trust, public life, and the bonds of social life. At the same time, politics has become intensely educative in terms of how it constructs the ways in which people understand themselves, their relations to others, and the wider society. Doreen Massey is right in arguing that "it is the internalization of the system that can potentially corrode our ability to imagine that things could be otherwise."[94] And that is precisely why, as the late Pierre Bourdieu argued, progressive intellectuals can no longer underestimate "the symbolic and pedagogical dimensions of struggle" if they are going to forge "appropriate weapons to fight on this front."[95]

If intellectuals are going to address the legacy of Hiroshima and the ongoing threat of nuclear annihilation, they will have to recognize that the struggle for a democratic formative culture will need to come from below; it will simply not take place at the behest of prevailing economic and political power. Moreover, they will have to acknowledge that matters of subjectivity, culture, and identity cannot be separated from material circumstances and commanding institutions, however complex that relationship often is. On the contrary, for such institutions and relations to be challenged collectively, they must be viewed as inextricably related, and they also have to be made visible—connected to the dynamics of everyday life—in order to become part of a transformative consciousness and struggle in which pedagogy becomes central to politics.

The need for a democratic formative culture in which critical intellectuals can thrive raises crucial questions about the educative nature of politics, and how the public pedagogy produced by the old and new media can be used to expand rather than close down democratic relations. Central to such a task is the attempt on the part of educators, intellectuals, artists, and other cultural workers to address what agents, conditions, contents, and structural transformations are necessary to rethink the importance of both the new media and a democratic formative culture within an advanced society so as to configure social practices within rather than outside of the realm of a substantive democracy.

If American intellectuals are to confront the horrors of Hiroshima, the long shadow of nuclear warfare that has developed since the rise of the atomic age and the memory of the horrors visited upon thousands of civilians must be revisited and made discernible. This is especially necessary if intellectuals are going to remember and condemn the bombing of Hiroshima and Nagasaki, call for the elimination of nuclear weapons and the oligarchic militarized governments that profit from them, and renounce the killing of civilians in the name of military necessity—a legacy that extends from Hiroshima to the slaughter of civilians in present-day Gaza.

But such struggles will succeed only if they are understood within a new political discourse and a new sense of crisis informed by an awareness of the world of images, digital technologies, the Internet, and alternative pedagogical spaces and cultural apparatuses so that they can be used in the struggle for a new type of agency, new modes of collective resistance, and an organized and long-term transformative struggle for a radical democracy. The struggles for justice and a radically new, democratically inspired society in which nuclear weapons and the dictates of perpetual war will no longer exist will only come when intellectuals and the wider public both understand and feel connected to the struggles of which they are asked to be a part. This is what Stuart Hall has called the "educative nature of politics." Hall spells this out in his claim that such a politics is sorely lacking on the left. He writes:

The left has no sense of politics being educative, of politics changing the way people see things. . . . The left is in trouble. It's not got any ideas, it's not got any independent analysis of its own, and therefore it's got no vision. It just takes the temperature: "Whoa, that's no good, let's move to the right." It has no sense of politics being educative, of politics changing the way people see things.[96]

Hall is arguing rightly in my view that the left and its intellectuals need to take seriously what it means to change the subjectivities, desires, and consciousness of people so that they can act as critically informed and engaged agents, capable of learning how to lead and govern rather than simply be assailed, subjugated, and ruthlessly controlled.

Democracy is under assault and appears to have fallen over the edge into what Hannah Arendt once called "dark times." But, once again, as Catherine Clément has noted, "Every culture has an imaginary zone for what it excludes, and it is that zone that we must remember today."[97] Such memory work can start with the seventieth anniversary of Hiroshima so that its horrible legacy and effects are no longer part of a purposeful zone of forgetting. I believe that such zones of exclusion are crucial to remember because they make evident the long history of struggle by labor, unions, workers, young people, feminists, civil rights advocates, gay activists, progressive educators, and others who believe in the promise of a radical democracy along with the necessity to struggle with a renewed sense of urgency and collective strength. Such historical memories also make it easier for intellectuals and others to dispute the myth that governments should be trusted because they always act in the best interest of the people.

The time is ripe for the long historical struggle to ban nuclear weapons technology to come alive once more so as to shake off the authoritarian nightmare now engulfing the globe. It is time for intellectuals once again to question the deadly missions of the sixth and ninth of August. As Howard Zinn observed, if we "declare nuclear weapons an unacceptable means, even if it ends a war a month or two earlier," then it may lead to larger questions regarding what role intellectuals might play in creating the conditions for questioning political leaders and stopping monstrous acts before they happen.[98] The old familiar ways of defining and engaging politics no longer work. It is time to reclaim the struggles and movements of resistance to nuclear weapons and once again take up the quest for global nuclear disarmament, on a different terrain, under new conditions, and with a renewed sense of urgency and hope.

I want to conclude by recalling Hannah Arendt's notion of "instants of truth" discussed in the epigraph of this chapter. Such instants often come in the form of images, narratives, and stories that shock. They don't accommodate reality as much as they turn it upside down, eviscerating commonsense assumptions a culture has about itself while revealing an intellectual and emotional chasm that runs through established modes of rationality and understanding. Such flashpoints not only rupture dominant modes of consciousness; they give rise to heated passion and debates, sometimes leading to massive displays of collective anguish and resistance, even revolutions. We have seen such "instants of truth" in Ferguson, Missouri; Staten Island, New York; and Cleveland, Ohio, where images of African American males being killed by the police helped to inspire huge waves of protests throughout the United States. These images of violence and human suffering inflamed a society to connect heated emotional investments to a politics in which unthinkable acts of violence are confronted as part of a larger "commitment to political accountability, community, and the importance of positive affect for both belonging and change."[99] Hiroshima provides another "instant of truth" through which intellectuals can confront the sins of the past in order to develop a collective struggle and an energized politics for a democratically inspired present and future. There may be no greater challenge than this one facing intellectuals in the twenty-first century.

13
Neoliberalism's War against
the Radical Imagination

⌀

Democracy is on life support in the United States. Throughout the social order, the forces of predatory capitalism are on the march. Their ideological and material traces are visible everywhere—in the dismantling of the welfare state, the increasing role of corporate money in politics, the assault on unions, the expansion of the corporate-surveillance-military state, widening inequalities in wealth and income, the defunding of higher education and the privatization of public education, and the war on women's reproductive rights. As David Harvey, Wendy Brown, and others have observed, neoliberalism's permeation is achieved through various guises that collectively function to undercut the public faith in the defining institutions of democracy.[1] As market mentalities and moralities tighten their grip on all aspects of society, public institutions and public spheres are first downsized, then eradicated. When these important sites of democratic expression vanish—from public universities to community health care centers—what follows is a serious erosion of the discourses of community, justice, equality, public values, and the common good. Moreover, as Stefan Collini has argued, under the regime of neoliberalism, the "social self" has been transformed into the "disembedded individual," just as the notion of the university as a public good is now repudiated by the privatizing and atomistic values at the heart of a hyper-market-driven society.[2]

We live in a society that appears to embrace the vocabulary of "choice," which is ultimately rooted in a denial of reality. In fact, most people daily experience an increasing limitation of choices, as they bear the heavy burden of massive inequality, social disparities, the irresponsible concentration of power in relatively few hands, a racist justice and penal system, the conversion of schools into detention centers, and a pervasive culture of violence and cruelty—all of which portends a growing machinery of social death, especially for those disadvantaged by a ruthless capitalist economy.[3] Renowned economist Joseph Stiglitz is one of many public intellectuals who has repeatedly alerted Americans to the impending costs of gross social inequality. Inequality is not simply about disproportionate amounts of wealth and income in fewer hands; it is also about the monopolization of power by the financial and corporate elite.

As power becomes global and is removed from local and nation-based politics, what is even more alarming are the sheer numbers of individuals and groups who are being defined by a free-floating class of ultrarich and corporate powerbrokers as disposable, redundant, or a threat to the forces of concentrated power. Power, particularly the power of the largest corporations, has become more unaccountable, and "the subtlety of illegitimate power makes it hard to identify."[4] Disposability has become the new measure of a neoliberal society in which the only value that matters is exchange value. Compassion, social responsibility, and justice are relegated to the dustbin of an older modernity that now is viewed as either quaint or a grim reminder of a socialist past.

A regime of repression, corruption, and dispossession has become the organizing principle of a society in which an ironic doubling takes place. Corporate bankers and powerbrokers trade with terrorists, bankrupt the economy, and commit all manner of crimes that impact on millions, yet they go free. Meanwhile, across the United States, citizens are being criminalized for all sorts of behaviors ranging from dress code infractions in public schools to peaceful demonstrations in public parks. As Michelle Alexander has thoroughly documented in her book *The New Jim Crow,* young men and women of color are being jailed in record numbers for nonviolent offenses as it becomes clear that justice is on the side of the rich, wealthy, and powerful. And when the wealthy are actually convicted of crimes, they are rarely sent to prison, even though millions languish under a correctional system aimed at punishing immigrants, low-income whites, and poor minorities.

An egregious example of how the justice system works in favor of the rich was recently on full display in Texas. Instead of being sent to prison, Ethan Couch, a wealthy teen who killed four people while driving inebriated, was given ten years of probation and ordered by the judge to attend an expensive rehabilitation facility that cost $450,000 a year, which will be paid for by his parents. The defense argued that he had "affluenza," a "disease" in which children of privilege are allegedly never given the opportunity to learn how to be responsible. In other words, irresponsibility is now an acceptable hallmark of having wealth, enabling the rich actually to kill people and escape the reach of justice. Under such circumstances, "justice" becomes synonymous with privilege, as wealth and power dictate who benefits and who doesn't by a system of law that enshrines lawlessness. In addition, moral and political outrage is no longer animated by the fearful consequences of an unjust society. Fear now trumps justice and has been redirected away from critiques of an authoritarian government and is now defined almost exclusively in reference to overcoming conditions of impoverishment and exclusion, which makes survival more important than the quest for the good life. The American dream is no longer built on the possibility of social mobility or getting ahead. Instead, it has become for many a nightmare rooted in the desire simply to stay afloat and survive.

One consequence of the vicissitudes of injustice is the growing number of people, especially young people, who inhabit zones of hardship, suffering, exclusion, and joblessness. They live in fear as they struggle to survive social conditions and policies more characteristic of authoritarian governments than democratic states. Indeed, Americans appear caught in a sinister web of ethical and material poverty manufactured by a state that trades in suspicion, bigotry, state-sanctioned violence, and disposability. Democracy loses its character as a disruptive element, a force of dissent, an insurrectional call for responsible change; democracy all but degenerates into an assault on the radical imagination, reconfigured as a force for whitewashing all ethical and moral considerations. What is left is a new kind of authoritarianism that thrives in such a state of exception, which in reality is a state of permanent war. A regime of greed, dispossession, fear, and surveillance has now been normalized.

The ideological script recited by the disciples of neoliberalism is now familiar: there is no such thing as the common good; market values provide the template for governing all of social life, not just the economy; consumerism is the only obligation of citizenship; a survival-of-the-fittest ethic should govern how we think and behave; militaristic values should trump democratic ideals; the welfare state is the archenemy of freedom; private interests should be safeguarded, while public values wane; law and order is the preferred language for mobilizing shared fears rather than shared responsibilities; and war becomes the all-embracing organizing principle for developing society and the economy.

As individual responsibility is promoted as a weapon in order to tear up social solidarities, experiences that once resonated with public purpose and meaning have been transformed into privatized spectacles and fragmented modes of consumption, and increasingly subjected to the surveillance tactics of the military-security state. The end point is the emergence of what the late Tony Judt called an "eviscerated society"—"one that is stripped of the thick mesh of mutual obligations and social responsibilities" integral to any viable democracy.[5] This grim reality has produced a failure in the power of the civic imagination, political will, and open democracy.[6] It is also part of a politics that strips society of any democratic ideals and renders its democratic character inoperative.

Neoliberalism succeeds, much like authoritarian regimes of the past, through the efforts it expends in the production of desires, identities, values, and modes of identification aligned with its worldview and values. Its adherents are increasingly produced by, and in turn reproduce, forms of neoliberal public pedagogy. These new modes of pedagogy are distributed through a variety of educational sites and cultural apparatuses that call into being subjects defined exclusively by market-driven values and the prioritization of commercial values over public values. This is why it is crucial that American educators continue to address important social issues and to defend democratic modes of pedagogy, which must include mounting a spirited defense of higher education as a democratic public sphere or public good. The power of the imagination and critical reasoning, the willingness to dissent, and the capacity to hold power accountable—historically fostered by sites of higher learning—constitute a major threat to authoritarian regimes. Yet it is increasingly the case that many institutions of higher education fail to take a position against the neoliberal state, instead defining themselves as part of a larger neoliberal rationality and social order.

Under the reign of neoliberalism, the university is turning into a modern-day version of the sweatshop for adjunct and nontenured faculty. A university without a proper faculty and governance structure cannot be a university wedded to democratic values and education for empowerment and autonomy. On the contrary, it is a site of reactionary power where all vestiges of critical thinking and exchange are wiped out. Under such circumstances, education becomes an obsession with accountability schemes, redefining students as consumers, deskilling faculty, governing through the lens of a business culture, and dumbing down the curriculum by substituting training for a critically informed education. How else to explain the attempts in Florida, Texas, and other states to defund the humanities and reward those disciplines and programs that blatantly serve corporate interests? Increasingly, it appears that the ideological assault waged by a range of religious, economic, and political fundamentalists on the university, which began during the radicalization of US colleges in the 1960s, is now almost complete.

As J. M. Coetzee puts it: "This assault on the [independence of universities] commenced in the 1980s as a reaction to what universities were doing in the 1960s and 1970s, namely, encouraging masses of young people in the view that there was something badly wrong with the way the world was being run and supplying them with the intellectual fodder for a critique of Western civilisation as a whole."[7] What has become clear in the last forty years is that illegitimate corporate rule has moved from occupying the state to dismantling all those public spheres over which it does not have full control, including higher education. Harnessing higher education to the demands of the warfare state and the needs of corporations has become normalized, fixated in the fog of common sense. If neoliberalism succeeds in reducing higher education to nothing more than job training, then the imagination will be effectively banished from a once vibrant site of critical engagement.

The current crisis in public and higher education has made it alarmingly clear that educators, artists, intellectuals, and youth need a new political and pedagogical language for addressing the changing contexts and issues facing a world in which capital draws upon an unprecedented convergence of resources—financial, cultural, political, economic, scientific, military, and technological—to exercise powerful and diverse forms of control. If educators and other cultural workers are to counter global capitalism's increased ability to separate the traditional sphere of politics from the now transnational reach of power, it is crucial to develop educational approaches that reject the deliberate blurring of market liberties and civil liberties, a market economy and a market society. Nothing will change unless the left and progressives take seriously the subjective underpinnings of neoliberal oppression. In the current historical moment, politics must involve the struggle over power and economics, but also the struggle over particular modes of subjectivity and agency.

Resisting the neoliberal assault on politics, education, and culture means developing forms of subjectivity capable of challenging casino capitalism and other antidemocratic forces, including the growing trend simply to criminalize social problems such as homelessness. What is needed is a radical democratic project that provides the basis for imagining a life beyond the "dreamworld" of capitalism. In opposition to the conservative assaults on critical thinking and the power of the imagination, it is crucial for educators, intellectuals, young people, artists, and others to resurrect the formative cultures necessary to challenge the various threats being mobilized against the very ideas of justice and democracy, while also fighting for those public spheres, ideals, values, and policies that offer alternative modes of identity, social relations, and politics. At stake here is the educative nature of politics itself, and the development and protection of those institutions that make such a politics possible.

In both conservative and progressive discourses today, pedagogy is often narrowed to the teaching of prespecified subject matter and stripped-down skills that can be assessed through standardized testing. The administration of education and its ensuing pedagogical practices are similarly confined to a set of corporate strategies rooted in an approach that views schooling as merely a private act of consumption. In opposition to the instrumental reduction of education to an adjunct of corporate and neoliberal interests—which have no language for relating the self to public life, social responsibility, or the demands of citizenship—a critical approach to education illuminates the relationships among knowledge, authority, and power. Critical forms of pedagogy raise questions regarding who has control over the conditions for the production of knowledge. Is the production of knowledge and curricula in the hands of teachers, textbook companies, corporate interests, the elite, or other forces? Central to the perspective informing critical pedagogy is the recognition that education is always implicated in power relations because it offers particular versions and visions of civic life, community, the future, and how we might construct representations of ourselves, others, and our physical and social environment. Critical pedagogy matters because it questions everything and complicates one's relationship to oneself, others, and the larger world. This unsettling process is what Kristen Case has called "moments of classroom grace." She writes:

> There is difficulty, discomfort, even fear in such moments, which involve confrontations with what we thought we knew, like why people have mortgages and what "things" are. These moments do not reflect a linear progress from ignorance to knowledge; instead they describe a step away from a complacent knowing into a new world in which, at least at first, everything is cloudy, nothing is quite clear. We cannot be a democracy if this power to reimagine, doubt, and think critically is allowed to become a luxury commodity.[8]

Education has always been part of a broader political, social, and cultural struggle over knowledge, subjectivities, values, and the future. Public and higher education is currently under a massive assault in Greece, the United States, and the United Kingdom because it represents one of the few places left that are capable of teaching young people to be critical, thoughtful, and engaged citizens who are willing to take risks, stretch their imaginations, and, most important, hold power accountable. The consequence of turning universities into sites that commodify both knowledge and people is a broader social order that embraces neoliberalism's methodical ruthlessness toward others, its hatred of democracy, and its fear of young people, who will increasingly lack the self-awareness and social consciousness to realize how they have been shut out of the language of democracy, justice, and hope.

One of the most serious challenges facing teachers, artists, journalists, writers, youth, and other cultural workers is the challenge of developing a discourse of both critique and possibility. This means insisting that democracy begins to fail and political life becomes impoverished in the absence of those vital public spheres such as higher education in which civic values, public scholarship, and social engagement allow for a more imaginative grasp of a future that takes seriously the demands of justice, equity, and civic courage. Democratic processes should always involve thinking about education—a kind of education that thrives on connecting equity to excellence, learning to ethics, and agency to the imperatives of social responsibility and the public good. Violence in its symbolic and material forms cannot be separated from the public pedagogies that produce them. Pedagogy is a moral and political practice rooted in the educational function of the larger culture and produced and disseminated through a wide variety of cultural apparatuses. The struggle against such violence must be rooted in developing emancipatory pedagogies and critical formative cultures both in public and higher education and in those cultural apparatuses that offer the promise of alternative public spheres dedicated to the production of critical agents who have the capacity to expand and deepen the promise of a substantive democracy. Democracy needs a Marshall Plan in which funding is sufficient to make all levels of education free, while also providing enough social support to eliminate poverty, hunger, inadequate health care, and the destruction of the environment. Democracy needs a politics and critical formative culture that not just restores hope, but envisions a different future, one in which the struggle for justice is never finished and the highest of values is caring for and being responsible to others. This is as much a pedagogical issue as it is a rethinking of the nature of politics itself.

Neoliberalism is a toxin that is generating a predatory class of the walking dead who are producing what might be called dead zones of the imagination. They are waging a fierce battle against the possibilities of a world in which the promise of justice and democracy is worth fighting for, but the future is still open. The time has come to develop a political language and critical pedagogy in which critical understanding, civic values, and social responsibility—and the institutions that support them—become central to invigorating and fortifying a new era of civic imagination, a renewed sense of social agency, and an impassioned international social movement with the vision, organization, and set of strategies capable of challenging the neoliberal nightmare engulfing the planet.

14
Protesting Youth in an Age of Neoliberal Savagery

⊕

Reality always has this power to surprise. It surprises you with an answer that it gives to questions never asked—and which are most tempting. A great stimulus to life is there, in the capacity to divine possible unasked questions.

—*Eduardo Galeano*

Neoliberalism's Assault on Democracy

Fredric Jameson has argued "that it is easier to imagine the end of the world than to imagine the end of capitalism." He goes on to say: "We can now revise that and witness the attempt to imagine capitalism by way of imagining the end of the world."[1] One way of understanding Jameson's comment is that within the ideological and affective spaces in which the neoliberal subject is produced and market-driven ideologies are normalized, there are new waves of resistance, especially among young people, who are insisting that casino capitalism is driven by a kind of mad violence and form of self-sabotage and that if it does not come to an end what we will experience in all probability is the destruction of human life and the planet itself. Certainly, more recent scientific reports on the threat of ecological disaster from researchers at the University of Washington, NASA, and the Intergovernmental Panel on Climate Change reinforce this dystopian possibility.[2]

As the latest stage of predatory capitalism, neoliberalism is part of a broader economic and political project of restoring class power and consolidating the rapid concentration of capital, particularly financial capital.[3] As a political project it includes "the deregulation of finance, privatization of public services, elimination and curtailment of social welfare programs, open attacks on unions, and routine violations of labor laws."[4] As an ideology, it casts all dimensions of life in terms of market rationality, construes profit-making as the arbiter and essence of democracy, consuming as the only operable form of citizenship, and upholds the irrational belief that the market can both solve all problems and serve as a model for structuring all social relations. As a mode of governance, it produces identities, subjects, and ways of life driven by a survival-of-the-fittest ethic, grounded in the idea of the free, possessive individual, and committed to the right of ruling groups and institutions to exercise power removed from matters of ethics and social costs. As a policy and political project, it is wedded to the privatization of public services, the dismantling of the connection of private issues and public problems, the selling off of state functions, liberalization of trade in goods and capital investment, the eradication of government regulation of financial institutions and corporations, the destruction of the welfare state and unions, and the endless marketization and commodification of society.

As I have pointed out in previous chapters, neoliberalism has put an enormous effort into creating a commanding cultural apparatus and public pedagogy in which individuals can view themselves only as consumers, embrace freedom as the right to participate in the market, and supplant issues of social responsibility for an unchecked embrace of individualism and the belief that all social relations be judged according to how they further one's individual needs and self-interests. Matters of mutual caring, respect, and compassion for the other have given way to the limiting orbits of privatization and unrestrained self-interest, just as it has become increasingly difficult to translate private troubles into larger social, economic, and political considerations. As the democratic public spheres of civil society have atrophied under the onslaught of neoliberal regimes of austerity, the social contract has been either greatly weakened or replaced by savage forms of casino capitalism, a culture of fear, and the increasing use of state violence. One consequence is that it has become more difficult for people to debate and question neoliberal hegemony and the widespread misery it produces for young people, the poor, middle class, workers, and other segments of society—now considered disposable under neoliberal regimes that are governed by a survival-of-the-fittest ethos, largely imposed by the ruling economic and political elite. Unable to make their voices heard and lacking any viable representation in the process makes clear the degree to which young people and others are suffering under a democratic deficit producing what Chantal Mouffe calls "a profound dissatisfaction with a number of existing societies" under the reign of neoliberal capitalism.[5]

This is one reason why so many youth, along with workers, the unemployed, and students, have been taking to the streets in Greece, Mexico, Egypt, the United States, and England.

The Rise of Disposable Youth

What is particularly distinctive about the current historical conjuncture is the way in which young people, particularly low-income and poor minority youth across the globe, have been increasingly denied any place in an already weakened social order and the degree to which they are no longer seen as central to how a number of countries across the globe define their future. The plight of youth as disposable populations is evident in the fact that millions of them in countries such as England, Greece, and the United States have been unemployed and denied long-term benefits. The unemployment rate for young people in many countries such as Spain, Italy, Portugal, and Greece hovers between 40 and 50 percent. To make matters worse, those with college degrees either cannot find work or are working at low-skill jobs that pay paltry wages. In the United States young adjunct faculty constitute one of the fastest growing populations on food stamps. Suffering under huge debts, a jobs crisis, state violence, a growing surveillance state, and the prospect that they would inherit a standard of living far below that enjoyed by their parents, many young people have exhibited a rage that seems to deepen their resignation, despair, and withdrawal from the political arena.

This is the first generation, as sociologist Zygmunt Bauman argues, in which the "plight of the outcast may stretch to embrace a whole generation."[6] Youth no longer occupy the hope of a privileged place that was offered to previous generations. They now inhabit a neoliberal notion of temporality marked by a loss of faith in progress along with the emergence of apocalyptic narratives in which the future appears indeterminate, bleak, and insecure. Heightened expectations and progressive visions pale and are smashed next to the normalization of market-driven government policies that wipe out pensions, eliminate quality health care, raise college tuition, and produce a harsh world of joblessness, while giving millions to banks and the military. Students, in particular, find themselves in a world in which unrealized aspirations have been replaced by dashed hopes and a world of onerous debt.[7]

The Revival of the Radical Imagination

Within the various regimes of neoliberalism that have emerged particularly in North America and Europe since the late 1970s, the ethical grammars that drew attention to the violence and suffering withered or, as in the United States, seemed to disappear altogether, while dispossessed youth continued to lose their dignity, bodies, and material goods to the machineries of disposability. The fear of losing everything, the horror of an engulfing and crippling precarity, the quest to merely survive, the rise of the punishing state and police violence along with the impending reality of social and civil death became a way of life for the 99 percent in the United States and other countries. Under such circumstances, youth were no longer the place where society reveals its dreams but increasingly hid its nightmares. Against the ravaging policies of austerity and disposability, "zones of abandonment" appeared in which the domestic machinery of violence, suffering, cruelty, and punishment replaced the values of compassion, social responsibility, and civic courage.[8] In opposition to such conditions, a belief in the power of collective resistance and politics emerged once again in 2010 as global youth protests embraced the possibility of deepening and expanding democracy rather than rejecting it. Such movements produced a new understanding of politics based on horizontal forms of collaboration and political participation. In doing so, they resurrected and revitalized much-needed questions about class power, inequality, financial corruption, and the shredding of the democratic process. They also explored what it meant to create new communities of mutual support, democratic modes of exchange and governance, and public spheres in which critical dialogue and exchanges could take place.[9]

A wave of youth protests starting in 2010 in Tunisia and spreading across the globe to the United States and Europe eventually posed a direct challenge to neoliberal modes of domination and the corruption of politics, if not democracy itself.[10] The legitimating, debilitating, and depoliticizing notion that politics could only be challenged within established methods of reform and existing relations of power was rejected outright by students and other young people across the globe. For a couple of years, young people transformed basic assumptions about what politics is and how the radical imagination could be mobilized to challenge the basic beliefs of neoliberalism and other modes of authoritarianism. They also challenged dominant discourses ranging from deficit reduction and taxing the poor to important issues that included poverty, joblessness, the growing unmanageable levels of student debt, and the massive spread of corporate corruption. As Jonathan Schell argued, youth across the globe were enormously successfully in unleashing "a new spirit of action," an expression of outrage fueled less by policy demands than by a cry of collective moral and political indignation whose message was "'Enough!' to a corrupt political, economic and media establishment that hijacked the world's wealth for itself . . . sabotaging the rule of law, waging interminable savage and futile wars, plundering the world's finite resources, and lying about all this to the public [while] threatening Earth's life forms into the bargain."[11] Yet, some theorists have recently argued that little has changed since 2011 in spite of this expression of collective rage and accompanying demonstrations by youth groups across the globe.

The Collapse or Reconfiguration of Youthful Protests?

Costas Lapavitsas and Alex Politaki, writing in *The Guardian,* argue that as the economic and social disaster unfolded in 2012 and 2013, youth in Greece, France, Portugal, and Spain have largely been absent from "politics, social movements and even from the spontaneous social networks that have dealt with the worst of the catastrophe."[12] Yet, at the same time they insist that more and more young people have been "attracted to nihilistic ends of the political spectrum, including varieties of anarchism and fascism."[13] This indicates that young people have hardly been absent from politics. On the contrary, those youth moving to the right are being mobilized around needs that simply promise the swindle of fulfillment. This does not suggest that youth are becoming invisible. On the contrary, the move on the part of students and others to the right implies that the economic crisis has not been matched by a crisis of ideas, one that would propel young people toward left political parties or social formations that effectively articulate a critical understanding of the present economic and political crisis. Missing here is also a strategy to create and sustain a radical democratic political movement that avoids cooptation of the prevailing economic and political systems of oppression now dominating the United States, Greece, Turkey, Portugal, France, and England, among other countries.

This critique of youthful protesters as a suspect generation is repeated in greater detail by Andrew R. Myers in *Student Pulse.*[14] He argues that deteriorating economic and educational conditions for youth all over Europe have created not only a profound sense of political pessimism among youth but also a dangerous, if not cynical, distrust of established politics. Regrettably, Myers seems less concerned about the conditions that have written young people out of jobs and a decent education, imposed a massive debt on them, and offers up a future of despair and dashed hopes, than the alleged unfortunate willingness of young people to turn their backs on traditional parties. Myers argues rightly that globalization is the enemy of young people and is undermining democracy, but he wrongly insists that traditional social democratic parties are the only vehicles and hope left for real reform. As such, Myers argues that youth who exhibit a distrust of established governments and call for the construction of another world symbolize political defeat, if not cynicism itself. Unfortunately, his lament about how little youth are protesting today and their lack of engagement in the traditional forms of politics he endorses is in the end a defense of those left/liberal parties that embrace social democracy and the new labor policies of centrist-left coalitions. His rebuke borders on bad faith, given his criticism of young people for not engaging in electoral politics and joining with unions, both of which for many youth rightfully represent elements of a reformist politics they reject in the first place.

It is ironic that both of these critiques of the alleged passivity of youth and the failure of their politics have nothing to say about the generations of adults that failed these young people—that is, what disappears in these narratives is the fact that an older generation accepted the "realization that one generation no longer holds out a hand to the next."[15] What is lacking here is any critical sense regarding the historical conditions and dismal lack of political and moral responsibility of an adult generation who shamefully bought into and reproduced, at least since the 1970s, governments and social orders wedded to war, greed, political corruption, xenophobia, and willing acceptance of the dictates of a ruthless form of neoliberal globalization.

In fact, what was distinctive about the protesting youth across the globe was their rejection of the injustices of neoliberalism and their attempts to redefine the meaning of politics and democracy while fashioning new forms of revolt.[16] Among their many criticisms, youthful protesters argued vehemently that traditional social democratic left and liberal parties suffered from an "extremism of the center" that made them complicitous with the corporate and ruling political elites, resulting in their embrace of the inequities of a form of casino capitalism, which assumed that the market should govern the entirety of social life, not just the economic realm.[17]

Resurrecting the Radical Imagination

Michael Hardt and Antonio Negri have argued that what united the Occupy movement in the United States with other movements globally was their emphasis on direct action and their rejection of modernist structures of representation and politics, including support for elections and traditional political parties, which they considered corrupt. As such, they did not reject the project of democracy but asked where it had gone and how could they "engage with it again" and win back "the political power of the citizen worker."[18] Commenting on the radical nature of such youth protests, David Graeber argues that the potential of the new youth movements, if not their threat to both conservatives and liberals alike, is that they were more "willing to embrace positions more radical than anything seen, on a mass scale" in a number of countries, particularly "their explicit appeal to class politics, a complete reconstruction of the existing political system, [and] a call (for many at least) not just to reform capitalism but to begin dismantling it entirely."[19]

What recent critics of the current state of youth protests miss is that the real issue is not whether the Occupy movements throughout Europe and the United States have petered out, but what have we learned from them, how have they been transformed, and what are we going to do about it? More specifically, what can be done to revitalize these rebellions into an international movement capable of effecting real change? Rather than claiming that youth have failed protesting the politics of austerity, neoliberal economies of stagnation, and the corrupt rule of finance capital, it is more important to recognize the ways in which such actions are undermined by the continued struggle for survival and the threat and realty of state violence. The great "crime" of the youthful protesters is that they have embraced the utopian notion that there is an alternative to capitalism and in doing so are fighting back against a systemic war on the radical imagination, the belief that everything is for consumption, and that the only value that matters is exchange value.

The protesters in various countries have not failed. On the contrary, they realize that they need more time to fully develop the visions, strategies, cultural apparatuses, infrastructures, organizations, and alliances necessary to more fully realize their attempts to replace the older, corrupt social orders with new ones that are not simply democratic but have the support of the people who inhabit them. Rather than disappearing, many protesters have focused on more specific struggles, such as getting universities to disinvest in coal industries, fighting the rise of student debt, organizing against the Trans-Pacific Partnership, protesting austerity cuts, creating free social services for the poor and excluded, preventing home foreclosures, and developing educational spaces that can provide the formative culture necessary for creating the needs, identities, and modes of agency capable of democratic relations.[20] At the same time, they are participating in everyday struggles that, as Thomas Piketty points out in *Capital in the Twenty-First Century*, make clear that free-market capitalism is not only responsible for "terrifying" inequalities in both wealth and income, but also produces antidemocratic oligarchies.[21] And it is precisely through various attempts to create spaces in which democratic culture can be cultivated that the radical imagination can be liberated from the machinery of social and political death produced by casino capitalism. What was once considered impossible becomes possible through the development of worldwide youth protests that speak to a future that is being imagined but waiting to be brought to fruition.

Challenges for Dark Times

New rights, demands, visions, and modes of political representation dedicated to the public and social good need time to grow and involve long-term commitments to develop. How the construction of alternative forms of power, strategies, and organization will be developed that can both challenge established powers and become more fully realized is not clear. Needless to say, while youth movements around the globe have provided and are providing what Hardt and Negri call "a scaffolding" in preparation for an unforeseen event that would provide the ground for a radical social break out of which a new society can be built, there is much to be done in preparation for such an event.[22] The challenge young protesters face centers on developing visions, tactics, and strong organizations that enable strategies for change that become more than what Stanley Aronowitz calls ephemeral protests reduced to "signs without organization," incapable of making a real difference.[23]

Youth in various countries need to cultivate a radical imagination capable of providing alternatives to capitalism that will offer a challenge not only to neoliberalism and its destructive austerity policies, but also a vision that speaks to people's needs for a radical democracy, one that is capable of convincing diverse elements of a broader public that change is possible, and that existing systems of globalization and casino capitalism can be overcome. While the crisis of financial capital, among other dominant modes of oppression, must be challenged, there is also the urgent need for youth protesters to articulate "the broader dimensions of alienation beyond income disparity."[24] Issues of existential despair, meaninglessness, hopelessness, and a retreat into the orbits of privatization must be addressed if subjectivities and modes of agency are to be mobilized capable of engaging in the long struggle for a radical democracy. Moreover, as long as these protest groups are fragmented, no significant change will take place. Planning effective strategies and building sustainable organizations will not work as long as there are divisions around authority, race, gender, class, sexuality, and identity. When these divisions function so as to fragment demands, create multiple organizations, and fail to provide some form of united leadership, politics dissolves into a jumble of competing discourses and power becomes pathologized. As Sarah Jaffee points out:

> The paradox of Occupy is that many of the things that made it succeed also made it splinter. The attraction to a "leaderless" movement was palpable, and the lack of demands made it possible for anyone to join in as long as they agreed with the basic premise that a tiny elite has too much power. Yet the idea of leaderlessness, as so many have written, masks the ways power continues to operate, and the lack of demands wound up as a refusal, oftentimes, to deal at all with existing systems.[25]

Alliances among different groups, especially with workers and labor unions, must take place across national boundaries motivated by a comprehensive understanding of global politics and its mechanics of power, ideology, corporate sovereignty, and its devastating effects on people's lives and the reality and ideal of a radical democracy and more just world. The possibility for such alliances, unity, and comprehensive understanding of politics among the youth of the world is greater than ever before, given the new technologies and the growing consciousness that power is now global and has generated a need for new modes of politics.[26] It is time for authentic rage to transform itself into an international movement for the creation of a genuinely democratic formative culture and an effective strategy for social, political, and economic change.

15

Noam Chomsky and the Public Intellectual in Dark Times

From Hope to Confrontation

⊷

In a market-driven system in which economic and political decisions are removed from social costs, the flight of critical thought and social responsibility is accentuated by what Zygmunt Bauman calls "ethical tranquillization."[1] One result is a form of depoliticization that works its way through the social order, removing social relations from the configurations of power that shape them, substituting what Wendy Brown calls "emotional and personal vocabularies for political ones in formulating solutions to political problems."[2] Consequently, it becomes difficult for young people too often bereft of a critical education to translate private troubles into public concerns. As private interests trump the public good, public spaces are corroded and short-term personal advantage replaces any larger notion of civic engagement and social responsibility. Under *the restricted rationality of the market,* pubic spheres and educational realms necessary for students to imagine alternative futures and horizons of possibility begin to disappear, as do the public intellectuals who embrace "the idea of a life dedicated to values that cannot possibly be realized by a commercial civilization [which rejects the idea that] loyalty, not truth, provides the social condition by which the intellectual discovers his new environment."[3]

In a dystopian world shaped by twenty-five years of neoliberal savagery, with its incessant assault on public values, the common good, and social responsibility, it has become difficult to remember what a purposeful and substantive democracy looks like or for that matter what even the idea of democracy might suggest. Democracy as both an ideal and working practice is under assault just as a number of antidemocratic educational, market, military, and religious fundamentalisms are gaining ascendency in American society. Increasingly, it becomes more difficult to inhabit those public spheres where politics thrives—where thinking, speaking, and acting subjects engage and critically address the major forces and problems bearing down on their lives. In this new moment in history, the symbiotic relationship among cultural institutions, political power, and everyday life has taken on a new register. As I have stressed throughout this book, the educative nature of politics has now become one of the most important elements shaping how people think, desire, act, and behave. The question of how society should imagine itself or what its future might hold has become more difficult given the eradication of social formations that place an emphasis on cooperation, trust, honesty, and compassion. As a robust democratic sociality is lost to the imperatives of commerce and a harsh, winner-take-all Social Darwinism, there has emerged what Richard Sennett calls a new character type: "an uncooperative self, ill-disposed for dealing with complexity and difference."[4] This character type is increasingly embodied in a new type of intellectual that has become entirely beholden to corporate power and whose ideas, values, and interaction with the American people is bereft of any sense of equality, justice, or ethical considerations. The American people are now beholden pedagogically to what might be called the antipublic intellectual.

Under such circumstances, to cite C. W. Mills, we are witnessing the breakdown of democracy, the infantilization of thought, the disappearance of critical intellectuals, and "the collapse of those public spheres which offer a sense of critical agency and social imagination."[5] Mills's prescient comments amplify what has become a tragic reality. Missing from neoliberal market societies are those public intellectuals who connect scholarship to larger public issues, provide a model of moral witnessing for young people, and embody the struggle to deepen and energize the civic imagination. Neoliberalism has produced and supported over the last forty years a host of foundations, institutes, and cultural apparatuses in which to produce a new kind of public intellectual—that is, an antipublic intellectual who rails against the social state, social wage, unions, and any other public sphere that offers the populace a discourse and mode of subjectivity that operates in the public interest, in support of what might be called the democratic commons. From Bill Gates to Bill Kristol, the American public is inundated with arguments that privilege the market over social needs, individualize the social, and make exchange value the only value that counts. These antipublic intellectuals now dominate the mainstream media and have been waging a war against higher education, public transportation, social provisions such as food stamps and social security. As Chomsky points out:

There are major efforts being made to dismantle Social Security, the public schools, the post office—anything that benefits the population has to be dismantled. Efforts against the U.S. Postal Service are particularly surreal. I'm old enough to remember the Great Depression, a time when the country was quite poor but there were still postal deliveries. Today, post offices, Social Security, and public schools all have to be dismantled because they are seen as being based on a principle that is regarded as extremely dangerous.[6]

These subsidized antipublic intellectuals are not driven by the search for truth but by loyalty to corporate power, all the while producing and legitimating policy that is as authoritarian as it is cruel and stupid, whether it is curbing the reproductive rights of women and preventing environmental reforms or the teaching of creationism in the schools. For example, in the last few decades, we have seen market mentalities attempt to strip education of its public values, critical content, and civic responsibilities as part of its broader goal of creating new subjects wedded to consumerism, risk-free relationships, and the disappearance of the social state in the name of individual, expanded choice. Tied largely to instrumental ideologies and measurable paradigms, many institutions of higher education are now committed almost exclusively to economic goals, such as preparing students for the workforce—all done as part of an appeal to rationality, one that eschews matters of inequality, power, and the ethical grammars of suffering.[7]

In what follows, I want to address the work of Noam Chomsky and his role as a public intellectual. I argue that Chomsky's role intellectually, educationally, and politically is more relevant now than ever, given the need for a display of civic courage, theoretical rigor, and a willingness to translate private troubles into public concerns. Moreover, he provides a model for young people and others to understand the importance of using ideas and knowledge to intervene politically in civic, political, and cultural life in order to make clear that democracy has to be struggled over, if it is going to survive.

Noam Chomsky is a world-renowned academic best known not only for his pioneering work in linguistics but also for his ongoing work as a public intellectual in which he has addressed a number of important social issues that include and often connect oppressive foreign and domestic policies—a fact well illustrated in his numerous pathbreaking books.[8] In fact, Chomsky's oeuvre includes too many exceptionally important books, making it all the more difficult to single out any one of them from his extraordinary and voluminous archive of work. Moreover, as political interventions, his many books often reflect both a decisive contribution and an engagement with a number of issues that have and continue to dominate a series of specific historical moments over the course of fifty years. His political interventions have been historically specific while continually building on the power relations he has engaged critically. For instance, his initial ideas about the responsibility of intellectuals cannot be separated from his early criticisms of the Vietnam

War and the complicity of intellectuals in brokering and legitimating that horrendous act of military intervention.[9] Hence, it becomes trying to compare his 1988 book, *Manufacturing Consent*, coauthored with Edward S. Herman, with his 2002 best seller, *9/11*. Yet, what all of these texts share is a luminous theoretical, political, and forensic analysis of the functioning of the current global power structure, new and old modes of oppressive authority, and the ways in which neoliberal economic and social policies have produced more savage forms of global domination and corporate sovereignty.

His many recent books, articles, and interviews have addressed how the new reign of neoliberal capital is normalized not only through military and economic relations but also through the production of new forms of subjectivity organized around the enslavement of debt, the security-surveillance state, the corporatization of higher education, the rise of finance capital, and the powerful corporate-controlled cultural apparatuses that give new power and force to the simultaneously educative and repressive nature of politics. Chomsky does not subscribe to a one-dimensional notion of power that one often finds among many on the left who view power as driven exclusively by economic forces. He keenly understands that power is multifaceted, operating through a number of material and symbolic registers, and he is particularly astute in pointing out that power also has a pedagogical function and must include a historical understanding of the public relations industry, existing and emerging cultural apparatuses, and that central to matters of power, agency, and the radical imagination are modes of persuasion, the shaping of identities, and the molding of desire.

Rooted in the fundamentals of anarcho-syndicalism and democratic socialism, he has incessantly exposed the gap between the reality and the promise of a radical democracy, particularly in the United States, though he has also provided detailed analysis of how the deformation of democracy works in a number of countries that hide their diverse modes of oppression behind the false claims of democratization. Chomsky has attempted to refigure both the promise of democracy and develop new ways to theorize agency and the social imagination outside of the neoliberal focus on individualization, privatization, and the assumption that the only value that matters is exchange value. Unlike many intellectuals who are trapped in the discourse of academic silos and a sclerotic professionalism, he writes and speaks from the perspective of what might be called contingent totalities. In so doing, he connects a wide variety of issues as part of a larger understanding of the diverse and specific economic, social, and political forces that shape people's lives in particular historical conjunctures. He is one of the few North American theorists who embrace modes of solidarity and collective struggle less as an afterthought than as central to what it means to connect the civic, social, and ethical as the foundation for global resistance movements. Implicit to his role as a public intellectual is the question of what a real democracy should look like, how are its ideals and practices subverted, and what are the forces necessary to bring it into being?

As someone who has been writing about youth, neoliberalism, disposability, the rise of the punishing state, the centrality of education to politics, and the notion that politics is about not only the struggle over power and economics but also the struggle over particular modes of culture, subjectivity, and agency, his work has been invaluable to me and many others. While it is often pointed out that he is one of the most influential left critics of American foreign policy, what is unique about his ongoing analyses is that his work is layered, complex, often connecting issues far removed from more narrow analyses of foreign policy. For Chomsky, crises are viewed as overlapping, merging into each other in ways that often go unrecognized. Accordingly, in this paradigm, the war on education cannot be understood if removed from the war on the social state, just as the rise of the punishing state cannot be removed from the harsh and punitive survival-of-the-fittest ethic that now characterizes a mode of savage neoliberalism in the United States in which the ruling classes no longer believe in political concessions because their power is global while politics is local and colonized by neoliberal geopolitical power relations. In fact, Chomsky often brings together in his work issues such as terrorism, corporate power, US exceptionalism, and other major concerns so as to provide maps that enable his readers to refigure the landscape of political, cultural, and social life in ways that offer up new connections and the possibility for fresh modes of theorizing potential resistance.

He has also written about the possibility of political and economic alternatives, offering a fresh language for a collective sense of agency and resistance, a new understanding of the commons, and a rewriting of the relations between the political and the up-to-date institutions of culture, finance, and capital. And, yet, he does not provide recipes but speaks to emerging modes of imaginative resistance always set within the boundaries of specific historical conjunctures. His work is especially important in understanding the necessity of public intellectuals in a time of utter tyranny, cruelty, financial savagery, and a mode of soft authoritarianism. His work should be required reading for all academics, students, and the wider public. Given that he is one of the most cited intellectuals in the world suggests strongly that his audience is general, diverse, and widespread, inhabiting many different sites, public spheres, and locations.

Chomsky is fiercely critical of fashionable conservative and liberal attempts to divorce intellectual activities from politics and is quite frank in his notion that education both in and out of institutional schooling should be involved in the practice of freedom and not just the pursuit of truth. He has strongly argued that educators, artists, journalists, and other intellectuals have a responsibility to provide students and the wider public with the knowledge and skills they need to be able to learn how to think rigorously, be self-reflective, and to develop the capacity to govern rather than be governed. But for Chomsky it is not enough to learn how to think critically. Engaged intellectuals must also develop an ethical imagination and sense of social responsibility necessary to make power accountable and to deepen the possibilities for everyone to live a life infused with freedom, liberty, decency, dignity, and justice. On higher education, Chomsky has been arguing since the 1960s that in a healthy society universities must press the claims for economic and social justice and that any education that matters must not merely be critical but also subversive. Chomsky has been unflinching in his belief that education should disturb the peace, and engage in the production of knowledge that is critical of the status quo, particularly in a time of legitimized violence. He has also been clear, as were his political counterparts the late Pierre Bourdieu and Edward Said, in asserting that intellectuals have to make their voices accessible to a wider public and be heard in all of those spheres of public life in which there is an ongoing struggle over knowledge, values, power, identity, agency, and the social imagination.

Capitalism may have found an honored place for many of its antipublic intellectuals, but it certainly has no room for the likes of Chomsky. Conservatives and liberals along with an army of unyielding neoliberal advocates have virtually refused to include him in the many discussions and publications on social issues that work their way into the various registers of the dominant media. In many ways, Chomsky's role as an intellectual and activist is a prototype of what may be called an American radical tradition and yet appears out of place. Chomsky appears to be an exile in his own country by virtue of his political interventions, the shock of his acts of translation, and his displays of fierce courage. As Zygmunt Bauman has argued, the "distinguishing mark" of the writer as exile "is the refusal to be integrated—the determination to ... conjure up a place of one's own, different from the place which those around are settled, a place unlike the places left behind and unlike the place of arrival."[10] This is not to suggest that he would make a claim to be in exile in the sense claimed by many intellectuals, though he might agree with the late Edward Said who was interested in what he called "traveling theory" in the sense of "being errant, provisional, intellectually on the hoof, [as one of] several ways in which he remained true to the exiled people to whom he lent his voice."[11] Exile in this sense suggests that as a "traveler" Chomsky is not interested staking out academic territory and consequently has no disciplinary sphere to protect.

Chomsky is interested in connecting intellectual competencies and critical independence with matters of social responsibility. His political and theoretical purview is capacious. Unlike many academics today who are caught in the cult of specialization and forms of disciplinary terror—forever excoriating those intellectuals who attempt to breach the steadfast rules of the discipline—Chomsky is committed to an intellectual vocation that questions authority, breaks down the dominant appeal to common sense, and exercises a "heighted sensitivity to oppression and injustice."[12]

Terry Eagleton offers a definition of how academics are different from public intellectuals that I think is useful in understanding Chomsky's work. He writes:

> Intellectuals are not only different from academics, but almost the opposite of them. Academics usually plough through a narrow disciplinary patch, whereas intellectuals ... roam ambitiously from one discipline to another. Academics are interested in ideas, whereas intellectuals seek to bring ideas to an entire culture. ... Anger and academia do not usually go together, except perhaps when it comes to low pay, whereas anger and intellectuals do. Above all, academics are conscious of the difficult, untidy, nuanced nature of things, while intellectuals take sides. ... In all the most pressing political conflicts which confront us, someone is going to have to win and someone to lose. It is this, not a deaf ear for nuance and subtlety, which marks them out from the liberal.[13]

While this description does not perfectly fit Chomsky, I think it is fair to say that his main role as a public intellectual is to lift ideas into the public realm in the hopes of exposing how power relations works for and against justice, how they are legitimated, and what can be done to challenge them. Many have commented on his staid delivery when he gives talks, but what they often fail to recognize is the sense of political and moral outrage that animates his diverse roles as a public intellectual. At the same time Chomsky is certainly an academic in terms of his rigorous intellectual work, but the point is that he is more than that. In the end, Chomsky's dialectical move between theory and practice, rigor and accessibility, critique and action offers up less a reason to praise him than to offer a noble vision of what we should all strive for.

As an engaged academic, Chomsky publicly argues against regimes of domination organized for the production of violence and social and civil death. His ghostly presence offers up the possibility of dangerous memories, alternative ways of imagining society and the future, and the necessity of public criticism as one important element of individual and collective resistance. And, yet, Chomsky's role as a public intellectual, given the huge audiences that he attracts when he lectures as well as his large reading public, suggests that there is no politics that matters without a sense of connecting meaningfully with others. Politics becomes emancipatory when it takes seriously that, as Stuart Hall has noted, "people have to invest something of themselves, something that they recognize is of them or speaks to their condition, and without that moment of recognition ... politics will go on, but you won't have a political movement without that moment of identification."[14] Chomsky has clearly connected with a need among the public for those intellectuals willing to make power visible, to offer an alternative understanding of the world, and to point to the hopes of a future that does not imitate the scurrilous present.

Chomsky has been relentless in reminding his audience that power takes many forms and that the production of ignorance is not merely about the crisis of test scores or a natural state of affairs—an idiotic argument if there ever was one—but about how ignorance is often produced in the service of power. According to Chomsky, ignorance is a pedagogical formation that is used to stifle critical thinking and promotes a form of antipolitics that undermines matters of judgment and thoughtfulness, which are central to politics. At the same time, neoliberalism's public pedagogy of ignorance is a crucial player in not just producing consent but also in squelching dissent. For Chomsky, ignorance is a political weapon that benefits the powerful, not a general condition rooted in some inexplicable human condition. One of his most insistent themes focuses on how state power functions in various forms as a mode of terrorism reigning violence, misery, and hardship often as a function of class warfare and American global imperialism and how people are often complicitous with such acts of barbarism. Chomsky has been particularly insightful in arguing that the state thrives on keeping the American public immersed in ignorance so that it can render its illegal practices invisible and protect the "security of state power from exposure."[15] He writes:

> There is, of course, a sense in which security is threatened by public awareness—namely, the basic insight was expressed well by the Harvard political scientist Samuel P. Huntington: "The architects of power in the United States must create a force that can be felt but not seen. Power remains strong when it remains in the dark; exposed to the sunlight it begins to evaporate."[16]

At the same time, Chomsky is an ardent defender of the poor, those populations considered disposable, the excluded, and those marginalized by class, race, gender, and other ideologies and structural relations considered threatening to tyrants both at home and abroad. There is no privileged, singularly oppressed group in Chomsky's work. He is capacious in making visible and interrogating oppression in its multiple forms, regardless of where it exists. Yet, while Chomsky has his critics, ranging from notables such as Sheldon Wolin and Martha Nussbaum to a host of less informed interlocutors, he rarely shies away from a reasoned debate, often elevating such exchanges to a new level of understanding and in some cases embarrassment for his opponents.[17] Some of his more illustrious and infamous debaters have included Michel Foucault, William Buckley, Jr., John Silber, Christopher Hitchens, and Alan Dershowitz. At the same time, he has refused, in spite of the occasional and most hateful and insipid of attacks, to mimic such tactics in responding to his less civil denigrators.[18] Some of

Chomsky's detractors have accused him of being too strident, not theoretical enough, or more recently of not understanding the true nature of ideology. These criticisms seem empty and baseless to me and appear irrelevant considering the impact Chomsky's work has had on a younger generation, including many in the Occupy movement, in calling into question the reckless mechanizations and dynamics of politics, power, and policies of the US government and other authoritarian regimes.

It is important to note that I am not suggesting that Chomsky is somehow an iconic figure who inhabits an intellectual version of celebrity culture. On the contrary, he deplores such a role and is an enormously humble and self-effacing human being. What I am contending, however, is that in an age when the models for political leadership and civic responsibility are put forth in American society for young people and others to learn from, they are largely drawn from the ranks of a criminal, if not egregiously anti-democratic class, of elite financers and the rich. Chomsky offers a crucial, though often unacknowledged, standard for how to be engaged with the world in ways in which issues of commitment and courage are tied to considerations of justice and struggle and not merely to the accumulation of capital regardless of the social costs. His decisive influence on a range of fields extending from linguistic theory to theories of the state and education have not only opened up new modes of inquiry but also give gravitas to the political impulse that underscores such contributions. The point here is neither to idolize nor demonize Chomsky—the two modalities that often mark reactions to his work. Rather the issue is to articulate the ways in which Chomsky as a public intellectual gives meaning to the disposition and characteristics that need to be in place for such critical work to thrive: a historical consciousness, civic courage, sacrifice, incisiveness, thoughtfulness, rigor, compassion, political interventions, the willingness to be a moral witness, and the ability to listen to others.

As a public intellectual, Chomsky offers academics a way to be both scholars and critical citizens, and calls upon them to use their talents and resources to promote public values, defend the common good, and connect education to social change. He strongly rejects the notion that academics are merely servants of the state and that students are nothing more than enterprising consumers. The role of academics as public intellectuals has a long history in Chomsky's work and is inextricably connected to defending the university as a public good and democratic public sphere. Chomsky made this clear in a talk he gave at the Modern Language Association in 2000 when he insisted that

> universities face a constant struggle to maintain their integrity, and their fundamental social role in a healthy society, in the face of external pressures. The problems are heightened with the expansion of private power in every domain,

in the course of the state-corporate social engineering projects of the past several decades. . . . To defend their integrity and proper commitments is an honorable and difficult task in itself, but our sights should be set higher than that. Particularly in the societies that are more privileged, many choices are available, including fundamental institutional change, if that is the right way to proceed, and surely including scholarship that contributes to and draws from the never-ending popular struggles for freedom and justice.[19]

Higher education is under attack not because it is failing, but because it is a potentially democratic public sphere. As such, conservatives and neo-liberals often see it as a threatening institution that reminds them of the rebellious legacy of the 1960s, when universities were the center of struggles over free speech, antiracist and feminist pedagogies, and the antiwar movement. Higher education has become a target for right-wing ideologues and the corporate elite because it is capable of teaching students how to think critically, and it offers the promise of new modes of solidarity to students outside of the exchange value proffered by neoliberal instrumentalism and the reduction of education to forms of training. Chomsky extends the democratic legacy of higher education by insisting that universities and faculty should press the broader claims for economic and social justice.

He also argues more specifically that while higher education should be revered for its commitment to disinterested truth and reason, it also has a crucial role to play in its opposition to the permanent warfare state, the war on the poor, the squelching of dissent by the surveillance state, the increasing violence waged against students, and the rise of an authoritarian state engaged in targeted assassination, drone warfare, and the destruction of the environment. Part of that role is to create an informed and reflective democratic citizenry engaged in the struggle for social justice and equality. Chomsky has no interest in rooting the practice of freedom in the narrow discourses of identity politics with its particularized notion of freedom, just as he has no interest in encouraging students to become apostles of fashionable intellectuals. This becomes clear when he writes about the need to go beyond fighting against the corporatization of the university. He stakes out a line of criticism that points to a general, not a particular, notion of freedom, refusing a politics and pedagogy largely defined within the parameters of a specialized academic discipline. For example, he writes:

> The processes of corporatization are a serious threat to the liberatory and subversive function that the universities should try to serve in a free and healthy society. To defend their integrity and proper commitments is an honorable and difficult task in itself, but our sights should be set higher than that. Particularly in the societies that are more privileged, many choices are available, including fundamental institutional change, if that is the right way to proceed, and surely including scholarship that contributes to and draws from the never-ending popular struggles for freedom and justice.[20]

Standing for truth is only one role the university can assume, but it isn't enough. It must also fulfill its role of being attentive to the needs of young people by safeguarding their interests while educating them to exercise their capacities to fulfill their social, political, economic, and ethical responsibilities to others, to broader publics, and the wider global social order. As Chomsky reminds us, caring about other people is a dangerous conception in America today, and signals the transformation of the United States from a struggling democracy to a full-fledged authoritarian state.[21] He writes:

> If you care about other people, that's now a very dangerous idea. If you care about other people, you might try to organize to undermine power and authority. That's not going to happen if you care only about yourself. Maybe you can become rich, but you don't care whether other people's kids can go to school, or can afford food to eat, or things like that. In the United States, that's called "libertarian" for some wild reason. I mean, it's actually highly authoritarian, but that doctrine is extremely important for power systems as a way of atomizing and undermining the public.[22]

Given the intensive attack that is currently being waged against higher education, Chomsky's defense of the latter as a democratic public sphere and his insistence on the responsibility of intellectuals—be they academics, students, artists, educators, or cultural workers, to name only a few—takes on a new urgency. Public intellectuals can play a crucial political role in not only translating private issues into public concerns, but also offering up a discourse of interrogation and possibility, one that understands the new historical configuration in which we find ourselves when power is separated from politics, demanding not only a new consideration of politics and power but also what it means to think otherwise in order to act otherwise. Chomsky is an important public intellectual because he has become a model for what it means to put a premium on social and economic justice, display a willingness to raise disquieting questions, make power accountable, defend democratic values, take political risks, and exhibit the moral courage necessary to address important social issues as part of an ongoing public conversation.

This is not an easy task at a time when many academics have removed themselves from engaging larger social issues and are all too willing to accommodate those in power, functioning as either entertainers or stenographers. Too many academics have become either uncritical servants of corporate interests, rendered invisible, if not irrelevant, behind a firewall of professional jargon, or have been reduced to a subaltern class of adjunct and part-time labor, with little time to think critically or address larger social issues. Consequently, they either no longer feel the need to communicate with a broader public, address important social problems, or they are deprived of the conditions that enable them to write, think, and function as public and engaged intellectuals. This is particularly troubling in an aspiring democracy where intellectuals above all should take seriously the notion that if democracy is to mean anything, it "requires its citizens to risk something, to test the limits of the acceptable."[23] This is particularly egregious when for many academics their working conditions no longer support their role as scholars and public intellectuals.

Noam Chomsky not only represents the antithesis of intellectual accommodation, he actually exemplifies a new kind of intellectual, one reminiscent of rigorous theorists such as Antonio Gramsci and Michelle Foucault, on the one hand, and C. Wright Mills, on the other, all of whom refused, as Mills put it, the role of "a sociological book-keeper," preferring instead to be "mutinous and utopian" rather than "go the way of the literary faddist and the technician of cultural chic."[24] Like C. Wright Mills, Chomsky addresses pressing social issues and painstakingly looks at how they are lived through the experiences of people who are often deeply affected, yet disappeared from such narratives. His work on political economy, regimes of authoritarianism, cultural domination, and global youth resistance is in my mind a pioneering work that examines the mechanisms of politics, and collective struggles globally within a larger matrix of economics, power, history, and culture. Chomsky is not content to focus on the perpetrators of global crime and the new forms of authoritarianism that are spreading in different ways across the globe; he also focuses on those who are now considered disposable, those who have been written out of the discourse of what he considers a tortured democracy, as a force for collective resistance capable of employing new modes of agency and struggle.

Whether he is talking about war, education, militarization, or the media, there is always a sense of commitment, civic courage, and a call for resistance in his work that is breathtaking and always moving. His interventions are always political, and yet he manages to avoid the easy mantle of dogmatism or a kind of humiliating clownish performance we see among some alleged leftist intellectuals. Like C. Wright Mills, he has revived the sociological imagination, connecting the totality and the historically specific, a broader passion for the promise of democracy, and a complex rendering of the historical narratives of those who are often marginalized and excluded. There is also a refusal to shield the powerful from moral and political critique. Chomsky has become a signpost for an emerging generation of intellectuals who are not only willing to defend the institutions, public spheres, and formative cultures that make democracy possible but also address those antidemocratic forces working diligently to dismantle the conditions that make an aspiring democracy meaningful.

We live at a time when the growing catastrophes that face Americans and the rest of the globe are increasingly matched by the accumulation of power by the rich and financial elite. Their fear of democracy is now strengthened by the financial, political, and corporate elite's intensive efforts to normalize their own power and silence those who hold them accountable. For many, we live in a time of utter despair. But resistance is not only possible, it may be more necessary now than at any other time in America's past, given the current dismantling of civil rights, democratic institutions, the war on women, labor unions, and the poor—all accompanied by the rise of a neoliberal regime that views democracy as an excess, if not dangerous, and an obstacle to implementing its ideological and political goals. What Noam Chomsky has been telling us for over fifty years is that resistance demands a combination of hope, vision, courage, and a willingness to make power accountable, all the while connecting with the desires, aspirations, and dreams of those who suffer under the apparatuses of regimes of violence, misery, fear, and terror. He has also reminded us again and again through numerous historical examples that public memory contains the flashpoints for remembering that such struggles are always collective and not merely a matter of individual resistance. There are always gaps in the work we do as intellectuals, and in Chomsky's case there is more to be said, as Archon Fung points out, regarding the role that public intellectuals can play in shaping "the democratic character of public policy," work with "popular movements and organizations in their efforts to advance justice and democracy," and while refusing to succumb to reformist practices "join citizens—and sometimes governments—to construct a world that is more just and democratic."[25]

He may be one of the few public intellectuals left of an older generation that offers a rare glimpse into what it means to widen the scope of the meaning of political and intellectual inquiry—an intellectual who rethinks in a critical fashion the educative nature of politics within the changed and totalizing conditions of a neoliberal global assault on all vestiges of democracy. He not only trades in ideas that defy scholastic disciplines and intellectual boundaries, he also makes clear that it is crucial to hold ideas accountable for the practices they legitimate and produce while at the same time refusing to limit critical ideas to simply modes of critique. In this instance, ideas not only challenge the normalizing discourses and representations of common sense and the power inequities they legitimate, but also open up the possibilities inherent in a discourse that moves beyond the given and points to new ways of thinking and acting about freedom, civic courage, social responsibility, and justice from the standpoint of radical democratic ideals.

16
The Specter of Authoritarianism
and the Future of the Left

‹⊝›

Henry A. Giroux Interviewed by C. J. Polychroniou

C. J. POLYCHRONIOU: *It is widely believed that the advanced liberal societies are suffering a crisis of democracy, a view you share wholeheartedly, although the empirical research, with its positivists bias, tends to be more cautious. In what ways is there less democracy today in places like the United States than there was, say, twenty or thirty years ago?*

HENRY GIROUX: What we have seen in the United States and a number of other countries since the 1970s is the emergence of a savage form of free-market fundamentalism, often called neoliberalism, in which there is not only a deep distrust of public values, public goods, and public institutions but also the embrace of a market ideology that accelerates the power of the financial elite and big business while gutting those formative cultures and institutions necessary for a democracy to survive.

The commanding institutions of society in many countries, including the United States, are now in the hands of powerful corporate interests, the financial elite, and right-wing bigots whose strangulating control over politics renders democracy corrupt and dysfunctional. Of course, what is unique about the United States is that the social contract and social wage are subject to a powerful assault by the right-wing politicians and antipublic intellectuals from both political parties. Those public spheres and institutions that support social provisions and the public good and keep public value alive are under sustained attack. Such attacks have not only produced a range of policies that have expanded the misery, suffering, and hardships of millions of people but have also put into place a growing culture of heartlessness in which those who suffer the misfortunes of poverty, unemployment, low-skill jobs, homelessness, and other social problems are the object of both humiliation and scorn.

Neoliberal societies, in general, are in a state of war—a war waged by the financial and political elite against youth, low-income groups, the elderly, poor minorities of color, the unemployed, immigrants, and others now considered disposable. Liberty and freedom are now reduced to fodder for inane commercials or empty slogans used to equate capitalism with democracy. At the same time, liberty and civil rights are being dismantled while state violence and institutional racism are spreading throughout the culture like wildfire, especially with regard to police harassment of young black and brown youth. A persistent racism can also be seen in the attack on voting rights laws, the mass incarceration of African American males, and the overt racism that has become prominent among right-wing Republicans and Tea Party types, most of which is aimed at President Obama. At the same time, women's reproductive rights are under assault and there is an ongoing attack on immigrants. Education at all levels is being defunded and defined as a site of training rather than as a site of critical thought, dialogue, and critical pedagogy. In addition, democracy has withered under the emergence of a national security and permanent warfare state. This is evident not only in endless wars abroad but also in the passing of a series of laws such as the Patriot Act, the Military Commission Act, the National Defense Authorization Act, and many other laws that shred due process and give the executive branch the right to hold prisoners indefinitely without charge or a trial, authorize a presidential kill list, and conduct warrantless wiretaps. Of course, both Bush and Obama claimed the right to kill any citizens considered to be a terrorist or who have come to the aid of terrorism. Moreover, targeted assassinations are now carried out by drones that are more and more killing innocent children, adults, and bystanders.

Another index of America's slide into barbarism and authoritarianism is the rise of the racial punishing state with its school-to-prison pipeline, criminalization of a range of social problems, a massive incarceration system, militarization of local police forces, and its use of ongoing state violence against youthful dissenters. The prison has now become the model for a type of punishment creep that has impacted upon public schools, where young children are arrested for violating something as trivial as doodling on a desk or violating a dress code. Under the dictates of the punishing state, incarceration has become the default solution for every social problem, regardless of how minor it may be. Discordant interactions between teacher and student, however minor, are now treated as a criminal offense. The long arm of punishment creep is also evident in a number of social services where poor people are put under constant surveillance and punished for petty infractions. It is also manifest in the militarization of everyday life, with its endless celebration of military, police, and religious institutions, all of which are held in high esteem by the American public, in spite of their undeniably authoritarian nature.

As Edward Snowden made clear, the hidden registers of authoritarianism have come to light in a trove of exposed NSA documents, which affirm that the United States has become a national security–surveillance state illegally gathering massive amounts of information from diverse sources on citizens who are not guilty of any crime. To justify such lawlessness, the American public is told that the rendering moot of civil liberties is justified in the name of security and defense against potential terrorists and other threats. In reality, what is being defended is the security of the state and the concentration of economic and political power in the hands of the controlling political and corporate elites. The real threat, in this case, is the American people and the possibility of their outrage and potential action against such dangerous Orwellian modes of surveillance. What is at risk and must be prevented at all costs is the possibility of dominant power and its machinery of civil and social death from becoming visible.

There is also the shameful exercise under Bush and to a lesser degree under Obama of state-sanctioned torture coupled with a refusal on the part of the government to prosecute those CIA agents and others who willfully engaged in systemic abuses that constitute war crimes. What this list amounts to is the undeniable fact that in the last forty years, the United States has launched an attack not only on the practice of justice and democracy itself, but on the very idea of justice and democracy.

Nowhere is this more obvious than in the realm of politics. Money now drives politics in the United States and a number of other countries. Congress and both major political parties have sold themselves to corporate power. Campaigns are largely financed by the financial elite such as the right-wing Koch brothers, Sheldon Adelson, major defense corporations such as Lockheed Martin, and major financial institutions such as Goldman Sachs. As a recent Princeton University report pointed out, policy in Washington, DC, has nothing to do with the wishes of the people but is almost completely determined by the wealthy, big corporations and a corrupt class of bankers and hedge fund managers, made even easier thanks to Citizens United and a number of other laws being enacted by a conservative Supreme Court majority. Hence, it should come as no surprise that Princeton University researchers Martin Gilens and Benjamin Page came to the conclusion that the United States is basically an oligarchy in which power is wielded by a small number of elites.

C. J. P.: *In other words, you do not think we have an existential crisis of democracy, the result of an economic crisis, with unforeseen and unintended consequences, but an actual corrosion of democracy, with calculated effects? Is this correct?*

H. G.: I think we have both. Not only has democracy been undermined and transformed into a form of authoritarianism unique to the twenty-first century, but there is also an existential crisis that is evident in the despair, depoliticization, and crisis of subjectivity that has overtaken much of the population, particularly since 9/11 and the economic crisis of 2007. The economic crisis is not matched by a crisis of ideas, and many people have surrendered to a neoliberal ideology that limits their sense of agency by defining them primarily as consumers, subjects them to a pervasive culture of fear, blames them for problems that are not of their doing, and leads them to believe that violence is the only mediating force available to them, just as the pleasure quotient is colonized and leads people to assume that the spectacle of violence is the only way in which they can feel anything anymore. How else to interpret polls that show that a majority of Americans support the death penalty, government surveillance, drone warfare, the prison-industrial complex, and zero-tolerance policies that punish children. Trust, honor, intimacy, compassion, and caring for others are now viewed as liabilities, just as self-interest has become more important than the general interest and common good. Selfishness, self-interest, and an unchecked celebration of individualism have become, as Joseph E. Stiglitz has argued, "the ultimate form of selflessness." One consequence of neoliberalism is that it makes a virtue of producing a collective existential crisis, a crisis of agency and subjectivity, one that saps democracy of its vitality. There is nothing about this crisis that suggests it is unrelated to the internal working of casino capitalism. The economic crisis intensified its worst dimensions, but the source of the crisis lies in the roots of capitalism and its most predatory form, a savage form of neoliberalism, whose inception since the 1970s found its most complete and ruthless expression when social democracy proved unable to curb the crisis of capitalism and economics became the driving force of politics. The existential crisis is further intensified in the brutal and degrading manner in which those marginalized by poverty, joblessness, and other constructed forms of misery are demeaned and humiliated in the dominant discourse of conservatives and other right-wing fundamentalists. Despair now disavows politics and turns into a kind of sadomasochistic knot seeking a kind of revenge on those deemed disposable, while demeaning those who thrive in such an emotional wasteland.

C. J. P.: *In your writings, you refer frequently to the specter of authoritarianism. Are you envisioning Western liberal democracies turning to authoritarian-style capitalism, as in China, Russia, Singapore, and Malaysia, to "friendly fascism," or to oligarchic democracy?*

H. G.: Each country will develop its own form of authoritarianism rooted in the historical, pedagogical, and cultural traditions best suited for it to reproduce itself. In the United States there will be an increase in military-style repression to deal with the inevitable economic, ecological, political crisis that will intensify under the new authoritarianism. In this instance, the appeal will largely be to security, reinforced by a culture of fear and an intensified appeal to nationalism. At the same time, this "hard war" against the American people will be supplemented by a "soft war" produced with the aid of the new electronic technologies of surveillance and control, but there will also be a full-fledged effort through the use of the pedagogical practices of various cultural apparatuses, extending from the schools and older forms of media, on the one hand, to the new media and digital modes of communication, on the other, to produce elements of the authoritarian personality while crushing as much as possible any form of collective dissent and struggle. State sovereignty has been replaced by corporate sovereignty, and this constitutes what might be called a new form of totalitarianism, which Michael Halberstam once stated "haunts the modern ideal of political emancipation." As Chris Hedges has argued: "There is no national institution left that can accurately be described as democratic." What is unique about this form of authoritarianism is that it is driven by a criminal class of powerful financial and political elites who refuse to make political concessions. The new elites have no allegiances to nation-states and don't care about the damage they do to workers, the environment, or the rest of humanity. They are unhinged sociopaths, far removed from what the Occupy movement called the 99 percent. They are the new gated class who float above national boundaries, laws, and forms of regulation. They are a global elite whose task is to transform all nation-states into instruments to enrich their wealth and power. The new authoritarianism is not just tantamount to a crisis of democracy; it is also about the limits now being placed on the very meaning of politics and the erasure of those institutions capable of producing critical, engaged, and socially responsible agents.

C. J. P.: *The role of neoliberalism in reducing democracy and destroying public values is an undeniable fact as the economics of neoliberal capitalism seek to establish the supremacy of corporate and market values over all political and social values. Many of your books represent a systematic attack on the neoliberal project. Do you treat neoliberalism as policy paradigm congruent with a certain stage in the evolution of capitalism, or as a particular philosophy of capitalism?*

H. G.: Neoliberalism is both an updated and more ruthless stage in predatory capitalism and its search for the consolidations of class power globally, buttressed by the free-market fundamentalism made famous by Friedrich Hayek and Milton Friedman, without any regard for the social contract. As Robert McChesney has argued, it is classical liberalism with the gloves off, or shall we say, liberalism without the guilt—a more predatory form of market fundamentalism that is as ruthless as it is orthodox in its disregard for democracy. The old liberalism believed in social provisions and partly pressed the claims for social and economic justice. Neoliberalism considers the discourse of equality, justice, and democracy quaint, if not dangerous, and must be either trivialized, turned into its Orwellian opposite, or eviscerated from public life. It certainly represents more than an intensification of classical liberalism, and in that sense it represents a confluence, a historical conjuncture in which the most ruthless elements of capitalism have come together to create something new and more predatory, amplified by the financialization of capital and the development of a mode of corporate sovereignty that takes no prisoners.

C. J. P.: *Some years ago, in an attempt to analyze the tragedy of Hurricane Katrina, you invented the term "the politics of disposability." Do you consider "disposability" to be a systemic element of global neoliberal capitalism?*

H. G.: Neoliberalism's war against the social state has produced new forms of collateral damage. As security nets are destroyed and social bonds undermined, casino capitalism relies on a version of Social Darwinism to both punish its citizens and legitimate its politics of exclusion, violence, and to convince people that the new normal is a constant state of fear, insecurity, and precarity. By individualizing the social, all social problems and their effects are coded as individual character flaws, a lack of individual responsibility, and often a form of pathology. Life is now a war zone and as such the number of people considered disposable has grown exponentially, and this includes low-income whites, poor minorities, immigrants, the unemployed, the homeless, and a range of people who are viewed as a liability to capital and its endless predatory quest for power and profits. Under the regime of neoliberalism, Americans now live in a society where ever-expanding segments of the population are subject to being spied on, considered potential terrorists, and subject to a mode of state and corporate lawlessness in which the arrogance of power knows no limits. As American society becomes increasingly militarized and political concessions become relics of a long-abandoned welfare state, hollowed out to serve the interests of global markets, the collective sense of ethical imagination and social responsibility toward those who are vulnerable or in need of care has become the central source of societal scourge. What has emerged under the regime of neoliberalism is a notion of disposability in which entire populations are now considered excess, relegated to zones of social death and abandonment, surveillance, and incarceration. The death-haunted politics of disposability is a systemic element of neoliberal capitalism actively engaged in forms of asset stripping, as is evident in the wave of austerity policies at work in North America and Europe. The politics of disposability is also one of neoliberalism's most powerful organizing principles, rendering millions who are suffering under its market-driven policies and practices as excess, rendered redundant according to the laws of a market that wages violence against the 99 percent for the benefit of the new financial elite. Disposable populations are now consigned to zones of terminal exclusion, inhabiting a space of social and civil death. These are students, unemployed youth, and members of the working poor as well as the middle class who have no resources, jobs, or hope. They are the voiceless and powerless who represent the ghostly presence of the moral vacuity and criminogenic nature of neo-liberalism. The expanding ranks of those considered disposable are also its greatest fear and potential threat. What is particularly distinctive about this neoliberal historical conjuncture is the way in which young people, particularly low-income and poor minority youth, are increasingly denied any place in an already weakened social contract and the degree to which they are no longer seen as central to how the many neoliberal societies define their future.

C. J. P.: *Adjusting themselves to the neoliberal reality, universities worldwide are turning increasingly toward corporate management models and marketization. What impact are these shifts likely to have on the traditional role of the university as a public sphere?*

H. G.: The increasing corporatization of higher education poses a dire threat to its role as a democratic public sphere and a vital site where students can learn to address important social issues, be self-reflective, and learn the knowledge, values, and ideas central to deepening and expanding the capacities they need to be engaged and critical agents. Under neoliberalism, higher education is dangerous because it has the potential to educate young people to think critically and learn how to hold power accountable. Unfortunately, with the rise of the corporate university, which now defines all aspects of governing, curriculum, financial matters, and a host of other academic policies, education is now largely about training, creating an elite class of managers, and eviscerating those forms of knowledge that conjure up what might be considered dangerous forms of moral witnessing and collective political action. Any subject or mode of knowledge that does not serve the instrumental needs of capital is rendered disposable, suggesting that the only value of any worth is exchange value, the only pedagogical practice of any value must be reduced to a commercial transaction. The corporate university is the ultimate expression of a disimagination machine, which employs a top-down authoritarian style of power, mimics a business culture, infantilizes students by treating them as consumers, and depoliticizes faculty by removing them from all forms of governance. As William Boardman argues, the destruction of higher education "by the forces of commerce and authoritarian politics is a sad illustration of how the democratic ethos (educate everyone to their capacity, for free) has given way to exploitation (turning students into a profit center that has the serendipitous benefit of feeding inequality)."

Particularly disturbing here is the corporate university's attempt to wage a war on higher education by reducing the overwhelming number of faculty to part-time help with no power, benefits, or security. Many part-time and nontenured faculty in the United States qualify for food stamps and are living slightly above the poverty level. The slow death of the university as a center of critique, a fundamental source of civic education, and a crucial public good make available the fundamental framework for the emergence of a formative culture that produces and legitimates an authoritarian society. The corporatization of higher education constitutes a serious strike against democracy and gives rise to the kind of thoughtlessness that Hanna Arendt believed was at the core of totalitarianism. A glimpse of such thoughtlessness was on display recently at Rutgers University when the university offered an honorary degree to Condoleezza Rice, while offering to pay her $35,000 to give a commencement speech. There is no honor in giving such a prestigious degree to a war criminal. Too many universities have become captives of corporate power. For instance, New York University, in its attempt to expand the reach of neoliberal academic globalization, constructed a campus in Abu Dhabi, the capital of the United Arab Emirates, in which, as the *New York Times* pointed out, workers were beaten and deported for going on strike, forced to pay recruitment fees that added up to a year's wages, and had their passports held in order to squelch dissent. But, then again, higher education is now firmly entrenched in what President Eisenhower once called the Military-Industrial-Academic Complex.

C. J. P.: *What role does popular culture play in contemporary democratic life?*

H. G.: Popular culture is largely colonized by corporations and is increasingly used to reproduce a culture of consumerism, stupidity, and illiteracy. Mainstream popular culture is a distraction and disimagination machine in which mass emotions are channeled toward an attraction for spectacles while suffocating all vestiges of the imagination, promoting the idea that any act of critical thinking is an act of stupidity, and offering up the illusion of agency through gimmicks like voting on *American Idol.* What is crucial to remember about popular culture is that it is not simply about entertainment; it also functions to produce particular desires, subjectivities, and identities. It has become one of the most important and powerful sites of education, or what I have called an oppressive form of public pedagogy. Film, television, talk radio, video games, newspapers, social networks, and online media do not merely entertain us, they are also teaching machines that offer interpretations of the world and largely function to produce a public with limited political horizons. They both titillate and create a mass sensibility that is conducive to maintaining a certain level of consent while legitimating the dominant values, ideologies, power relations, and policies that maintain regimes of neoliberalism. There are a number of registers through which popular culture produces a subject willing to become complicit with their own oppression. Celebrity culture collapses the public into the private and reinforces a certain level of stupidity. Surveillance culture undermines notions of privacy and is largely interested in locking people into strangulating orbits of privatization and atomization. A militarized popular culture offers up the spectacle of violence and a hypermasculine image of agency as both a site of entertainment and as a mediating force through which to solve all problems. Violence now becomes the most important element of power and mediating force in shaping social relationships. Market culture functions largely to turn people into consumers, suggesting that the only obligation of citizenship is to shop. This is largely a way to depoliticize the population and distract them from recognizing their capacities as critically engaged agents and to empty out any notion of politics that would demand thoughtfulness, social responsibility, and the demands of civic courage.

There is also a subversive side to popular culture, as Stuart Hall implied when he argued that the left "has no sense of politics being educative, of politics changing the way people see things." In a similar fashion, the late Pierre Bourdieu argued that the left "has underestimated the symbolic and pedagogical dimensions of struggle and have not always forged appropriate weapons to fight on this front." Both theorists were pointing in part to the failure of the left to take seriously the political unconscious and the need to use alternative media, theater, online journals, and news outlets. At the same time, there is enormous pedagogical value in bringing attention in the rare oppositional representations offered within the dominant media. In this instance, popular culture can be a powerful resource to map and critically engage the everyday, mobilize alternative narratives to capitalism, activate those needs vital to producing more critical and compassionate modes of subjectivity. Film, television, news programs, social media, and other instruments of culture can be used to make education central to a politics that is emancipatory and utterly committed to developing a democratic formative culture. At stake here is the need for progressives to not only understand popular culture and its cultural apparatuses as modes of dominant ideology but also to take popular culture seriously as a tool to revive the radical imagination and to make education central to politics, so as to change the way people think, desire, and dream. Stanley Aronowitz is right in arguing that "education would be one of the crucial tasks of a radical political formation" and would need to launch a comprehensive educational program extending from the creation of online journals and magazines to the development of alternative schools. Everything must be done to offer an educational and political counteroffensive to what Cornelius Castoriadis called "the shameful degradation of the critical function."

C. J. P.: *While we speak of a crisis in democracy, some writers speak of a crisis in neoliberalism, probably influenced by the recent global crisis in neoliberal capitalism. Do you believe that neoliberalism is in a crisis?*

H. G.: I think it is more appropriate to argue that neoliberalism creates and thrives on crises. Crises provide the opening for radical neoliberal reforms, for suspending all government regulations, and for building support for extreme policies that under normal conditions would not be allowed to be put in place. One only has to think about Hurricane Katrina and how the Bush administration used this tragic event to destroy the public school system and replace it with charter schools. This was a classic example of disaster capitalism at work in which a tragic happening makes it easier for right-wing governments to push through neoliberal reforms such as the privatization of schools, public housing, and public transit as part of an ongoing war against low-income people and poor minorities. Another classic example is how 9/11 offered up an opportunity for the Bush-Cheney administration to go to war with Iraq and drastically curtail civil liberties that benefited the rich and powerful defense corporations.

C. J. P.: *The "retreat of the intellectuals" is not a recent phenomenon, yet it has become quite pervasive, partly due to the collapse of socialism and partly due to the marketization of contemporary society as well as the neoliberal restructuring of the university. In your view, how critical is the "retreat of the intellectuals" to the struggle for radical social change?*

H. G.: The seriousness of the retreat of intellectuals from addressing important social issues, aiding social movements, and using their knowledge to create a critical formative culture cannot be overstated. Unfortunately, the retreat of the intellectuals in the struggle against neoliberalism and other forms of domination is now matched by the rise of antipublic intellectuals who have sold themselves to corporate power. More specifically, neoliberalism has created not only a vast apparatus of pedagogical relations that privileges deregulation, privatization, commodification, and the militarization of everyday life, but also an army of antipublic intellectuals who function largely in the interest of the financial elite. Rather than show what is wrong with democracy, they do everything they can to destroy it. These intellectuals are bought and sold by the financial elite and are nothing more than ideological puppets using their skills to destroy the social contract, critical thought, and all those social institutions capable of constructing noncommodified values and democratic public spheres. They are the enemies of democracy and are crucial in creating subjectivities and values that buy into the notion that capital rather than people is the subject of history and that consuming is the only obligation of citizenship. Their goal is to normalize the ideologies, modes of governance, and policies that reproduce massive inequities and suffering for the many and exorbitant and dangerous privileges for the corporate and financial elite. Moreover, such intellectuals are symptomatic of the fact that neoliberalism represents a new historical conjuncture in which cultural institutions and political power have taken on a whole new life in shaping politics. What this suggests is that the left in its various registers has to create its own public intellectuals in higher education, the alternative media, and all of those spaces where meaning circulates. Intellectuals have a responsibility to connect their work to important social issues, work with popular movements, and engage in the shaping of policies that benefit all people and not simply a few. At the heart of this suggestion is the need to recognize that ideas matter in the battle against authoritarianism and that pedagogy must be central to any viable notion of politics and collective struggle. Public intellectuals have an obligation to work for global peace, individual freedom, care of others, economic justice, and democratic participation, especially at a time of legitimized violence and tyranny. I completely agree with the late Pierre Bourdieu when he insisted that there is enormous political importance "to defend the possibility and necessity of the intellectual, who is firstly critical of the existing state of affairs. There is no genuine democracy without genuine opposing critical power." The very notion of being an engaged public intellectual is neither foreign to nor a violation of what it means to be an academic scholar, but central to its very definition. Put simply, academics have a duty to enter into the public sphere unafraid to take positions and generate controversy, functioning as moral witnesses, raising political awareness, and making connections to those elements of power and politics often hidden from public view.

C. J. P.: *One final question. Are you optimistic about the future of the left and of progressive politics in general?*

H. G.: It is impossible to be on the left and at the same time surrender to the normalization of a dystopian vision. One has to be optimistic, but also realistic. This means that there is no room for a kind of romanticized utopianism. Instead, one has to be motivated by a faith in the willingness of young people principally to fight for a future in which dignity, equality, and justice matter and at the same time recognize the forces that are preventing such a struggle. More specifically, hope has to be fed by the need for collective action. Power is never completely on the side of domination, and resistance is not a luxury but a necessity.

As Stanley Aronowitz has argued, the left has to engage the issue of economic inequality, overcome its fragmentation, develop an international social formation for radical democracy and the defense of the public good, undertake ways to finance itself, take seriously the educative nature of politics and the need to change the way people think, and develop a comprehensive notion of politics and a vision to match. History is open, though the gates are closing fast. The issue for me personally is not whether I am pessimistic, but how I am going to use whatever intellectual resources I have to make it harder to prevent various events and problems from getting worse while at the same time struggling for a society in which the promise of democracy appears on the horizon of possibility.

Notes

><

Chapter 1

1. Neil Postman, *Amusing Ourselves to Death: Public Discourse in the Age of Show Business* (New York: Penguin Books, 1985, 2005).

2. Antonio Gramsci, *Prison Notebooks,* ed. and trans. Quintin Hoare and Geoffrey Nowell Smith (New York: International Publishers, 1971), 275–276.

3. I take up elsewhere, in great detail, the nature of the surveillance state and the implications that the persecution of these whistleblowers has for undermining any viable understanding of democracy. See Henry A. Giroux, "Totalitarian Paranoia in the Post-Orwellian Surveillance State," *Truthout,* February 10, 2014, available at www.truth-out.org/opinion/item/21656-totalitarian-paranoia-in-the -post-orwellian-surveillance-state.

4. For an excellent description of the new surveillance state, see Glenn Greenwald, *No Place to Hide* (New York: Signal, 2014); and Julia Angwin, *Dragnet Nation: A Quest for Privacy, Security, and Freedom in a World of Relentless Surveillance* (New York: Times Books, 2014).

5. Zygmunt Bauman and David Lyon, *Liquid Surveillance: A Conversation* (Cambridge: Polity Press, 2013).

6. Zygmunt Bauman, *Wasted Lives* (London: Polity, 2004), 132–133.

7. Heidi Boghosian, *Spying on Democracy: Government Surveillance, Corporate Power, and Public Resistance* (San Francisco: City Lights Books, 2013).

8. Instructive here is Manuel Castells, *Networks of Outrage and Hope: Social Movements in the Internet Age* (Cambridge: Polity, 2012).

9. Marjorie Cohn, "Beyond Orwell's Worst Nightmare," *Huffington Post,* January 31, 2014.

10. See, for example, Manuel Castells, *The Rise of the Network Society* (Malden, MA:

Wiley-Blackwell, 1996); and Zygmunt Bauman, *Collateral Damage: Social Inequalities in a Global Age* (Cambridge: Polity Press, 2011).

11. Postman, *Amusing Ourselves to Death*, xix–xx.

12. Postman, *Amusing Ourselves to Death*.

13. Ariel Dorfman, "Repression by Any Other Name," *Guernica*, February 3, 2014.

14. Boghosian, *Spying on Democracy*, 32.

15. Pete Cashmore, "Why 2012, Despite Privacy Fears, Isn't Like Orwell's 1984," *CNN*, January 23, 2012, available at www.ireport.cnn.com/docs/DOC-770499.

16. Greenwald, *No Place to Hide*, 108.

17. Spencer Ackerman, "US Tech Giants Knew of NSA Data Collection, Agency's Top Lawyer Insists," *The Guardian*, March 19, 2014, available at www.theguardian .com/world/2014/mar/19/us-tech-giants-knew-nsa-data-collection-rajesh-de.

18. Boghosian, *Spying on Democracy*, 22.

19. Jonathan Crary, *24/7* (London: Verso, 2013), 16.

20. Mark Karlin, "From Spying on 'Terrorists Abroad' to Suppressing Domestic Dissent: When We Become the Hunted," *Truthout*, August 21, 2013.

21. Boghosian, *Spying on Democracy*, 22–23.

22. Arun Gupta, "Barrett Brown's Revelations Every Bit as Explosive as Edward Snowden's," *The Guardian*, June 24, 2013.

23. Bruce Schneier, "The Public-Private Surveillance Partnership," *Bloomberg*, July 31, 2013.

24. David Graeber, "Dead Zones of the Imagination," *HAU: Journal of Ethnographic Theory* 2 (2012): 119.

25. The quotation by Karl Jaspers is cited in Hannah Arendt, *The Last Interview and Other Conversations* (Brooklyn, NY: Melville House Publishing, 2013), 37.

26. Ibid., 48.

27. Theodor W. Adorno, "Aldous Huxley and Utopia," *Prisms* (Cambridge, MA: MIT Press, 1967), 106–107.

28. Tom Engelhardt, "Tomgram: Engelhardt, a Surveillance State Scorecard," November 12, 2013, available at *Tom Dispath.com*.

29. I take up many of these issues in Henry A. Giroux, *The Violence of Organized Forgetting* (San Francisco: City Lights, 2014), *The Twilight of the Social* (Boulder, CO: Paradigm Publishers, 2012), and *Zombie Politics and Culture in the Age of Casino Capitalism* (New York: Peter Lang, 2011).

30. Quoted in Quentin Skinner and Richard Marshall, "Liberty, Liberalism and Surveillance: A Historic Overview," *Open Democracy*, July 26, 2013, available at www.opendemocracy.net/ourkingdom/quentin-skinner-richard-marshall/liberty -liberalism-and-surveillance-historic-overview.

31. Charles Derber, private correspondence with the author, January 29, 2014.

Chapter 2

1. See the 2012 Republican Party platform, available at http://s3.amazonaws .com/texasgop_pre/assets/original/2012Platform_Final.pdf.

2. Chris Kirk, "Map: Publicly Funded Schools That Are Allowed to Teach Creationism," *Slate*, January 26, 2014, available at www.slate.com/articles/health

_and_science/science/2014/01/creationism_in_public_schools_mapped_where _tax_money_supports_alternatives.html.

3. Amy Goodman, "After Censorship of History Course, Colorado Students and Teachers Give a Lesson in Civil Disobedience," *Democracy Now,* October 1, 2014, available at www.democracynow.org/2014/10/1/after_censorship_of_history _course_denver.

4. Emmanuel Felton, "Is the New AP U.S. History Really Anti-American?" *Huffington Post,* October 1, 2014, available at www.huffingtonpost.com/2014/10/01 /ap-us-history-anti-american_n_5914326.html.

5. Ibid.

6. John Pilger, "The World We've Constructed Is Far Beyond George Orwell's Worst Nightmare," *AlterNet,* July 11, 2014, available at www.alternet.org/culture /our-world-far-beyond-george-orwells-worst-nightmare.

7. This theme is taken up in Henry A. Giroux, *Neoliberalism's War on Higher Education* (Chicago: Haymarket, 2014); Diane Ravitch, *Reign of Error* (New York: Vintage, 2013); Henry A. Giroux, *Education and the Crisis of Public Values* (New York: Peter Lang, 2012); Kenneth Saltman, *The Gift of Education: Public Education and Venture Philanthropy* (New York: Palgrave, 2010), and Stanley Aronowitz, *Against Schooling: For an Education that Matters* (Boulder, CO: Paradigm Publishers, 2008).

8. Glenn Greenwald, *No Place to Hide: Edward Snowden, the NSA, and the U.S. Surveillance State* (New York: Metropolitan Books, 20014).

9. Sonali Kolhatkar, "Orwell's Dystopian Future Is Almost Here: A Conversation with Glenn Greenwald," *TruthDig,* July 3, 2014, available at www.truthdig.com/report /item/orwells_dystopian_future_is_almost_here_a_conversation_20140703.

10. Henry A. Giroux, *The University in Chains: Confronting the Military-Industrial-Academic Complex* (Boulder, CO: Paradigm Publishers, 2007).

11. See, for example, David Palumbo-Liu, "Why the 'Unhiring' of Steven Salaita Is a Threat to Academic Freedom," *The Nation,* August 27, 2014, available at www.the nation.com/article/181406/why-unhiring-steven-salaita-threat-academic-freedom#.

12. I take up these issues in detail in Giroux, *The University in Chains.*

13. Thomas Friedman, "Giving the Hatemongers No Place to Hide," *New York Times,* July 22, 2005, available at www.nytimes.com/2005/07/22/opinion /22friedman.html?ex=1279684800&en=17fb5beb19b09d86&ei=5090&partner =rssuserland&emc=rss.

14. Malinda Smith, ed., "Preface: Post-9/11: Thinking Critically, Thinking Dangerously," in *Securing Africa: Post-9/11 Discourses on Terrorism* (Burlington, VT: Ashgate, 2010), xiii–xiv.

15. Igor Volsky, "Arizona Bill to Force Students to Take Loyalty Oath," *AlterNet,* January 26, 2013, available at www.alternet.org/arizona-bill-force-students-take -loyalty-oath.

16. See Noam Chomsky, "Corporations and the Richest Americans Viscerally Oppose the Common Good," *AlterNet,* September 29, 2014, available at www.alternet .org/visions/chomsky-corporations-and-richest-americans-viscerally-oppose -common-good-0; Steve Horn, "ALEC Bill in Three States to Require Climate Change Denial In Schools," *CounterPunch,* February 1–3, 2013, available at www .counterpunch.org/2013/02/01/alec-bill-in-three-states-to-require-climate-change -denial-in-schools/.

17. John Atcheson, "Dark Ages Redux: American Politics and the End of the Enlightenment," *CommonDreams,* June 18, 2012, available at www.commondreams .org/view/2012/06/18-2.

18. Steve Peoples and Ken Thomas, "Jindal: GOP Must Stop Being 'Stupid Party,'" *Yahoo News,* January 24, 2013, available at http://news.yahoo.com/jindal-gop-must -stop-being-stupid-party-014220693—election.html.

19. Chomsky, "Corporations and the Richest Americans Viscerally Oppose the Common Good," www.alternet.org/visions/chomsky-corporations-and-richest -americans-viscerally-oppose-common-good-0

20. Ibid.

21. Helen Gao, "Tiananmen, Forgotten," *New York Times,* June 3, 2014, available at www.nytimes.com/2014/06/04/opinion/tiananmen-forgotten.html ?hp&rref=opinion&_r=0.

22. Ibid.

23. Ibid.

24. Fred Inglis, "Today's intellectuals: Too Obedient?" *Times Higher Education,* August 22, 2014, available at www.timeshighereducation.co.uk/features/feature -todays-intellectuals-too-obedient/2015328.fullarticle.

25. Ibid.

26. Ibid.

27. Robert Pogue Harrison, "The Children of Silicon Valley," *New York Review of Books,* July 17, 2014, available at www.nybooks.com/blogs/nyrblog/2014/jul/17 /children-silicon-valley/.

28. Michiko Kakutani, "Texts without Context," *New York Times,* March 21, 2010, available at www.nytimes.com/2010/03/21/books/21mash.html?pagewanted=all.

29. Guy Standing, *The Precariat: The New Dangerous Class* (London: Bloomsbury Academic, 2011), 18–19.

30. A. O. Scott, "The Death of Adulthood in American Culture," *New York Times,* September 11, 2014, available at www.nytimes.com/2014/09/14/magazine/the -death-of-adulthood-in-american-culture.html.

31. Ibid.

32. Brad Evans and Julien Reid, "The Promise of Violence in the Age of Ca-tastrophe," *Truthout,* January 5, 2014, available at http://truth-out.org/opinion /item/20977-the-promise-of-violence-in-the-age-of-catastrophe.

33. Steven Pinker, "Why Academics Stink at Writing," *Chronicle of Higher Educa-tion,* September 26, 2014, available at http://chronicle.com/article/Why-Academics -Writing-Stinks/148989.

34. For a truly egregious example of this kind of anti-intellectualism and self-promoting, masturbatory performance, see Paul Kirk, "Opposing the Elite Oppos-ers," *Dissident Voice,* August 28, 2014, available at http://dissidentvoice.org/2014/08 /opposing-the-elite-opposers/.

35. Arundhati Roy, *Power Politics* (Cambridge, MA: South End Press, 2001), 1.

36. Stuart Hall and Les Back, "In Conversation: At Home and Not at Home," *Cultural Studies* 23, no. 4 (July 2009): 664–665.

37. I have taken this phrase from an interview with Homi Bhaba, in Gary Olson and Lynn Worsham, "Staging the Politics of Difference: Homi Bhaba's Critical Literacy," *JAC* (1999): 9.

38. Zygmunt Bauman, *Liquid Life* (London: Polity Press, 2005), 139.

39. Michael Payne, "What Difference Has Theory Made? From Freud to Adam Phillips," *College Literature* 32, no. 2 (Spring 2005): 7.

40. Lawrence Grossberg, *Cultural Studies in the Future Tense* (Durham, NC: Duke University Press, 2010).

41. The notion that theory is a pedagogical and political resource is taken up in great detail in Jeffrey Nealon and Susan Searls Giroux, *The Theory Toolbox*, 2nd ed. (Boulder, CO: Rowman and Littlefield, 2012).

42. Bauman, *Liquid Life*, 151.

43. Salman Rushdie, "Whither Moral Courage?" *New York Times*, April 28, 2013, available at www.nytimes.com/2013/04/28/opinion/sunday/whither-moral -courage.html?pagewanted=all.

44. Jonathan Crary, *24/7: Late Capitalism and the Ends of Sleep* (London: Verso, 2013), 71.

45. Kate Murphy, "No time to Think," *New York Times,* July 25, 2014, available at www.nytimes.com/2014/07/27/sunday-review/no-time-to-think.html?_r=0.

46. Judith Butler, *Precarious Life: The Powers of Mourning and Violence* (London: Verso Press, 2004), 126.

47. On the political and democratic importance of being able to think and communicate clearly and critically, see Robert Jensen, *Arguing for Our Lives* (San Francisco: City Lights Books, 2013).

48. Cornelius Castoriadis, *The Rising Tide of Insignificancy,* March 1996, p. 4, available at www.notbored.org/RTI.pdf.

49. Zygmunt Bauman, "Critical Theory," in Peter Beilharz, ed., *The Bauman Reader* (Malden, MA: Blackwell, 2001), 139.

50. Robert W. W. McChesney, *Blowing the Roof off the Twenty-First Century: Media, Politics, and the Struggle for Post-Capitalist Democracy* (New York: Monthly Review Press, 2015).

51. Herbert Marcuse, cited in Jürgen Habermas, "Psychic Thermidor and Re-birth of Rebellious Subjectivity," in Robert Pippin, Andrew Feenberg, and Charles P. Webel, eds., *Marcuse: Critical Theory and the Promise of Utopia* (South Hadley, MA: Bergin and Garvey, 1988), 11.

Chapter 3

1. Yose Hayim Yerushalmi, *Zakhor: Jewish History and Jewish Memory* (New York: Schocken Books, 1989), 105.

2. Herbert Marcuse, *The Aesthetic Dimension* (Boston: Beacon Press, 1978), 73.

3. See, for example, Mark Danner, "In the Darkness of Dick Cheney," *New York Review of Books,* March 6, 2014, available at www.nybooks.com/articles/archives /2014/mar/06/darkness-dick-cheney/; and Mark Danner, "He Remade Our World," *New York Review of Books,* April 3, 2014, available at www.nybooks.com/articles /archives/2014/apr/03/dick-cheney-he-remade-our-world/.

4. Thom Hartman, "Dick Cheney Should Be Rotting in a Prison Cell, Not Opining about Iraq," *AlterNet,* June 19, 2014.

5. I have taken this phrase from Mary Gordon, "Late Reinforcements," *New York Times Sunday Book Review,* June 20, 2014.

6. Glenn Greenwald, *No Place to Hide* (New York: Metropolitan, 2014).

Notes

7. Charles Lewis, *935 Lies: The Future of Truth and the Decline of America's Moral Integrity* (New York: Public Affairs, 2014).

8. Susan Jacoby, *The Age of American Unreason* (New York: Pantheon, 2008); Robert N. Proctor and Londa Schiebinger, eds., *Agnotology: The Making and Unmaking of Ignorance* (Stanford, CA: Stanford University Press, 2008). The classic text here is Richard Hofstadter, *Anti-Intellectualism in America Life* (New York: Knopf, 1963).

9. Hannah Arendt, *Hannah Arendt: The Last Interview and Other Conversations* (Brooklyn, NY: Melville House Publishing, 2013), 31.

10. Ibid., 37. See also the brilliant essay by Leo Lowenthal, "Atomization of Man," in *False Prophets: Studies in Authoritarianism* (New Brunswick, NJ: Transaction Books, 1987), 181–191.

11. Jonathan Crary, *24/7: Late Capitalism and the Ends of Sleep* (Brooklyn, NY: Verso Press, 2013), 5.

12. Christian Marazzi, The Violence of Financial Capitalism (New York: Semiotext(e), 2011), 96.

13. Doreen Massey, "Vocabularies of the Economy," *Soundings*, 2013, available at http://lwbooks.co.uk/journals/soundings/pdfs/Vocabularies%20of%20the%20economy.pdf.

14. Zygmunt Bauman and Leonidas Donskis, *Moral Blindness: The Loss of Sensitivity in Liquid Modernity* (Cambridge: Polity Press, 2013), 7.

15. George Will, "Colleges Become the Victims of Progressivism," *Washington Post,* June 6, 2014.

16. Ibid.

17. Ibid.

18. See, for instance, Walt Bogdanich, "Reporting Rape, and Wishing She Hadn't: How One College Handled a Sexual Assault Complaint," *New York Times,* July 12, 2014, available at www.nytimes.com/2014/07/13/us/how-one-college-handled-a-sexual-assault-complaint.html?_r=0. See also Angus Johnson, "Yet Another College under Fire for Mishandling Rape Case," *AlterNet,* July 17, 2014, available at www.alternet.org/education/yet-another-college-under-fire-mishandling-rape-case?akid=12025.40823.uPtm51&rd=1&src=newsletter1011618&t=18.

19. Henry A. Giroux, *Zombie Politics in the Age of Casino Capitalism* (New York: Peter Lang, 2014), 84.

20. John Pilger, "'Good' and 'Bad' War and the Struggle of Memory against Forgetting," *Truthout,* February 14, 2014.

21. Lowenthal, "Atomization of Man," 183.

22. On the economics of contempt, see Jeffrey St. Claire, "The Economics of Contempt," *CounterPunch,* May 23–25, 2014.

23. C. J. Werleman, "Americans Are Dangerously Politically Ignorant—The Numbers Are Shocking," *AlterNet,* June 17, 2014.

24. Herbert Marcuse, cited in Peter Marcuse, "The Baran-Marcuse Letters: 'The Truth Is in the Whole,'" *Monthly Review Zine,* June 20, 2014, available at http://mrzine.monthlyreview.org/2014/marcuse200614.html.

25. Evgeny Morozov, "The Rise of Data and the Death of Politics," *The Guardian,* July 20, 2014, available at www.theguardian.com/technology/2014/jul/20/rise-of-data-death-of-politics-evgeny-morozov-algorithmic-regulation.

26. Ibid.

27. Brad Evans and Julian Reid, *Resilient Life: The Art of Living Dangerously* (London: Polity, 2014), 38.

28. Henry A. Giroux, *The Violence of Organized Forgetting* (San Francisco: City Lights Publishers, 2014), 30.

29. For a sustained critique of resilience, see Evans and Reid, *Resilient Life.*

30. William Easterly, *The Tyranny of Experts* (New York: Basic Books, 2014), 6.

31. Bruce Feiler, "The United States of Metrics," *New York Times,* May 16, 2014.

32. Max Horkheimer, *Eclipse of Reason* (New York: Martino Fine Books, 2013 [1947]). I have discussed the Frankfurt School critique in great detail in Henry A. Giroux, *Theory and Resistance in Education* (New York: Greenwood Publishing, 2001), esp. ch. 1, "Critical Theory and Educational Practice."

33. Feiler, "The United States of Metrics."

34. John Steppling, "Sort of Awake," McMaster Centre for Scholarship in the Public Interest, December 15, 2013.

35. Bauman and Donskis, *Moral Blindness,* 9–10.

36. Zygmunt Bauman and David Lyons, *Liquid Surveillance* (Cambridge: Polity Press, 2013).

37. Bauman and Donskis, *Moral Blindness,* 7.

38. See John Feffer's interesting notion of "participatory totalitarianism": Feffer, "Participatory Totalitarianism," *CommonDreams,* June 4, 2014.

39. Jaron Lanier, *You Are Not a Gadget: A Manifesto* (New York: Vintage, 2011).

40. Cited in Michiko Kakutani, "Texts without Context," *New York Times,* March 21, 2010, available at www.nytimes.com/2010/03/21/books/21mash.html ?pagewanted=all.

41. Lanier, *You Are Not a Gadget.*

42. Madeleine Bunting, "From Buses to Blogs, a Pathological Individualism Is Poisoning Public Life," *The Guardian/UK,* January 28, 2008, available at www.guardian .co.uk/commentisfree/2008/jan/28/comment.society.

43. Howard W. French, "Spare the Advice," *New York Times Book Review,* April 20, 2014, available at www.nytimes.com/2014/04/20/books/review/the-tyranny-of -experts-by-william-easterly.html?ref=bookreviews&_r=0.

44. Bauman and Donskis, *Moral Blindness,* 57.

45. Stanley Aronowitz, *False Promises* (New York: McGraw-Hill, 1973), 278.

46. The Editors of Rethinking Schools, "The Trouble with the Common Core," *Rethinking Schools* 27, no. 4 (Summer 2013).

47. M. Merleau-Ponty, *The Structure of Behavior* (Boston: Beacon Press, 1967), 175.

48. Paulo Freire, *Pedagogy of the Oppressed* (New York: Seabury Press, 1973), 101.

49. Jean-Paul Sartre, *Sartre by Himself,* trans. Michael Seaver (New York: Urizen Books, 1977), 54.

50. Arendt, *Hannah Arendt.*

51. Marcuse, *The Aesthetic Dimension.*

Chapter 4

1. David Theo Goldberg, "In Our Collective Name," *Truthout,* July 15, 2014, available at http://truth-out.org/opinion/item/24972-in-our-collective-name.

2. Bernie Sanders, "The Cost of War," *Boston Globe,* July 22, 2014, available at www.bostonglobe.com/opinion/2014/07/22/podium-sanders/OFhN279p30QIxV V44rWdwO/story.html.

3. Finian Cunningham, "Killing Children Is the All-American Way," *Dissident Voice,* December 22, 2012, available at http://dissidentvoice.org/2012/12/killing -children-is-the-all-american-way/.

4. Amy Goodman, "Report: U.S. Drone Strikes Kill 28 Unnamed People for Every 1 Target," *Democracy Now,* November 25, 2014, available at http://www.democracy now.org/2014/11/25/headlines#11253.

5. Peter Beilharz, *Zygmunt Bauman: Dialect of Modernity* (London: Sage, 2000), 164.

6. See, for instance, Sheldon S. Wolin, *Democracy Incorporated: Managed Democracy and the Specter of Inverted Totalitarianism* (Princeton, NJ: Princeton University Press, 2008); Jonathan Turley, "10 Reasons the U.S. Is No Longer the Land of the Free," *Washington Post,* January 13, 2012, available at http://articles.washingtonpost.com/2012-01-13 /opinions/35440628_1_individual-rights-indefinite-detention-citizens; and the recent Princeton study deducing the United States is no longer a democracy but an oligarchy: Tom McKay, "Princeton Concludes What Kind of Government America Really Has, and It's Not a Democracy," *Popular Resistance,* April 16, 2014, available at www.policymic.com/articles/87719/princeton-concludes-what-kind-of-government -america-really-has-and-it-s-not-a-democracy.

7. Ibid., 162.

8. Andrew J. Bacevich, *The New American Militarism* (New York: Oxford University Press, 2005), 7.

9. Ibid., 5.

10. Catherine Lutz, "Making War at Home in the United States: Militarization and the Current Crisis," *American Anthropologist* 104, no. 3 (2002): 725.

11. Chris Hedges, "Military Metaphysics: How Militarism Mangles the Mind," *Truthout,* February 3, 2014, available at www.truth-out.org/opinion/item/21624 -military-metaphysics-how-militarism-mangles-the-mind.

12. For a commentary on the absurdity of this overabundance of military-grade weapons, see Lyle Jeremy Rubin, "A Former Marine Explains All the Weapons of War Being Used by Police in Ferguson," *The Nation,* August 20, 2014, available at www.thenation.com/article/181315/catalog-ferguson-police-weaponry?utm_source =Sailthru&utm_medium=email&utm_term=email_nation&utm_campaign=Email %20Nation%20%28NEW%29%20-%20Most%20Recent%20Content%20Feed%20 20140821&newsletter=email_nation#.

13. Glenn Greenwald, "The Militarization of U.S. Police: Finally Dragged into the Light by the Horrors of Ferguson," *Dispatches,* August 14, 2014, available at https://firstlook.org/theintercept/2014/08/14/militarization-u-s-police-dragged -light-horrors-ferguson/.

14. Cited in Hanqing Chen, "The Best Reporting on Federal Push to Militarize Local Police," *ProPublica,* August 19, 2014, available at www.propublica.org/article /the-best-reporting-on-the-federal-push-to-militarize-local-police#.

15. David Theo Goldberg, "Revelations from Ferguson," *Truthout* (in press).

16. For the history of the military transfer programs, see Radley Balko, *Rise of*

the Warrior Cop: The Militarization of America's Police Forces (New York: Public Affairs, 2013); and Jill Nelson, ed., *Police Brutality* (New York: Norton, 2000).

17. Matt Apuzzo, "War Gear Flows to Police Departments," *New York Times*, June 8, 2014, available at www.nytimes.com/2014/06/09/us/war-gear-flows-to-police -departments.html. As Hanquing Chen writes in *ProPublica*, "The militarization of St. Louis and other local police departments can be traced to two major sources— the 1033 Program, a section of the National Defense Authorization Act passed in the 1990s, as well as federal homeland security grants to states." Chen, "The Best Reporting on Federal Push to Militarize Local Police."

18. Greenwald, "The Militarization of U.S. Police."

19. Chen, "The Best Reporting on Federal Push to Militarize Local Police."

20. Ibid.

21. Ibid.

22. Cited in Chris Womack, "Anthropologies of Empire and Militarization: A New Anthropology of Empire," *New York Academy of Sciences*, March 18, 2004, available at www.nyas.org/ebriefreps/print.asp?intEbriefID=252. See also John Gillis, ed., *The Militarization of the Western World* (New York: Rutgers University Press, 1989).

23. Kevin Johnson, Meghan Hoyer, and Brad Heath, "Local Police Involved in 400 Killings per year," *USA Today*, August 15, 2014, available at http://www.usatoday .com/story/news/nation/2014/08/14/police-killings-data/14060357/.

24. Mariame Kaba, "For Blacks, America Is Dangerous by Default," *Washington Post*, August 22, 2014, available at www.washingtonpost.com/news/the-watch/wp /2014/08/22/for-blacks-america-is-dangerous-by-default/.

25. Ibid.

26. Ibid.

27. Ibid.

28. Zygmunt Bauman, *Living on Borrowed Time: Conversations with Citlali Rovirosa-Madrazo* (Cambridge: Polity Press, 2010), 8.

29. Zygmunt Bauman and Leonidas Donskis, *Moral Blindness: The Loss of Sensitivity in Liquid Modernity* (Cambridge: Polity Press, 2013), 59–60.

30. Slavoj Žižek, *Demanding the Impossible*, ed. Yong-June Park (Cambridge: Polity Press, 2013), 58.

31. Ibid., 68.

32. Tamara K. Nopper and Mariame Kaba, "Itemizing Atrocity," *Truthout*, August 17, 3014, available at www.truth-out.org/opinion/item/25612-itemizing-atrocity.

33. Kevin Zeese and Margaret Flowers, "Ferguson Exposes the Reality of Militarized, Racist Policing," *Truthout*, August 18, 2014, available at http://truth-out.org/news /item/25645-ferguson-exposes-the-reality-of-militarized-racist-policing.

34. Greenwald, "The Militarization of U.S. Police."

35. Rand Paul, "We Must Demilitarize the Police," *Time* magazine, August 14, 2014, available at http://time.com/3111474/rand-paul-ferguson-police/.

36. Kevin Baker, "Barack Hoover Obama: The Best and the Brightest Blow It Again," *Harper's Magazine*, July 2009, available at www.harpers.org/archive /2009/07/0082562.

37. Danielle M. LaSusa, "In a Profession Plagued by Homogeneity, a Philosophy Conference Delivers Diversity," *Truthout*, August 16, 2014, available at http://

truth-out.org/news/item/25589-in-a-profession-plagued-by-homogeneity-a
-philosophy-conference-delivers-diversity.

38. See, esp., Balko, *Rise of the Warrior Cop*; Michelle Alexander, *The New Jim Crow* (New York: New Press, 2010); and Nelson, ed., *Police Brutality*.

39. Cited in Carol Becker, "The Art of Testimony," *Sculpture* (March 1997): 28.

40. David Swanson, "Militarism Is a Public Safety Crisis," *CounterPunch,* August 19, 2014, available at www.counterpunch.org/2014/08/19/militarism-is-a-public -safety-crisis/print.

41. Editorial, "Two Very Troubled Jets," *New York Times,* July 14, 2014, available at www.nytimes.com/2012/07/15/opinion/sunday/two-very-troubled-fighter-jets .html?_r=2&ref=opinion&.

42. Jordan Weissmann, "Here's Exactly How Much the Government Would Have to Spend to Make Public College Tuition-Free," *Atlantic,* January 3, 2014, available at www.theatlantic.com/business/archive/2014/01/heres-exactly-how-much-the -government-would-have-to-spend-to-make-public-college-tuition-free/282803/.

43. Carl Gibson, "6 Easy Ways to Make College Free for All Americans," *Reader Supported News,* November 23, 2014, available at http://readersupportednews.org /opinion2/277-75/27113-focus-6-easy-ways-to-make-college-free-for-all-americans.

44. I take up this issue in great detail in Henry A. Giroux, *Zombie Politics and Culture in the Age of Casino Capitalism,* 2nd ed. (New York: Peter Lang, 2014).

45. A video of the interview can be found at www.liveleak.com/view ?i=b63_1355548664.

46. Noam Chomsky, "Noam Chomsky: Our Govt. Is Capable of Creating Total Catastrophe for Humankind," *AlterNet,* July 1, 2014, available at www.alternet.org/world /noam-chomsky-our-govt-capable-creating-total-catastrophe-humankind.

47. Rick Perlstein, *The Invisible Bridge: The Fall of Nixon and the Rise of Reagan* (New York: Simon and Schuster, 2014).

48. Alexander, *The New Jim Crow*; and Nelson, ed., *Police Brutality.*

Chapter 5

1. This article draws on a number of ideas in Henry A. Giroux, *Beyond the Spectacle of Terrorism: Global Uncertainty and the Challenge of the New Media* (Boulder, CO: Paradigm Publishers, 2006).

2. Cited in Alice Speri, "ISIS Fighters and Their Friends Are Total Social Media Pros," *Vice News,* January 17, 2014, available at https://news.vice.com/article/isis -fighters-and-their-friends-are-total-social-media-pros.

3. David Carr, "With Videos of Killings, ISIS Sends Medieval Message by Modern Method," *New York Times,* September 7, 2014, available at www.bing.com/search ?q=Eddard%20Stark&pc=cosp&ptag=A01EC74C9980D4C0F8BF&form=CONBD F&conlogo=CT3210127.

4. Ibid.

5. Ibid.

6. This issue is taken up in detail in Brad Evans and Henry A. Giroux, *Disposable Futures: The Seduction of Violence in the Age of the Spectacle* (San Francisco: City Lights, 2015).

7. President George W. Bush, "President Welcomes President Chirac to the

White House," White House News Release, November 6, 2001, available at www
.whitehouse.gov/news/releases/2001/11/print/20011106-4.html.

8. Roger Cohen, "Here There Is No Why: For ISIS, Slaughter Is an End in Itself,"
New York Times, September 30, 2014, available at www.nytimes.com/2014/09/30
/opinion/roger-cohen-for-isis-slaughter-is-an-end-in-itself.html?ref=opinion.

9. See, for instance, Henry A. Giroux, "Disturbing Pleasures: Murderous Images and the Aesthetics of Depravity," *Third Text,* no. 116 (May 2012): 259–273.

10. Brian Massumi, "Preface," in Massumi, ed., *The Politics of Everyday Fear* (Minneapolis: University of Minnesota Press, 1993), viii.

11. Andrew J. Bacevich, *Washington Rules: America's Path to Permanent War* (New
York: Metropolitan Books, Henry Holt and Company, 2010).

12. Robert W. McChesney, "This Isn't What Democracy Looks like," *Monthly
Review* 64, no. 6 (2012); Robert McChesney, *Digital Disconnect: How Capitalism Is
Turning the Internet against Democracy* (New York: New Press, 2013).

13. I take this up in detail in Henry A. Giroux, *The Violence of Organized Forgetting*
(San Francisco: City Lights Books, 2014).

14. Hannah Tennant-Moore, "The Awakening," *New York Times Book Review,* June
19, 2014, 9.

15. Helene Cixous and Catherine Clement, *The Newly Born Woman,* trans. Betsy
Wing, Theory and History of Literature Series 24 (Minnesota: University of Minnesota Press, 1986), ix.

16. See Stanley Aronowitz's brilliant analysis of this issue in "What Kind of Left
Does America Need?" *Tikkun,* April 14, 2014, available at www.tikkun.org/nextgen
/what-kind-of-left-does-america-need.

17. I take up the issue of soft and hard war in Henry A. Giroux, *Youth in a Suspect
Society: Democracy or Disposability?* (New York: Palgrave, 2010).

18. "Neoliberalism's War against the Radical Imagination," *Tikkun* (Summer
2014): 9–12, 59–60.

19. Allen Feldman, "On the Actuarial Gaze from 9/11 to Abu Ghraib," *Cultural
Studies* 19, no. 2 (March 2005): 212.

20. Retort (Iain Boal, T. J. Clark, Joseph Matthews, and Michael Watts), *Afflicted
Powers: Capital and Spectacle in a New Age of War* (London: Verso Press, 2005), 17.

21. The concept of necropolitics is taken from Achille Mbembe, "Necropolitics,"
trans. Libby Meintjes, *Public Culture* 15, no. 1 (2003): 11–40.

22. Jürgen Habermas, *Theory of Communicative Action,* vol. 2: *Lifeworld and System:
A Critique of Functionalist Reason,* trans. Thomas McCarthy (Cambridge: Polity Press,
1987), 390.

23. Lewis H. Lapham, "Tentacles of Rage—The Republican Propaganda Mill,
A Brief History," *Harper's Magazine* (September 2004), 31–41.

24. Sharon Sliwinski, "A Painful Labour: Responsibility and Photography," *Visual
Studies* 19, no. 2 (August 2004): 148.

25. Dilip Parameshwar Gaonkar and Elizabeth A. Povinelli, "Technologies of
Public Forms: Circulation, Transfiguration, Recognition," *Public Culture* 15, no. 3
(2003): 385–397.

26. See Roger I. Simon, Mario DiPaolantoni, and Mark Clamen, "Remembrance
as Praxis and the Ethics of the Inter Human," *Culture Machine* 24 (October 2004):
1–33.

27. Daniel Leighton, "Searching for Politics in an Uncertain World: Interview with Zygmunt Bauman," *Renewal: A Journal of Labour Politics* 10, no. 1 (Winter 2002): 14.

28. Edward W. Said, *Power, Politics, and Culture: Interviews with Edward W. Said,* ed. Gauri Viswanathan (New York: Vintage Books, 2001), 65.

29. James Baldwin, *The Price of the Ticket: Collected Non-Fiction 1948–1985* (New York: Saint Martin's Press, 1985).

Chapter 7

1. See, for instance, Tom Engelhardt, *Shadow Government* (Chicago: Haymarket Press, 2014); Mike Lofgren, "The 'Deep State'—How Much Does It Explain?" *Truthout,* February 26, 2014, available at www.truth-out.org/opinion/item/22075 -anatomy-of-the-deep-state.

2. A. J. Vicens, "How Dark Money Is Taking Over Judicial Elections," *Mother Jones,* November-December 2014, available at http://www.motherjones.com/politics /2014/10/judicial-elections-dark-money.

3. Peter Beilharz, *Zygmunt Bauman: Dialect of Modernity* (London: Sage, 2000), 162.

4. Martin Gilens and Benjamin I. Page, "Testing Theories of American Politics: Elites, Interest Groups, and Average Citizens," *Perspectives on Politics* 12, no. 3 (September 2014): 581.

5. Tom McKay, "Princeton Concludes What Kind of Government America Really Has, and It's Not a Democracy," *Popular Resistance,* April 16, 2014, available at www.policymic.com/articles/87719/princeton-concludes-what-kind-of-government -america-really-has-and-it-s-not-a-democracy.

6. Bill Blunden, "Why the Deep State Always Wins: The Zero-Sum Game of Perpetual War," *CounterPunch,* September 2, 2014, available at www.counterpunch .org/2014/09/02/the-zero-sum-game-of-perpetual-war/.

7. Jonathan Turley, "10 Reasons the U.S. Is No Longer the Land of the Free," *Washington Post,* January 13, 2012, available at http://articles.washingtonpost .com/2012-01-13/opinions/35440628_1_individual-rights-indefinite-detention -citizens.

8. For a clear exposé of the emerging surveillance state, see Glenn Greenwald, *No Place to Hide* (New York: Signal, 2014); Julia Angwin, *Dragnet Nation: A Quest for Privacy, Security, and Freedom in a World of Relentless Surveillance* (New York: Times Books, 2014); Heidi Boghosian, *Spying on Democracy: Government Surveillance, Corporate Power, and Public Resistance* (San Francisco: City Lights Books, 2013).

9. Giles Deleuze, "Societies of Control," *October* 59 (1992): 3–7.

10. Michelle Alexander, "The Age of Obama as a Racial Nightmare," *Tom-Dispatch,* March 25, 2012, available at www.tomdispatch.com/post/175520/best _of_tomdispatch%3A_michelle_alexander,_the_age_of_obama_as_a_racial _nightmare/.

11. Robin D. G. Kelley, "Why We Won't Wait: Resisting the War against the Black and Brown Underclass," *CounterPunch,* November 25, 2014, available at http://www .counterpunch.org/2014/11/25/75039/.

12. Orville Schell, "Follies of Orthodoxy," in *What Orwell Didn't Know: Propaganda and the New Face of American Politics* (New York: Perseus Books Group, 2007), xviii.

13. Stuart Hall, Doreen Massey, and Michael Rustin, "After Neoliberalism: Analysing the Present," *Soundings,* Spring 2013, available at www.lwbooks.co.uk /journals/soundings/pdfs/s53hallmasseyrustin.pdf.

14. John Feffer, "Participatory Totalitarianism," *CommonDreams,* June 4, 2014, available at www.commondreams.org/view/2014/06/04-10.

15. Hannah Arendt, *Hannah Arendt: The Last Interview and Other Conversations* (Brooklyn, NY: Melville House Publishing, 2013), 33–34.

16. Radley Balko, *The Rise of the Warrior Cop: The Militarization of America's Police Forces* (Jackson, TN: Perseus Books, 2013).

17. Chase Madar, "Everyone Is a Criminal: On the Over-Policing of America," *Huffington Post,* December 13, 2013, available at www.huffingtonpost.com/chase -madar/over-policing-of-america_b_4412187.html.

18. Paul Buchheit, "The Carnage of Capitalism," *AlterNet,* August 17, 2014, available at www.commondreams.org/views/2014/08/18/carnage-capitalism.

19. Adolph Reed, Jr., "Nothing Left: The Long, Slow Surrender of American Liberals," *Harper's Magazine* (March 2014): 29.

20. Lorenzo Del Savio and Matteo Mameli, "Anti-representative Democracy and Oligarchic Capture," *Open Democracy,* August 16, 2014, available at www.open democracy.net/lorenzo-del-savio-matteo-mameli/antirepresentative-democracy -and-oligarchic-capture.

21. Chris Hedges, "The Last Gasp of American Democracy," *TruthDig* (January 6, 2014). Online: www.truthdig.com/report/item/the_last_gasp_of_american _democracy_20140105?utm_source=feedburner&utm_medium=feed&utm _campaign=Feed%2525253A+Truthdig%2525252FChrisHedges+Chris+Hedges +on+Truthdig.

22. Ibid.

23. Stuart Hall and Les Back, "In Conversation: At Home and Not at Home," *Cultural Studies* 23, no. 4 (July 2009): 680–681.

24. Pierre Bourdieu and Gunter Grass, "The 'Progressive' Restoration: A Franco-German Dialogue," *New Left Review* 14 (March–April 2002): 2.

25. Pierre Bourdieu, *Acts of Resistance* (New York: Free Press, 1998), 11.

26. Stanley Aronowitz, "What Kind of Left Does America Need?" *Tikkun,* April 14, 2014, available at www.tikkun.org/nextgen/what-kind-of-left-does-america-need.

27. Ibid.

28. Ibid.

29. Ibid.

Chapter 8

1. João Biehl, *Vita: Life in a Zone of Social Abandonment* (Los Angeles: University of California Press, 2005), 4.

2. Ibid.

3. See Robert B. Reich, "McCutcheon Took Us Back in Time, But It Might Just Birth the Next Occupy," *The Guardian,* April 6, 2014, available at www.theguardian.com /commentisfree/2014/apr/06/mccutcheon-conservative-supreme-court-next -occupy; Doug Henwood, "Our Gilded Age," *The Nation* (June 30, 2008): 14, 17; Paul Krugman, "Why We're in a New Gilded Age," *New York Review of Books,* May

8, 2014, available at www.nybooks.com/articles/archives/2014/may/08/thomas
-piketty-new-gilded-age/.

4. Robert Jay Lifton, *Death in Life: Survivors of Hiroshima* (Chapel Hill: University
of North Carolina Press, 1987), 479.

5. As indicated by a report from the Corporation for Enterprise Development,
"Nearly half of Americans are living in a state of 'persistent economic security,'
that makes it 'difficult to look beyond immediate needs and plan for a more secure
future.' . . . The CFED . . . report finds that 44 percent of Americans are living with
less than $5,887 in savings for a family of four." Christopher Mathews, "Nearly Half
of America Lives Paycheck-to-Paycheck," *Time* magazine, June 30, 2014, available at
http://time.com/2742/nearly-half-of-america-lives-paycheck-to-paycheck/.

6. Zygmunt Bauman, *Liquid Times: Living in an Age of Uncertainty* (Cambridge:
Polity Press, 2007), 14.

7. The quotation by Karl Jaspers is cited in Hannah Arendt, *The Last Interview
and Other Conversations* (Brooklyn, NY: Melville House Publishing, 2013), 37.

8. Ibid., 48.

9. Peter Beilharz, *Zygmunt Bauman: Dialect of Modernity* (London: Sage, 2000), 160.

10. Jason Deparle and Robert M. Gebeloff, "Living on Nothing but Food Stamps,"
New York Times, January 3, 2010, A1.

11. Editor, "75 Economic Numbers from 2012 That Are Almost Too Crazy to
Believe," *Economic Collapse Blog,* December 20, 2012, available at http://theeconomic
collapseblog.com/archives/75-economic-numbers-from-2012-that-are-almost-too
-crazy-to-believe.

12. David DeGraw, "Meet the Global Financial Elites Controlling $46 Trillion
in Wealth," *AlterNet,* August 11, 2011, available at www.alternet.org/story/151999
/meet_the_global_financial_elites_controlling_$46_trillion_in_wealth.

13. Zygmunt Bauman, "Downward Mobility Is Now a Reality," *The Guardian,*
May 31, 2012, available at www.guardian.co.uk/commentisfree/2012/may/31
/downward-mobility-europe-young-people; Bauman develops this theme in detail
in both Bauman, *On Education* (Cambridge: Polity Press, 2012), and Bauman, *This
Is Not a Diary* (Cambridge: Polity Press, 2012).

14. Zygmunt Bauman, *Wasted Lives* (London: Polity, 2004), 76.

15. See Steve Fraser, "The Politics of Debt in America: From Debtor's Prison to
Debtor Nation," *TomDispatch,* January 29, 2013, available at www.tomdispatch.com
/dialogs/print/?id=175643. On the history of debt, see David Graeber, *Debt: The
First 5,000 Years* (New York: Melville House, 2012).

16. Bauman, *On Education,* 47.

17. I have borrowed the term "zones of social abandonment" from Biehl, *Vita;* see
also Henry A. Giroux, *Disposable Youth* (New York: Routledge, 2012); and Michelle
Alexander, *The New Jim Crow* (New York: Free Press, 2012).

18. Angela Y. Davis, "State of Emergency," in Manning Marable, Keesha Middle-
mass, and Ian Steinberg, eds., *Racializing Justice, Disenfranchising Lives* (New York:
Palgrave, 2007), 324.

19. Biehl, *Vita,* 14.

20. Alexandra Politaki, "The Cultural Poison of Europe's Immigration Policies,"
Huffington Post, November 7, 2014, available at http://www.huffingtonpost.co.uk
/alexandra-politaki/europe-immigration_b_6232364.html.

Notes

21. Kyle Bella, "Bodies in Alliance: Gender Theorist Judith Butler on the Occupy and Slut Walk Movements," *Truthout,* December 15, 2011, available at www.truth-out.org/bodies-alliance-gender-theorist-judith-butler-occupy-and-slutwalk-movements/1323880210.

22. Daniel Bell, *The End of Ideology: On the Exhaustion of Political Ideas in the Fifties* (New York: Free Press, 1966); and the more recent Francis Fukuyama, *The End of History and the Last Man* (New York: Free Press, 2006).

23. Steve Herbert and Elizabeth Brown, "Conceptions of Space and Crime in the Punitive Neoliberal City," *Antipode* (August 4,2006): 757.

24. John Van Houdt, "The Crisis of Negation: An Interview with Alain Badiou," *Continent* 1, no. 4 (2011): 234–238, available at http://continentcontinent.cc/index.php/continent/article/viewArticle/65.

25. This position has been taken up recently by former labor secretary Robert Reich; see Reich, "McCutcheon Took Us Back in Time, but It Might Just Birth the Next Occupy."

26. Ulrich Beck, *Democracy without Enemies* (London: Polity Press, 1998), 38.

Chapter 9

1. For the war on academics, see Henry A. Giroux, *The University in Chains: Confronting the Military-Industrial-Academic Complex* (Boulder, CO: Paradigm Publishers, 2007), and *Neoliberalism's War on Higher Education* (Chicago: Haymarket, 2014); For an analysis of the war on journalists, see Jesselyn Radack, "Obama Targets Journalists," *Salon,* April 9, 2012, available at www.salon.com/2012/04/09/journalists_casualties_in_the_war_on_whistleblowers/. For the war on whistleblowers, see Glenn Greenwald, *No Place to Hide* (New York: Signal, 2014).

2. There is nothing new about the squashing of dissent in the United States and the complicity of liberals in such acts of repression. While I have not focused on this history, it is well to remember that the suppression of dissent is not a recent phenomenon. The sordid attacks against Scott Nearing, Paul Sweezy, and dozens of leftists who were fired just before and after World War II represent a glaring indictment of a history that is being repeated. As a number of intellectuals such as Robert Lynd and I. F. Stone have pointed out, it is hard to overlook the morally and politically poisonous role that liberals such as Schlesinger, Reuther, almost the entire group of "New York Intellectuals," as well as most universities, unions, and liberal organizations played in suppressing dissent in a wide variety of fields.

3. Marina Warner, "Dairy," *London Review of Books* 36, no. 17 (September 11, 2014), available at www.lrb.co.uk/v36/n17/marina-warner/diary.

4. Keith Bradsher and Chris Buckley, "Hong Kong Leader Reaffirms Tough Stance on Elections and Economic Discontent," *New York Times,* October 20, 2014, available at www.nytimes.com/2014/10/21/world/asia/leung-chun-ying-hong-kong-china-protests.html?hp&action=click&pgtype=Homepage&version=HpSumSmallMedia&module=first-column-region&region=top-news&WT.nav=top-news.

5. Ibid.

6. J. M. Coetzee, "JM Coetzee: Universities Head for Extinction," *Mail and Guardian,* November 1, 2013, available at http://mg.co.za/article/2013-11-01-universities-head-for-extinction.

7. For an excellent analysis of the conservative reaction to the growing democratization of the university from the 1960s on, see Christopher Newfield, *Unmaking the Public University: The Forty-Year Assault on the Middle Class* (Cambridge, MA: Harvard University Press, 2008).

8. Ellen Schrecker, *The Lost Soul of Higher Education* (New York: New Press, 2010), 3.

9. Zygmunt Bauman and Leonidas Donskis, *Moral Blindness: The Loss of Sensitivity in Liquid Modernity* (Cambridge: Polity Press, 2013), 139.

10. Joshua Kurlantzick, *Democracy in Retreat* (New Haven: Yale University Press, 2013).

11. Cited in Mark Fisher, *Capitalist Realism* (Washington, DC: Zero Books, 2009), 11.

12. Morris Berman, "Slouching towards Nuremberg," *CounterPunch,* July 25, 2012, available at www.counterpunch.org/2012/07/25/slouching-towards-nuremberg/.

13. Ibid.

14. Carol Matlack, "Bubble U.: High Point University," *Bloomberg Business Week,* April 19, 2012, available at www.businessweek.com/articles/2012-04-19/bubble-u -dot-high-point-university#p3.

15. Terry Eagleton, "The Death of Universities," *The Guardian,* December 17, 2010, available at www.theguardian.com/commentisfree/2010/dec/17/death-universities -malaise-tuition-fees.

16. Michael Snyder, "You Won't Believe Who Is Getting Away with Paying Zero Taxes while the Middle Class Gets Hammered," *InfoWars.com,* February 19, 2013, available at www.infowars.com/abolish-the-income-tax-you-wont-believe-who-is -getting-away-with-paying-zero-taxes-while-the-middle-class-gets-hammered/.

17. Ben Armbruster, "Study: Iraq War Cost U.S. $2.2 Trillion, Claimed Nearly 200,000 Lives," *ThinkProgress,* March 14, 2013, available at http://thinkprogress .org/security/2013/03/14/1721961/study-iraq-war-cost-2-triillion/. The publication by the Watson Institute of the March 14, 2013, Costs of War Project, "Iraq War: 190,000 Lives, $2.2 Trillion," can be found online at http://news.brown.edu /articles/2013/03/warcosts.

18. For *Tikkun*'s Marshall Plan, see http://spiritualprogressives.org/newsite /?page_id=114.

19. Susan George, "State of Corporations: The Rise of Illegitimate Power and the Threat to Democracy," in Transnational Institute and Occupy.com., *State of Power 2014: Exposing the Davos Class,* February 2014, available at www.tni.org/sites/www .tni.org/files/download/state_of_power-6feb14.pdf.

20. Radley Balko, *Rise of the Warrior Cop: The Militarization of America's Police Forces* (New York: Public Affairs, 2013); and Jill Nelson, ed. *Police Brutality* (New York: Norton, 2000).

21. Michelle Alexander, *The New Jim Crow* (New York: New Press, 2010).

22. Henry A. Giroux, *Youth in a Suspect Society* (New York: Palgrave, 2012).

23. David DeGraw, "Meet the Global Financial Elites Controlling $46 Trillion in Wealth," *AlterNet,* August 11, 2011, available at http://www.alternet.org /story/151999/meet_the_global_financial_elites_controlling_%2446_trillion_in _wealth?akid=7394.40823.3WyUYz&rd=1&t=5.

24. Senator Bernie Sanders, "A Threat to American Democracy," *RSN,* April 1,

2014, available at http://readersupportednews.org/opinion2/277-75/22830-focus
-a-threat-to-american-democracy.

25. Tom McKay, "Princeton Concludes What Kind of Government America Really Has, and It's Not a Democracy," *Popular Resistance,* April 16, 2014, available at www.policymic.com/articles/87719/princeton-concludes-what-kind-of-government
-america-really-has-and-it-s-not-a-democracy.

26. Jennifer M. Silva, *Coming up Short: Working-Class Adulthood in an Age of Uncertainty* (New York: Oxford University Press, 2013), 10.

27. Ibid.

Chapter 10

1. Gene R. Nichol, "Public Universities at Risk Abandoning Their Mission," *Chronicle of Higher Education* 55, no. 10 (October 31, 2008): A50.

2. Debra Leigh Scott, "How Higher Education in the US Was Destroyed in 5 Basic Steps," *AlterNet,* October 16, 2012, available at www.alternet.org/how-higher
-education-us-was-destroyed-5-basic-steps.

3. Benjamin Ginsberg, *The Fall of the Faculty: The Rise of the All-Administrative University and Why It Matters* (New York: Oxford University Press, 2011).

4. Hart Research Associates, *American Academics: Survey of Part Time and Adjunct Higher Education Faculty* (Washington, DC: AFT, 2011), available at www.aft.org
/pdfs/highered/aa_partimefaculty0310.pdf; Steve Street, Maria Maisto, Esther Merves, and Gary Rhoades, *Who Is Professor "Staff" and How Can This Person Teach So Many Classes?* (Los Angeles: Center for the Future of Higher Education, 2012), available at http://futureofhighered.org/uploads/ProfStaffFinal.pdf.

5. Michael Hardt and Antonio Negri, *Declarations* (Boulder, CO: Argo Navis, 2012); see also David Graeber, *The Democracy Project: A History, A Crisis, A Movement* (New York: Spiegel and Grau, 2013).

6. Cited in Andrew Martin and Andrew W. Lehren, "A Generation Hobbled by the Soaring Cost of College," *New York Times,* May 12, 2012, A1.

7. Paul Buchheit, "Five Ugly Extremes of Inequality in America—The Contrasts Will Drop Your Chin to the Floor," *AlterNet,* March 24, 2013, available at www.alternet
.org/economy/five-ugly-extremes-inequality-america-contrasts-willdrop-your-chin
-floor.

8. Paul Buchheit, "4 Ways the Koch Brothers' Wealth is Incomprehensible," *Salon* November 27, 2013, available at www.salon.com/2013/11/27/4_ways_the
_koch_brothers_wealth_is_incomprehensible_partner.

9. For an excellent defense of critical thinking not merely as a skill but as a crucial foundation for any democratic society, see Robert Jensen, *Arguing for Our Lives* (San Francisco: City Lights Books, 2013).

10. Cited in Richard J. Bernstein, *The Abuse of Evil: The Corruption of Politics and Religion since 9/11* (London: Polity Press, 2005), 7–8.

11. Paul Buchheit, "Now We Know Our ABCs and Charter Schools Get an F," *CommonDreams,* September 24, 2012, available at www.commondreams.org
/view/2012/09/24-0.

12. See Henry A. Giroux, *The University In Chains: Confronting the Military-Industrial-Academic Complex* (Boulder, CO: Paradigm Publishers, 2007).

13. See, for instance, Robert B. Reich, "Slashed Funding for Public Universities Is Pushing the Middle Class toward Extinction," *AlterNet*, March 5, 2012, available at www.alternet.org/education/154410/slashed_funding_for_public_universi ties_is_pushing_the_middle_class_toward_extinction. For a brilliant argument regarding the political and economic reasons behind the defunding and attack on higher education, see Christopher Newfield, *Unmaking the Public University: The Forty-Year Assault on the Middle Class* (Cambridge, MA: Harvard University Press, 2008).

14. Les Leopold, "Crazy Country: 6 Reasons America Spends More on Prisons Than on Higher Education," *AlterNet*, August 27, 2012, available at www.alternet .org/education/crazy-country-6-reasons-america-spends-more-prisons-higher education. On this issue, see also the classic work by Angela Y. Davis, *Are Prisons Obsolete?* (New York: Open Media, 2003); and Michelle Alexander, *The New Jim Crow: Mass Incarceration in the Age of Colorblindness* (New York: New Press, 2012).

15. Leopold, "Crazy Country."

16. Zygmunt Bauman, *The Individualized Society* (London: Polity, 2001), 4.

17. See, for instance, Rebecca Solnit, "Rain on Our Parade: A Letter to the Dismal Left," *TomDispatch*, September 27, 2012, available at www.tomdispatch.com/blog /175598/tomgram%3A_rebecca_solnit,_we_could_be_he.roes/. *TomDispatch* refers to this article as a call for hope over despair. It should be labeled as a call for accommodation over the need for a radical democratic politics. For an alternative to this politics of accommodation, see the work of Stanley Aronowitz, Chris Hedges, Henry Giroux, Noam Chomsky, and others.

18. This term comes from Daniel Bainsaid. See Sebastian Budgen, "The Red Hussar: Daniel Bensaïd, 1946–2010," *International Socialism* 127 (June 25, 2010), available at www.isj.org.uk/?id=661.

19. Michael Halberstam, "Introduction," in *Totalitarianism and the Modern Conception of Politics* (New Haven, CT: Yale University Press, 1999), 1.

Chapter 12

1. Hannah Arendt, cited in Georges Didi-Huberman, *Images in Spite of All: Four Photographs from Auschwitz* (Chicago: University of Chicago Press, 2008), 31.

2. This reference refers to a collection of interviews with Michel Foucault originally published by Semiotext(e). Michel Foucault, "What Our Present Is?" in Sylvere Lotringer, ed., *Foucault Live: Collected Interviews, 1961–1984* (New York: Semiotext(e), 1989), 407–415.

3. Zygmunt Bauman and Leonidas Donskis, *Moral Blindness: The Loss of Sensitivity in Liquid Modernity* (Cambridge: Polity Press, 2013), 33.

4. Daniel Sandstrom, "My Life as a Writer," interview with Philip Roth, *New York Times*, March 2, 2014, available at www.nytimes.com/2014/03/16/books/review /my-life-as-a-writer.html.

5. Of course, the Occupy movement in the United States and the Quebec student movement are exceptions to this trend. More recently, we have seen massive protests against police brutality in a number of cities. See, for instance, David Graeber, *The Democracy Project: A History, a Crisis, a Movement* (New York: Random House, 2013); and Henry A. Giroux, *Neoliberalism's War on Higher Education* (Chicago: Haymarket, 2014).

6. Cited in Robert Jay Lifton and Greg Mitchell, *Hiroshima in America* (New York: Avon Books, 1995), 351.

7. Ibid., 345.

8. Jennifer Rosenberg, "Hiroshima and Nagasaki (Part 2)," *About.com—20th Century History* (accessed March 28, 2014), available at http://history1900s.about.com/od/worldwarii/a/hiroshima_2.htm. A more powerful atom bomb was dropped on Nagasaki on August 9, 1945, and by the end of the year an estimated 70,000 had been killed. For the history of the making of the bomb, see the monumental Richard Rhodes, *The Making of the Atomic Bomb* (New York: Simon and Schuster, repr. 2012).

9. The term "technological fanaticism" comes from Michael Sherry, who suggested that it produced an increased form of brutality. Cited in Howard Zinn, *The Bomb* (New York: City Lights, 2010), 54–55.

10. Oh Jung, "Hiroshima and Nagasaki: The Decision to Drop the Bomb," *Michigan Journal of History* 1, no. 2 (Winter 2002), available at http://michiganjournalhistory.files.wordpress.com/2014/02/oh_jung.pdf.

11. See, in particular, Ronald Takaki, *Hiroshima: Why America Dropped the Atomic Bomb* (Boston: Back Bay Books, 1996).

12. Peter Bacon Hales, *Outside the Gates of Eden: The Dream of America from Hiroshima to Now* (Chicago: University of Chicago Press, 2014), 17.

13. Paul Ham, *Hiroshima Nagasaki: The Real Story of the Atomic Bombings and Their Aftermath* (New York: Doubleday, 2011).

14. Kensaburo Oe, *Hiroshima Notes* (New York: Grove Press, 1965), 114.

15. Ibid., 117.

16. Jung, "Hiroshima and Nagasaki."

17. Lifton and Mitchell, *Hiroshima in America,* 314–315, 328.

18. Robert Jay Lifton, "American Apocalypse," *The Nation* (December 22, 2003): 12.

19. For an interesting analysis of how the bomb was defended by the *New York Times* and a number of high-ranking politicians, especially after John Hersey's *Hiroshima* appeared in *The New Yorker,* see Steve Rothman, "The Publication of 'Hiroshima' in *The New Yorker,*" *Herseyhiroshima.com,* January 8, 1997, available at www.herseyhiroshima.com/hiro.php.

20. Wilson, cited in Lifton and Mitchell, *Hiroshima in America,* 309.

21. Hales, *Outside the Gates of Eden,* 8.

22. Zinn, *The Bomb,* 26.

23. Lifton and Mitchell, *Hiroshima in America.*

24. For a more recent articulation of this argument, see Ward Wilson, *Five Myths about Nuclear Weapons* (New York: Mariner Books, 2013).

25. Takaki, *Hiroshima,* 39.

26. Zinn, *The Bomb,* 45.

27. Ham, *Hiroshima Nagasaki.* See, for example, Gar Alperowitz's *Atomic Diplomacy Hiroshima and Potsdam: The Use of the Atomic Bomb and the American Confrontation with Soviet Power* (London: Pluto Press, 1994), and *The Decision to Use the Atomic Bomb* (New York: Vintage, 1996).

28. John Hersey, *Hiroshima* (New York: Alfred A. Knopf, 1946), 68.

29. Giovanna Borradori, ed., "Autoimmunity: Real and Symbolic Suicides—A

Dialogue with Jacques Derrida," in *Philosophy in a Time of Terror: Dialogues with Jurgen Habermas and Jacques Derrida* (Chicago: University of Chicago Press, 2004), 85–136.

30. Mary McCarthy, "The Hiroshima '*New Yorker*,'" *New Yorker*, November 1946, available at http://americainclass.org/wp-content/uploads/2013/03/mccarthy _onhiroshima.pdf.

31. Ham, *Hiroshima Nagasaki*, 469.

32. George Burchett and Nick Shimmin, eds., *Memoirs of a Rebel Journalist: The Autobiography of Wilfred Burchett* (Sydney: UNSW Press, 2005), 229.

33. For an informative analysis of the deep state and a politics driven by corporate power, see Bill Blunden, "The Zero-Sum Game of Perpetual War," *Counterpunch*, September 2, 2014, available at www.counterpunch.org/2014/09/02/the-zero-sum -game-of-perpetual-war/.

34. The following section relies on the work of Lifton and Mitchell, Zinn, and M. Susan Lindee's *Suffering Made Real: American Science and the Survivors at Hiroshima* (Chicago: University of Chicago Press, 1994).

35. Greg Mitchell, "The Great Hiroshima Cover-up," *The Nation*, August 3, 2011, available at www.thenation.com/blog/162543/great-hiroshima-cover#. See also Mitchell, "Part 1: Atomic Devastation Hidden for Decades," *WhoWhatWhy*, March 26, 2014, available at http://whowhatwhy.com/2014/03/26/atomic-devastation-hidden- decades; Mitchell, "Part 2: How They Hid the Worst Horrors of Hiroshima," *WhoW- hatWhy*, March 28, 2014, available at http://whowhatwhy.com/2014/03/28/part -2-how-they-hid-the-worst-horrors-of-hiroshima/; and Mitchell, "Part 3: Death and Suffering, in Living Color," *WhoWhatWhy*, March 31, 2014, available at http://who whatwhy.com/2014/03/31/death-suffering-living-color/.

36. Lifton and Mitchell, *Hiroshima in America*, 321.

37. Ibid., 322.

38. Ibid., 322–323.

39. Ibid., 336.

40. The genealogy from anti-intellectualism in American life to the embrace of illiteracy as a virtue is analyzed in the following books: Richard Hofstadter, *Anti- Intellectualism in American Life* (New York: Vintage, 1966); Susan Jacoby, *The Age of American Unreason* (New York: Pantheon, 2008); Charles P. Piece, *Idiot America: How Stupidity Became a Virtue in the Land of the Free* (New York: Anchor Books, 2009).

41. George Monbiot, "Evidence Meltdown," *The Guardian*, April 5, 2011, available at www.monbiot.com/2011/04/04/evidence-meltdown/.

42. Patrick Allitt, *A Climate of Crisis: America in the Age of Environmentalism* (New York: Penguin, 2015); Horace Herring, *From Energy Dreams to Nuclear Nightmares: Lessons from the Anti-Nuclear Power Movement in the 1970s* (Chipping Norton, UK: Jon Carpenter, 2006); Alain Touraine, *Anti-Nuclear Protest: The Opposition to Nuclear Energy in France* (Cambridge: Cambridge University Press, 1983); Stephen Croall, *The Anti-Nuclear Handbook* (New York: Random House, 1979). On the decade that enveloped the antinuclear moment with a series of crises, see Philip Jenkins, *Decade of Nightmares: The End of the Sixties and the Making of Eighties America* (New York: Oxford University Press, 2008).

43. Jim McCluskey, "Nuclear Weapons—Hope at Last," *Truthout*, March 5, 2014, available at www.truth-out.org/opinion/item/22256-nuclear-weapons-hope-at-last.

44. James McCluskey, "Nuclear Deterrence: The Lie to End All Lies," *Truthout*, October 29, 2012, available at truth-out.org/opinion/item/12381.

45. For a list of crises, near misses, and nuclear warmongering that characterizes US foreign policy in the last few decades, see Noam Chomsky, "How Many Minutes to Midnight? Hiroshima Day 2014," *Truthout*, August 5, 2014, available at www.truth -out.org/news/item/25388-how-many-minutes-to-midnight-hiroshima-day-2014.

46. Patricia Lewis, Heather Williams, Benoît Pelopidas, and Sasan Aghlani, *Too Close for Comfort—Cases of Near Nuclear Use and Options for Policy* (London: Chatham House, 2014), available at www.chathamhouse.org/sites/files/chathamhouse/home /chatham/public_html/sites/default/files/20140428TooCloseforComfortNuclear UseLewisWilliamsPelopidasAghlani.pdf.

47. McCluskey, "Nuclear Deterrence: The Lie to End All Lies."

48. Amy Goodman, "Hiroshima and Nagasaki, 69 Years Later," *TruthDig*, August 6, 2014, available at www.truthdig.com/report/item/hiroshima_and_nagasaki_69 _years_later_20140806.

49. William J. Broad and David E. Sanger, "U.S. Ramping up Major Renewal in Nuclear Arms," *New York Times,* September 21, 2014, available at www.nytimes .com/2014/09/22/us/us-ramping-up-major-renewal-in-nuclear-arms.html.

50. Ibid.

51. Hales, *Outside the Gates of Eden,* 17.

52. See, esp., David Krieger, *Zero: The Case for Nuclear Weapons Abolition* (Santa Barbara, Ca: A Nuclear Age Peace Foundation Book, 2013), and Krieger and Richard Falk, *The Path to Zero: Dialogues on Nuclear Dangers* (Boulder, CO: Paradigm Publishers, 2012).

53. Jacques Derrida, "No Apocalypse, Not Now (Full Speed Ahead, Seven Missiles, Seven Missives)," *Diacritics* 14, no. 2 (Summer 1984): 22, 29.

54. Didi-Huberman, *Images in Spite of All.*

55. I have taken this term from Sandstrom, "My Life as a Writer."

56. Susan Sontag has famously pursued this theme in Susan Sontag, "The Imagination of Disaster," *Commentary* (October 1965): 42–48, available at http://american futuresiup.files.wordpress.com/2013/01/sontag-the-imagination-of-disaster.pdf.

57. Michael Levine and William Taylor, "The Upside of Down: Disaster and the Imagination 50 Years On," *M/C Journal* 16, no. 1 (March 2013), available at http:// journal.media-culture.org.au/index.php/mcjournal/article/viewArticle/586.

58. Sontag, "The Imagination of Disaster," 42.

59. Ibid.

60. Mark Fisher, *Capitalist Realism: Is There no Alternative* (Washington, DC: Zero Books, 2009), p. 2.

61. Ibid., 3.

62. Brad Evans, "The Promise of Violence in the Age of Catastrophe," *Truthout*, January 5, 2014, available at www.truth-out.org/opinion/item/20977-the-promise -of-violence-in-the-age-of-catastrophe.

63. Bauman and Donskis, *Moral Blindness.*

64. Zinn, *The Bomb,* 23–24.

65. I have taken up this issue in detail in Giroux, *Neoliberalism's War on Higher Education.*

Notes

66. João Biehl, *Vita: Life in a Zone of Social Abandonment* (Los Angeles: University of California Press, 2005), 2.

67. This theme is taken up extensively in Brad Evans and Henry A. Giroux, *Disposable Futures: Violence in the Age of the Spectacle* (San Francisco: City Lights, 2015).

68. Glenn Greenwald, *No Place to Hide* (New York: Macmillan, 2014); Henry A. Giroux, *Zombie Politics in the Age of Casino Capitalism,* 2nd edition (New York: Peter Lang, 2014).

69. Hales, *Outside the Gates of Eden.*

70. Graeber, *The Democracy Project,* 281.

71. Tom Englehardt, "Tomgram: Noam Chomsky, Why National Security Has Nothing to Do with Security," *TomDispatch,* August 5, 2014, available at www.tomdispatch.com/post/175877/tomgram%3A_noam_chomsky%2C_why_national_security_has_nothing_to_do_with_security/.

72. Susan Sontag, *Regarding the Pain of Others* (New York: Farrar, Straus and Giroux, 2003), 81.

73. Paul Virilio, *Art and Fear* (New York: Continuum, 2004), 28.

74. Lifton and Mitchell, *Hiroshima in America,* 338.

75. Evans and Giroux, *Disposable Futures.*

76. Étienne Balibar, "Outline of a Topography of Cruelty: Citizenship and Civility in the Era of Global Violence," in *We, the People of Europe? Reflections on Transnational Citizenship* (Princeton, NJ: Princeton University Press, 2004), 115–132.

77. Jeremy Scahill, "It's Official: Obama Will Not Prosecute CIA Torturers," *Common Dreams,* April 16, 2009, available at www.commondreams.org/news/2009/04/16/its-official-obama-will-not-prosecute-cia-torturers. On the state of exception, see Giorgio Agamben, *State of Exception,* trans. Kevin Attell (Chicago: University of Chicago Press, 2005).

78. Blunden, "The Zero-Sum Game of Perpetual War."

79. Ibid.

80. Ibid.

81. See Lifton and Mitchell, *Hiroshima in America.*

82. Bauman and Donskis, *Moral Blindness,* 39.

83. Blunden, "The Zero-Sum Game of Perpetual War."

84. Mark Memmott, "Let Teachers Carry Guns? Some State Lawmakers Say Yes," *npr.org,* December 19, 2012, available at www.npr.org/blogs/thetwo-way/2012/12/19/167622812/let-teachers-carry-guns-some-state-lawmakers-say-yes.

85. German Lopez, "The Shooting of Michael Brown Was the Final Straw for People in Ferguson," *Vox,* August 14, 2014, available at www.vox.com/2014/8/14/5999929/shooting-mike-brown-final-straw-ferguson-st-louis-missouri. See also Bryan Winston, "Ferguson in Context," *Counterpunch,* August 22, 2014, available at www.counterpunch.org/2014/08/22/ferguson-in-context/.

86. Antonio Thomas, "Petition-Stop Police Brutality against Black People," *Change.Org,* June 2010, available at www.change.org/p/stop-police-brutality-against-black-people.

87. Hannah Tennant-Moore, "The Awakening," *New York Times Book Review,* June 19, 2014, 9.

88. This theme is brilliantly explored in Hales, *Outside the Gates of Eden.*

89. Raymond Williams, "Preface to Second Edition," in *Communications* (New York: Barnes and Noble, 1967), 15.

90. Quoted in Zinn, *The Bomb,* 58.

91. Hannah Arendt, *Hannah Arendt: The Last Interview and Other Conversations* (Brooklyn, NY: Melville House, 2013), 37.

92. Charles P. Pierce, "Why Bosses Always Win if the Game Is Always Rigged," *Esquire,* October 18, 2012, available at www.esquire.com/blogs/politics/mitt-romney -boss-13852713.

93. Stanley Aronowitz has taken up this theme in a number of articles. See, for instance, "What Kind of Left Does America Need?" *Tikkun,* April 14, 2014, available at www.tikkun.org/nextgen/what-kind-of-left-does-america-need.

94. Doreen Massey, "Vocabularies of the Economy," *Soundings,* January 2013, available at http://lwbooks.co.uk/journals/soundings/pdfs/Vocabularies %20of%20the%20economy.pdf.

95. Pierre Bourdieu, *Acts of Resistance* (New York: Free Press, 1998), 11.

96. Zoe Williams, "The Saturday Interview: Stuart Hall," *The Guardian,* February 11, 2012, available at www.guardian.co.uk/theguardian/2012/feb/11/saturday -interview-stuart-hall.

97. Hélène Cixous and Catherine Clément, *The Newly Born Woman,* trans. Betsy Wing, Theory and History of Literature Series 24 (Minnesota: University of Minnesota Press, 1986), ix.

98. Howard Zinn, "The Bombs of August," *Progressive,* August 2000, available at www.commondreams.org/views/073000-108.htm.

99. Clare Hemmings, "Invoking Affect: Cultural Theory and the Ontological Turn," *Cultural Studies* 19, no. 5 (September 2005): 557–558.

Chapter 13

1. See, for example, David Harvey, *The New Imperialism* (New York: Oxford University Press, 2003); David Harvey, A Brief History of Neoliberalism (Oxford: Oxford University Press, 2005); Wendy Brown, *Edgework* (Princeton, NJ: Princeton University Press, 2005); Henry A. Giroux, *Against the Terror of Neoliberalism* (Boulder, CO: Paradigm Publishers, 2008); Manfred B. Steger and Ravi K. Roy, *Neoliberalism: A Very Short Introduction* (New York: Oxford University Press, 2010).

2. These two terms are taken from Stefan Collini, "Response to Book Review Symposium: Stefan Collini, What Are Universities For," *Sociology* 1–2 (February 5, 2014), available at http://soc.sagepub.com/content/early/2014 /02/14/0038038513518852.

3. See, for instance, on the rise of the racist punishing state, Michelle Alexander, *The New Jim Crow: Mass Incarceration in the Age of Colorblindness* (New York: New Press, 2010); on the severe costs of massive inequality, Joseph E. Stiglitz, *The Price of Inequality: How Today's Divided Society Endangers Our Future* (New York: Norton, 2012); on the turning of public schools into prisons, see Annette Fuentes, *Lockdown High: When the Schoolhouse Becomes a Jailhouse* (New York: Verso, 2011).

4. Susan George, "State of Corporations: The Rise of Illegitimate Power and the Threat to Democracy," in Transnational Institute and *Occupy.com., State of Power*

2014: Exposing the Davos Class, February 2014, available at www.tni.org/sites/www .tni.org/files/download/state_of_power-6feb14.pdf.

5. Terry Eagleton, "Reappraisals: What Is the Worth of Social Democracy?" *Harper's Magazine,* (October 2010): 78, available at www.harpers.org/archive /2010/10/0083150.

6. Alex Honneth, *Pathologies of Reason* (New York: Columbia University Press, 2009), 188.

7. J. M. Coetzee, "JM Coetzee: Universities Head for Extinction," *Mail and Guardian,* November 1, 2013, available at http://mg.co.za/article/2013-11-01-universities -head-for-extinction.

8. Kristen Case, "The Other Public Humanities," *Chronicle of Higher Education,* January 13, 2014, available at http://m.chronicle.com/article/Ahas -Ahead/143867/.

Chapter 14

1. Fredric Jameson, "Future City," *New Left Review,* May–June 21, 2003, available at http://newleftreview.Org/II/21/fredric-jameson-future-city.

2. See, for instance, the 5th Assessment Report by the Intergovernmental Panel on Climate Change, available at www.ipcc.ch/report/ar5/wg3/. See also the Obama administration's publication of the third US National Climate Assessment, which provides a comprehensive and dire "scientific assessment of generated climate change, focusing on its effects on the US economy as well as on various regions across the United States." The report can be found at http://nca2014.globalchange.gov/.

3. I have taken up the issue of neoliberalism extensively in Henry A. Giroux, *Against the Terror of Neoliberalism* (Boulder, CO: Paradigm Publishers, 2008), and in *Against the Violence of Organized Forgetting: Beyond America's Disimagination Machine* (San Francisco: City Lights, 2014).

4. Michael D. Yates, "Occupy Wall Street and the Significance of Political Slogans," *Counterpunch,* February 27, 2013, available at www.counterpunch .org/2013/02/27/occupy-wall-street-and-the-significance-of-political-slogans/.

5. Chantal Mouffe, *Agonistics: Thinking the World Politically* (London: Verso, 2013), 119.

6. Zygmunt Bauman, "Downward Mobility Is Now a Reality," *The Guardian,* May 31, 2012, available at www.guardian.co.uk/commentisfree/2012/may/31/downward -mobility-europe-young-people; Bauman develops this theme in detail in both *On Education* (Cambridge: Polity Press, 2012) and *This Is Not a Diary* (Cambridge: Polity Press, 2012).

7. See Steve Fraser, "The Politics of Debt in America: From Debtor's Prison to Debtor Nation," *TomDispatch,* January 29, 2013, available at www.tomdispatch.com /dialogs/print/?id=175643. On the history of debt, see David Graeber, *Debt: The First 5,000 Years* (New York: Melville House, 2012).

8. Joao Biehl, *Vita: Life in a Zone of Social Abandonment* (Berkeley: University of California Press, 2005), 2.

9. For an excellent analysis of neoliberal-induced financial corruption, see Perry Anderson, "The Italian Crisis," *London Review of Books,* May 22, 2004, available at www.lrb.co.uk/v36/n10/perry-anderson/the-italian-disaster.

10. Michael Hardt and Antonio Negri, *Declaration* (New York: Argo Navis Author Services, 2012).

11. Jonathan Schell, "Occupy Wall Street: The Beginning Is Here," *The Nation*, October 19, 2011, available at www.thenation.com/article/164078/occupy-wall -street-beginning-here.

12. Costas Lapavitsas and Alex Politaki, "Why Aren't Europe's Young People Rioting any More?" *The Guardian*, April 1, 2014, available at www.theguardian .com/commentisfree/2014/apr/01/europe-young-people-rioting-denied -education-jobs.

13. Ibid.

14. Andrew R. Myers, "Dissent, Protest, and Revolution: The New Europe in Crisis," *Student Pulse* 4, no. 3 (May 2012), available at www.studentpulse.com/articles /624/4/dissent-protest-and-revolution-the-new-europe-in-crisis.

15. Marie Luise Knott, *Unlearning with Hannah Arendt*, trans. David Dollenmayer (New York: Other Press, 2011), ix.

16. See, for example, Hardt and Negri, *Declaration*; and David Graeber, *The Democracy Project: A History, a Crisis, a Movement* (New York: Random House, 2013).

17. Hardt and Negri, *Declaration*, 88.

18. Ibid., 29.

19. Graeber, *The Democracy Project*, 69–70.

20. See, for instance, Kevin Zeese, "TPP Protesters Drop Banner from Trade Building to Bring Attention to Secretive Deal," *Real News*, October 2, 2013, available at www.theinnoplex.com/news/newssub/tpp-protestors-scale-trade-building -to-bring-attention-to-secretive-deal; Peter Taaffe, "Another Year of Mass Struggles Beckons," *Socialist World*, December 13, 2013, available at www.socialistworld.net /doc/6604; Joshua Brahinsky, Sara Smith, and Asad Haider, "Class Size and Class Struggle: Organizing Lessons from the UCSC Strike," *Viewpoint Magazine*, April 14, 2014, available at http://viewpointmag.com/2014/04/14/class-size-and-class -struggle-organizing-lessons-from-the-ucsc-strike/.

21. Thomas Piketty, *Capital in the Twenty-First Century* (Cambridge, MA: Harvard University Press, 2014), 571.

22. Hardt and Negri, *Declaration*, 103.

23. Stanley Aronowitz, "Where Is the Outrage?" *Situations* 5, no. 2 (2014), available at http://ojs.gc.cuny.edu/index.php/situations/article/view/1488/1524.

24. Stanley Aronowitz, "Notes on the Occupy Movement," *Logos*, Fall 2011, available at http://logosjournal.com/2011/fall_aronowitz/.

25. Sarah Jaffe, "Post-Occupied," *Truthout*, May 19, 2014, available at http:// truth-out.org/news/item/23756-post-occupied.

26. For an interesting analysis of this position, see Barbara Epstein, "Prospects for a Resurgence of the US Left," *Tikkun* 29, no. 2 (Spring 2014): 41–44. See also Stanley Aronowitz, "What Kind of Left Does America Need?" *Tikkun*, April 14, 2014, available at www.tikkun.org/nextgen/what-kind-of-left-does-america-need; and Aronowitz, "Where Is the Outrage?"

Chapter 15

1. Gerry McCarthy, "*The Social Edge* Interview: Zygmunt Bauman." *Social Edge*,

February 2007, available at http://webzine.thesocialedge.com/interviews/the-social-edge-interview-sociologist-and-author-zygmunt-bauman/.

2. Wendy Brown, *Regulating Aversion: Tolerance in the Age of Identity and Empire* (Princeton, NJ: Princeton University Press, 2006), 16.

3. Irving Howe, "This Age of Conformity," *Selected Writings 1950–1990* (New York: Harcourt Brace Jovanovich, 1990), 29. 32.

4. Richard Sennett, *Together: The Rituals, Pleasures and Politics of Cooperation* (New Haven: Yale University Press, 2012), 30.

5. C. Wright Mills, *The Politics of Truth: Selected Writings of C. Wright Mills* (New York: Oxford University Press, 2008), 200.

6. Chris Zuccotti, "Noam Chomsky: America Hates Its Poor," *Reader Supported News*, December 1, 2013, available at http://readersupportednews.org/opinion2/277-75/20712-focus-noam-chomsky-america-hates-its-poor.

7. Frank B. Wilderson III, "Introduction: Unspeakable Ethics," in *Red, White, & Black* (London: Duke University Press, 2012), 2.

8. For a list of Chomsky's books, see http://chomsky.info/books.htm.

9. See, for example, Noam Chomsky, "The Responsibility of Intellectuals," *New York Review of Books*, February 13, 1967, available at www.chomsky.info/articles/19670223.htm. See also an updated version of this essay in Noam Chomsky, "The Responsibility of Intellectuals, Redux: Using Privilege to Challenge the State," *Boston Review*, September 1, 2011, available at https://www.bostonreview.net/noam-chomsky-responsibility-of-intellectuals-redux.

10. Zygmunt Bauman, "Afterthought: On Writing; On Writing Sociology," *Cultural Studies/Critical Methodologies* 2, no. 3 (March 2002): 364.

11. Terry Eagleton, "The Last Jewish Intellectual," *New Statesman*, March 29, 2004, available at www.newstatesman.com/node/147614. Edward Said's notion of traveling theory can be found in Edward W. Said, "Traveling Theory," in *The Edward Said Reader*, ed. Moustafa Bayoumi and Andrew Rubin (New York: Vintage, 2007), 195–217.

12. Noam Chomsky, "Paths Taken, Tasks Ahead," *Profession* (2000): 32.

13. Eagleton, "The Last Jewish Intellectual."

14. Stuart Hall and Les Back, "In Conversation: At Home and Not at Home," *Cultural Studies* 23, no. 4 (July 2009): 680–681.

15. Noam Chomsky, "An Ignorant Public Is the Real Kind of Security Our Govt. Is After," *AlterNet*, March 3, 2014, available at www.alternet.org/chomsky-staggering-differences-between-how-people-and-powerful-define-security.

16. Ibid.

17. See, for instance, the list of published debates in which he has engaged: http://chomsky.info/debates.htm.

18. Over the course of his career, a number of false claims have been attributed to Chomsky, including the absurd notion published in the *Times Higher Education Supplement* that he was an apologist for the Pol Pot regime, and on another occasion the damaging charge that he was anti-Semitic, given his defense of freedom of speech, including that of the French historian Robert Faurisson, an alleged Holocaust denier. Chomsky's long-standing critique of totalitarianism in all of its forms seems to have been forgotten in these cases. More recently a well-known left critic, capitalizing on his own need for indulging the performative, challenged Chomsky

to a boxing match partly as a result of Chomsky's criticism of him. Granted this may be more ironic than literal, but in the end it reveals the collapse of serious dialogue into the dustbin of the heightened spectacle and a fatuous aesthetics. At issue in this instance is not an attempt at serious dialogue but a form of self-sabotage and a withdrawal from the serious engagement if not politics itself. Chomsky has never stooped to this level of self-immolation or overinflated grandiosity.

19. Chomsky, "Paths Taken, Tasks Ahead," 38.

20. Ibid.

21. See, for instance, Zuccotti, "Noam Chomsky: America Hates Its Poor."

22. Ibid.

23. Mark Slouka, "Dehumanized: When Math and Science Rule the School," *Harper's Magazine* (September 2009): 38.

24. C. Wright Mills, "Culture and Politics: The Fourth Epoch," *The Politics of Truth: Selected Writings of C. Wright Mills* (Oxford: Oxford University Press, 2008), 199.

25. Archon Fung, "The Constructive Responsibility of Intellectuals," *Boston Review,* September 9, 2011, available at www.bostonreview.net/BR36.5/archon _fung_noam_chomsky_responsibility_of_intellectuals.php.

Index

⟳

A

Abandonment, zones of. *See* Disposability

Academics: and assault on critical thought, 27–29; Chomsky's views on, 185–186; current crisis of, 187–188; issues needing to be addressed by, 113–117; new brutalism in academia, 108; versus public intellectuals, 183. *See also* Intellectuals

Administrative university, 119. *See also* Corporatization of higher education

Adorno, Theodor, 11, 14, 24

Aesthetics of catastrophe, 153–154

Affluenza, 163–164

African-Americans: deep state, violence of, 88–90; militarized racism directed at, 50–54, 56–57, 78–79; overt racism in law enforcement, 156. *See also* Disposability

Agency: and anti-intellectualism, 20–21; critical thinking and historical consciousness, 43–47; and disposability, 99–100; in new order of authoritarianism, 10–11; relation to hope, 80

Aghlani, Sasan, 146

Albright, Madeleine, 59

Alexander, Michelle, 88, 115, 163

Algorithmic authoritarianism. *See* Instrumental reason

Alliances, need for among protest groups, 176

Alobeid, Dinah, 62

American Deep State: challenging, 92–96; general discussion, 85–92. *See also* Authoritarianism, new order of

American Legislative Exchange Council (ALEC), 18

Amnesia, historical. *See* Historical memory; Oganized forgetting

Antidemocratic processes: consequences of, 79–80; in electoral politics, 92–93; unleashed by atomic age, 143–145; in various countries, 19–20. *See also* Authoritarianism, new order of; Democracy; Depoliticization; Neoliberalism

Anti-immigrant groups, 102

Anti-intellectualism, 14–21, 26–30, 108–113

Antipublic intellectuals, 27, 178–179, 199–200

Arendt, Hannah, 34; absolute meaninglessness, time of, 79; disposability, 98; humanity as not acquired in solitude, 158; instants of truth, 137, 160–161; prime importance of political, 90; root of totalitarianism, 11, 99, 120; society of ignorance, 43; thinking as dangerous activity, 14, 46–47; thoughtfulness, 24; totalitarianism, 48

Arming of police, 52–53, 57. *See also* Militarism

Q

R

S

About the Author

⊷

Henry A. Giroux currently holds the McMaster University Chair for Scholarship in the Public Interest in the English and Cultural Studies Department and a Distinguished Visiting Professorship at Ryerson University. His most recent books are *America's Educational Deficit and the War on Youth* (Monthly Review Press, 2013), *Neoliberalism's War on Higher Education* (Haymarket Press, 2014), and *The Violence of Organized Forgetting: Thinking beyond America's Disimagination Machine* (City Lights Books, 2014). His website is www.henryagiroux.com.